Game On!

GAMING AT THE LIBRARY

Beth Gallaway

Neal-Schuman Publishers, Inc.

New York   London

Don't miss the companion Web site for this book!
Download forms and get access to updated core collection lists at:
www.informationgoddess.info/go.html

Published by Neal-Schuman Publishers, Inc.
100 William St., Suite 2004
New York, NY 10038

Printed and bound in the United States of America.

The paper used in this publication meets the minimum requirements of American National Standard for Information Sciences—Permanence of Paper for Printed Library Materials, ANSI Z39.48-1992.

Library of Congress Cataloging-in-Publication Data

Gallaway, Beth, 1975–
    Game on! : gaming at the library / Beth Gallaway.
        p. cm.
    Includes bibliographical references and index.
    ISBN 978-1-55570-595-4 (alk. paper)
    1. Libraries—Special collections—Electronic games. 2. Video games. I. Title.

Z692.E4215G35 2009
025.2'84—dc22

2009014110

Table of Contents

Preface

The public library's computer area is deluged every day with adults playing chess and poker while chatting, e-mailing, and surfing the Web. The students in the school library media center who want to log on to *RuneScape* or care for their virtual penguin outnumber the students seeking homework help or book recommendations. Patrons at the special library are seeking multimedia training for their legal or health care positions. The local senior center is looking for an alternative venue for its Wii Bowling League. The children's librarian has just asked the director to consider circulating video games in the public library. The Teen Advisory Board suggests having a *Dance Dance Revolution* tournament. A group of concerned parents want to know more about video game ratings. A work–study student wants to have a LAN party in the college library's information commons. Several adult patrons come in regularly to download cheat codes for games. You haven't picked up a joystick since *Pong* and want to know a little more about how games have changed since 1972.

To some of you, these situations are familiar; others may be wondering: What's a LAN? What's a Wii? Don't panic! The purpose of *Game On!* is to educate the beginning gamer and support the master gamer, so, whether you want to develop links to Web sites for cheat codes, write a policy for the circulation of PlayStation 3 games, or just understand a little bit more about the games your patrons are most assuredly playing, this book is for you.

Why is there a need for an entire book about video games? According to researcher NDP Group, the video game industry netted over $21.33 billion in 2008,[1] surpassing box office ticket sales and CD sales. In fact, over 80 percent of the population under the age of 34 has played a game,[2] and the average age of the gamer continues to rise—28 in 2003, 29 in 2004, and 35 in 2007.[3] Gaming has become ubiquitous: it's something most people do, from 97 percent of teenagers[4] to 26 percent of adults over age 50.[5] Video games have become a permanent part of mainstream culture for all ages, classes, races, and genders. As media continue to converge into multiple formats, patrons will demand to have many options for information formats, and libraries that value excellence in customer service will be obligated to begin treating games as yet another medium format that patrons want to access.

The introduction of any new medium requires the same careful planning and justification that libraries undertook when adding videos, DVDs, CDs, the Internet, and graphic novels. These media formats were once thought to be outside the

ix

jurisdiction of libraries, yet, today, the library that does not provide them is viewed as archaic or incomplete.

This book, designed a bit like a video game, will bring librarians working in school, public, and academic libraries up to speed on the topic of video games. The premise? You, the Hero Librarian, are on a quest to provide a superior gaming experience to your patrons, including the best games, as well as the top gaming magazines, books, programs, and services related to gaming.

Level 1, "The Backstory," provides an overview of pivotal moments in the development of video game history and culture.

In Level 2, "Video Games at the Library," you face the challenge of advocating for library services, programs, and collections to serve gamers. Along the journey, we'll gain experience points as we gather definitions of the "need to know" terms, tie gaming to the Search Institute's Developmental Assets® for teens, and debate the controversies involving video games. The "Level 2 Strategy Guide: Gaming Resources" provides annotated lists of valuable online resources that you can consult in your quest to develop a comprehensive gaming library.

Level 3, "Providing Library Services to Gamers," challenges you to provide services that don't involve picking up a controller, once your advocacy mission is complete. The "Level 3 Strategy Guide: Recommended Gaming-related Literature" offers core lists of fiction titles based on gaming and popular magazines for gamers.

Level 4, "Games and Programs," provides model programs to duplicate at your library. Although the primary focus is young adult audiences, many programs can be customized to fit children, seniors, college students, and families. The "Level 4 Strategy Guide: Forms and Flyers for Video Gaming Programs" includes many useful "cheat sheets" for creating your own gaming programs.

Level 5, "Selecting, Collecting, and Circulating Video Games," adds evaluating and selecting games to your newfound skill set; once games are in the library, storage, marketing, and display are the next puzzles to solve. The "Level 5 Strategy Guide: Recommended Gaming Collections" presents comprehensive lists of the essential games for your gaming library.

Level 6, "The Future of Games," concludes with a look at the future of games and gaming; think of it as a preview to the sequel.

The core collections and ready-to-go programs included in *Game On!* will get your quest off on the right foot, but I encourage you to "hack" by modifying these lists and programs to fit the special needs of your patrons, libraries, and communities. Also, don't miss out on the companion Web site for this book: to download forms and handouts and get access to updated core collection lists, visit www.informationgoddess.info/go.html.

Consider this your call to adventure: You are standing in an open field west of a white house, with a boarded front door. There is a small mailbox here. The small mailbox contains a book,[6] which reads: "WELCOME TO GAMING! Gaming is filled with adventure, danger, learning and literacy, identity formation, role-playing, hand–eye coordination, and many, many other unique skills. While gaming, you will explore some of the most amazing territory ever seen by mortals. No library should be without games. Good luck, Adventurer!"

Notes

1. Konigkramer, Lisa. "NDP: US Videogame Sales Total 21.33 Bil in 2008, Wii Play Top Selling Game." El33t OnLine (2008). Available: www.el33tonLine.com/past/2009/1/16/ndp_us_videogame_sales_total/ (accessed April 16, 2009).
2. Beck, John C. and Mitchell Wade. 2004. *Got Game? How the Gamer Generation Is Reshaping Business Forever.* Cambridge, MA: Harvard Business School Press.
3. ESA. *Essential Facts About the Computer and Game Industry.* Washington, DC: Entertainment Software Association (2008). Available: www.theesa.com/facts/index.asp (accessed April 16, 2009).
4. Lenhart, Amanda. "Teens, Video Games and Civics." Pew Internet and American Life Project (September 2008). Available: www.pewinternet.org/PPF/r/263/report_display.asp (accessed April 16, 2009).
5. ESA. *Essential Facts About the Computer and Game Industry.* Washington, DC: Entertainment Software Association (2008). Available: www.theesa.com/facts/index.asp (accessed April 16, 2009).
6. Anderson, Tim, et al. *Zork.* Infocom, 1977. Video game.

Acknowledgments

T hanks to my husband Earl, a first person shooter gamer who put up with *DDR* in the living room ("it looks like you're trying to put a fire out!"), *Rock Band* (when he had a headache), and hours and hours of *World of Warcraft* (2-damage! 2-damage! 2-damage!). He "taught" me how to play *Halo 3* by mercilessly killing me over and over.

Linda Braun, library consultant, made gaming and libraries click for me when she presented a program on the topic at the Metrowest (MA) Regional Library System in the fall of 2004. I hadn't realized there was opposition to it; that supporting gaming was *not* the norm in many libraries. "Someone needs to champion this," I said. "*You* do it," she suggested, in that quiet, sincere, and empowering way of hers.

Thanks to Sunny Vandermark at Metrowest, for being an amazing mentor and encouraging my gaming pursuits, and to her husband Stu, who sent me articles about gaming; thanks to Jenny Levine, for providing many lucrative opportunities to get the word out about gaming.

Thanks to Michele Gorman, who introduced me to Migell Acosta, who recruited me to write this book for Neal-Schuman. While working with Neal-Schuman throughout the writing process, I've gone through many editors. Thanks to Michael Kelley, Elizabeth Lund, Paul Seeman, and Christopher Rivera for their supreme patience and insights. RoseMary Honnold has my heartfelt gratitude for asking the right questions and having an eagle eye for inconsistencies and missing data.

Several friends served as readers and fact-checkers. Thanks to Alissa Lauzon, Brian Robinson, Jami Schwarzwalder, and Chris Castaldi for superb editing and to Ralph Trentelman and Jason Mylott for bibliography/gameography assistance.

The model programs and collections described came from librarians in the field. Thanks to contributors Allison Angell, Christy Branston, Andrew Cherbas, Eric Currie, Kelly Czarnecki, Michelle Deschene, John Fischer, Matt Gullett, Gretchen Ipock, Ginny Konefal, Jessica R. Marie, Susy Moorhead, Eli Neiburger, Jennifer Nelson, John Scalzo, Karl G. Siewert, Sarah Sogigian, Kelli Staley, and Jeff Wyner for sharing their programs and collection lists. Also, thanks to Steven Bellotti for helping to increase the knowledge base about cataloging video games.

Thanks to all the libraries in New England that invited me in to do hands-on gaming with teens over the past three years. It's a special joy that many of the libraries were inspired to purchase their own equipment and host their own programs.

I hope the completion of this volume doesn't mean that I cannot include *World of Warcraft* as a business expense any longer. Thanks to my guild, the Pig & Whistle Society on Kirin Tor server, for all their support in the journey from levels 1 to 70 in 2008. Special thanks to my regular questing party, Arthanas, Aelfrida, and Albrect, and other drop-ins: Conan, Forgan, Malaficent, and Kastulo.

Finally, thanks to the artists and copyright holders who gave me permission to reprint their work: Snack or Die, Cables To Go, The DigiBarn Computer Museum, The ESRB, Penny Arcade, and John Beck.

CHAPTER 1

Level 1: The Backstory—Video Game Basics

W hat are video games? How are they different from other kinds of games? How have video games evolved? What are the important things to know about video game history to institute a successful gaming experience in the library?

What Are Video Games?

Throughout this book, the term "video game" refers to interactive, digital media created with specified goals played through an electronic medium. Emphasis is often on fun and fast-moving action, although some games have a serious intent and are educational or informational in nature (see Figure 1.1 for some of the more popular video games). The verb "gaming" as used in libraries refers to playing video games and tabletop games (board, card, dice, or miniatures), never to casino gambling.

Video games may be played:

- on a Web site or downloaded from a Web site;
- on a CD, CD-ROM, or DVD played on a computer;
- on a CD, CD-ROM, or DVD played on a computer with an Internet connection required;
- on a CD, CD-ROM, DVD, or cartridge on a standalone console, requiring a television or other monitor;
- on a CD, CD-ROM, DVD, or cartridge on a standalone console, requiring a television or other monitor and a live Internet connection; and
- on a handheld device such as a Palm Pilot, cell phone, smart phone, or other personal type of system.

When playing a video game, the player interacts with the game on a screen by using a controller. A controller might be a keyboard, joystick, mouse, floor pad, steering wheel, wand, or even a motion-sensitive camera that is activated by the player to control the game. Devices for playing video games come in a variety of shapes and sizes (see Figure 1.2).

Figure 1.1. Popular Current Games

Source: Photo by Beth Gallaway.

When one thinks about video games, competition comes to mind. Video games have a clear set of rules, and winners/losers emerge based on that set of rules. All video games have a goal for the player to achieve and obstacles that impede progress to the goal.[1] Tools to overcome the obstacles are provided but little to no instruction on how to use the tools—figuring it out is part of the challenge. Stephen Johnson, author of *Everything Bad Is Good for You*, explains that playing a video game is like learning to play a game of chess, except you don't know how the pieces move, and as soon as you figure them out, the rules change. "Most video games are different from traditional games like chess or Monopoly in the way they withhold information about the underlying rules of the system."[2]

The learning process of discovering how to use the tools is akin to the scientific method of formulating a hypothesis, testing your hypothesis through experimentation, evaluating the outcomes, and developing a theory or retesting. Because players learn by trial and error, there is a high failure rate, so multiple second chances are provided.[3] The game becomes harder as gameplay advances and the player learns how to beat the game.[4] The game design must provide a delicately balanced scale of difficulty: too easy, and the player becomes bored and quits playing; too difficult, and the player becomes frustrated and quits.

Figure 1.2. Video Game Devices

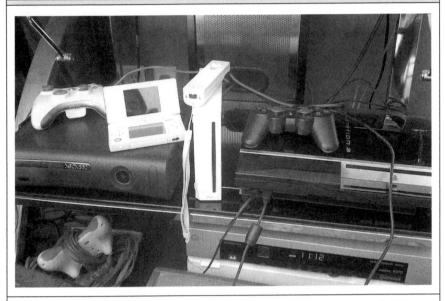

Source: Photo by Beth Gallaway.

There is a growing trend to incorporate content creation—designing levels—as part of the gameplay. *Little Big Planet* (Sony, 2008) for PlayStation 3, *Drawn to Life* (THQ, Inc., 2007) for the Nintendo DS, and *Ben 10: Alien Force* on the Cartoon Network's Web site are three examples. The annotated bibliography at the end of the book lists a number of wonderful resources about game design. How better to learn about the design of games than by playing a game about game design? In addition, take a look at *Understanding Games* (www.pixelate.de/games/understanding-games), a four-part series on game design that covers rules, interactivity, representation, simulation in games, player motivation, learning in video games, and identification in video games. You can also learn more about game design at: www.kongregate .com/games/pixelate/understanding-games-episode-1

Video Game Formats

"Platform" is a jargon term used to encompass all the formats that video games come in. Currently, there are three competing console systems on the market for home use that may be of interest to libraries: Microsoft's Xbox series, Nintendo's Wii, and the Sony PlayStation series. Some gamers have a strong preference for one console over another. Each console has a dedicated following of hardcore fans, similar to the way some readers are strong fans of a particular author, series, or genre. Unlike in publishing, competition is fierce among console manufacturers in terms of units sold and keeping up with new technologies. This competition is often referred to as the "console wars."

"Next-gen" (next-generation) consoles are the newest, most advanced game consoles. The Xbox 360 debuted in late fall 2005; Nintendo's Wii and Sony's PlayStation 3 hit the shelves in fall 2006. Next-gen consoles are covered in detail in Level 4 (programming), Level 5 (collections), and Level 6 (the future of gaming).

> "Games, like music, cinema, and the theatre, are experiences we can share."
> – Lucien King (2002), author of *Game On: The History and Culture of Videogames*[5]

Both Sony and Nintendo manufacture handheld versions of their video game console: Sony the PlayStation Portable and the Nintendo Game Boy, Nintendo DS, and Nintendo DS Lite, respectively.

In addition to consoles, video games can be played on personal computers (Mac, Windows, LINUX, etc.), Palm Pilots, iPods, and cell phones. Cell phone carrier Nokia designed one phone model, the N-Gage, to be both a phone and a handheld gaming device, while the Apple iPhone had success with offering games, including popular titles ported from consoles, to its library of downloadable software. Many cell phones now come with game demos; after an hour (or less) of playing time, users must purchase the full-length game from a cell phone service carrier.

Many other types of games are appropriate in libraries. Tabletop role-playing games (RPGs) involve roles based on archetypal characters and monsters, and gameplay follows probabilities based on dice rolling; libraries interested in this type of gaming can find resources on the Wizards of the Coast's Web site (www.wizards.com). Some card games feature illustrated cards that represent characters, weapons, and elements, and action flows according to the cards the players draw; in other card games, action is based solely on drawing, playing, and discarding cards. A variety of board games resemble the familiar "roll dice, move mice" type of family board games, but a slew of modern games (mostly originating from Germany and Europe) are widely available. Modern board games feature authentic play—the focus is creative thinking and having fun—player engagement and, often, multiple end-game scenarios. Finally, tabletop miniature games feature painstakingly painted miniatures of characters and creatures that model the gameplay. Resources for tabletop, board, and card games include the following:

- Board Game Geek. Available: www.boardgamegeek.com: Reviews, forums, and resources for finding local board game clubs
- Board Games with Scott. Available: http://boardgameswithscott.com: Online video tutorials on how to play board and card games
- Swift Six Games, hosted by the School Library System of Genesee Valley BOCES. Available: http://sls.gvboces.org/gaming/: Advocates for board games in education and discusses how board games support the American Association of School Librarians' (2008) *Standards for the 21st-Century Learner*

A History of Video Games

"Play" is the first form of ritual exploratory motor and sensory development a human engages in during life. Playing helps stimulate coordination, reflexes, situational awareness and event processing, confrontational logistics, and a myriad of other skills vital to adolescent development. Games of all types are a higher level, more sophisticated element of play to help children learn the skills they need as adults. Gaming has existed since hunter–gatherers played with mock bows and arrows to learn how to kill animals. War games in Germany were played with toy soldiers in the 1800s,[6] and these military games evolved into strategy games based on civil, revolutionary, and world wars, such as those released by Avalon Hill in the 1950s. Essentially, these were role-playing games with miniature props. Although this type of game continues to be popular, the digital revolution has brought us to the next natural succession in gaming technology—the electronic video game.

> The game company Avalon Hill has been producing strategy-based miniature and board games since 1958. It was acquired by Hasbro in 1998, a company that also owns Wizards of the Coast, affiliated with the *Dungeons & Dragons* franchise. For more information about Avalon Hill games, visit its Web site at www.wizards.com/.

Video Games and Computers

The first graphical interactive game simulated in a digital environment (that is, run on a computer) was *Tic-Tac-Toe*, which was developed on an EDSAC vacuum-tube computer with a cathode ray tube display.[7] Although not quite a video game by modern standards, it proved that electronic circuitry could make a viable platform for interactive media. In 1958, the first "real" video game, *Table Tennis for Two*, was developed by William Higinbotham using an oscilloscope.[8]

The most highly acclaimed game in the heritage of video gaming is *Spacewar!*, created by two students at MIT in 1962.[9] Widely misrepresented as the first video game, *Spacewar!* was merely the first popularized video game, which in turn attracted a vibrant community. Players competed in pairs or groups; gaming has been a social activity from the start.

Environmentalist and computer advocate Steward Brand, in a 1972 interview with *Rolling Stone* magazine, talked about the delight of *Spacewar!*:

> *Spacewar*…was the illegitimate child of the marrying of computers and graphic displays. It was part of no one's grand scheme. It served no grand theory. It was the enthusiasm of irresponsible youngsters. It was disreputably competitive.…It was an administrative headache. It was merely delightful. Yet *Spacewar!*, if anyone cared to notice, was a flawless crystal ball of things to come in computer science and computer use:
>
> 1. It was intensely interactive in real time with the computer.
> 2. It encouraged new programming by the user.
> 3. It bonded human and machine through a responsive broadband interface of live graphics display.
> 4. It served primarily as a communication device between humans.

5. It was a game.

6. It functioned best on stand-alone equipment (and disrupted multiple-user equipment).

7. It served human interest, not machine. (*Spacewar!* is trivial to a computer.)

8. It was delightful.[10]

Forty-five years later, these characteristics are still the hallmarks of the very best video games: engagement, user content creation, interaction with a machine, a social focus, and, most importantly, fun.

Storytelling Meets Video Gaming

In 1976, the first popular text adventure game, *Adventure* (also known as *ADVENT*, *Adventure*, and later as *Colossal Caves*), was written by Will Crowther.[11] It introduced humor and a word-based control schema that required players to use deductive reasoning instead of completing a motor coordination–dependent activity. Adventure games became increasingly complex. In 1979, *Zork* (designed by David Lebling at MIT; see Figure 1.3) brought natural language processing to video games.[12] The quality of writing was as important as plot and gameplay. At the other end of the adventure gaming spectrum, programmers reacted to the paper *Dungeons & Dragons* craze by creating video games that had simple line-drawn dungeon maps, such as *Oubliette* (Bear Systems, 1983) (the first group-oriented game)[13] and *DND* (R.O. Software, 1984).

Figure 1.3. *Zork* Screenshot

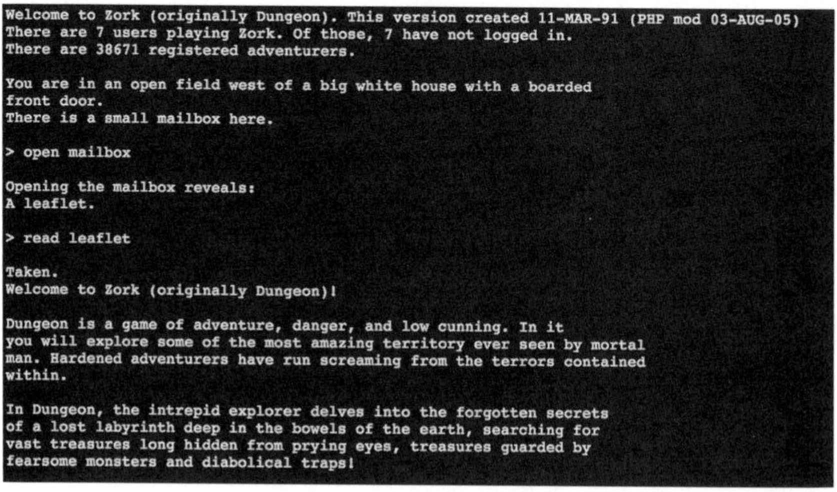

```
Welcome to Zork (originally Dungeon). This version created 11-MAR-91 (PHP mod 03-AUG-05)
There are 7 users playing Zork. Of those, 7 have not logged in.
There are 38671 registered adventurers.

You are in an open field west of a big white house with a boarded
front door.
There is a small mailbox here.

> open mailbox

Opening the mailbox reveals:
A leaflet.

> read leaflet

Taken.
Welcome to Zork (originally Dungeon)!

Dungeon is a game of adventure, danger, and low cunning. In it
you will explore some of the most amazing territory ever seen by mortal
man. Hardened adventurers have run screaming from the terrors contained
within.

In Dungeon, the intrepid explorer delves into the forgotten secrets
of a lost labyrinth deep in the bowels of the earth, searching for
vast treasures long hidden from prying eyes, treasures guarded by
fearsome monsters and diabolical traps!
```

The beginning of Zork is depicted in this screenshot. Many older text adventure games are archived on the Interactive Fiction Web site at http://ifarchive.org.

Source: Pot, Martin. "Zork I: The Great Underground Adventure." Play Infocom Adventures Online. 2005. www.xs4all.nl/~pot/infocom/zork1.html (accessed: February 3, 2009).

Dungeons & Dragons, created by Dave Arneson and Gary Gygax, was described as "*Chainmail* [a tabletop war game] in a Dungeon."[14] The video game version of *Dungeons & Dragons* was released by TSR in 1974, and 4–5 million copies were sold by the early 1980s. The fourth edition was released in 2008. It is interesting that Atari, the first home video game system, and *Dungeons & Dragons*, a pencil and dice role-playing game, were born in the same year, 1972.

The first multiplayer pseudo-three-dimensional (3D) game came out in 1977; *Maze War*, a first person shooter created in the NASA/Ames Research Center Computation Division by high school students Steve Colley, Howard Palmer, and Greg Thompson under the direction of their electronics teacher, John McCollum.[15] Sometimes known simply as *Maze*, eyeballs on the screen depicted players, and they chased each other through a maze (see Figure 1.4).

Figure 1.4. *Maze War* Screenshot

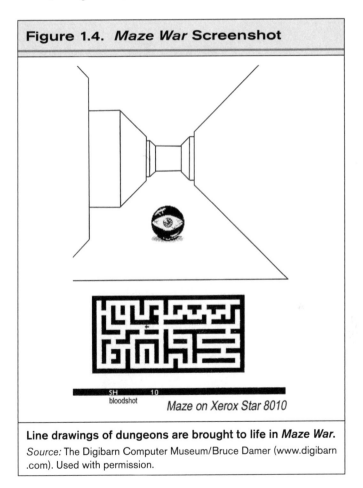

Maze on Xerox Star 8010

Line drawings of dungeons are brought to life in *Maze War*.
Source: The Digibarn Computer Museum/Bruce Damer (www.digibarn .com). Used with permission.

Computer gaming was becoming more popular as evidenced by record-breaking sales of both games and computer books, such as *Microcomputer BASIC Computer Games*, edited by David Ahl (Atari, 1978), which sold over one million copies. The book contained instructions for programming over 100 games into your computer.[16] Until then, computer games were the domain of the reclusive geek who had access to equipment still not commonly available at the time. The release of the Apple II in 1977 and of the Commodore 64 in 1983 gave mainstream consumers an affordable way to get in touch with the computing world and thus heralded an unprecedented era of innovation and creativity in video game development.

In the 1980s and early 1990s, computer gaming was a largely unregulated, "Wild West" style market that lacked any kind of standards. The science of video game development had just become comfortable enough to trivialize many of the technical challenges in producing a game. In 1993,[17] *Doom*, a first person shooter with 3D mazes and a fast-paced, "kill or be killed" premise, exploded onto the scene. The

TIMELINE OF SIGNIFICANT GAMES:

1958: *Table Tennis for Two*, first video game

1961: *Spacewar!*, first popular video game

1967: *Death Race*, first racing video game

1972: *Pong*, first Atari arcade game

1974: *Dungeons & Dragons*, pencil and dice role-playing game published

1975: *Adventure*, first multiplayer online game

1977: *Maze War*, first 3D simulated video game

1978: *Space Invaders*, Japanese arcade game

1979: *Zork*, popular interactive fiction (text adventure) video game

1980: *Pac-Man*, Japanese arcade game

1985: *Super Mario Brothers*, side-scrolling video game for the Nintendo Entertainment System

1992: *Mortal Kombat*, street fighting game, so violent it spurred Congressional hearings

1993: *Doom*, gleefully violent 3D first person shooter for the personal computer that introduced online gaming via LAN (local area network)

1995: *The Sims*, dollhouse simulation game, first to incorporate player beta testing

1996: *Quake*, first MMOG to encourage clan-style play

1997: *UltimaOnline*, first 3D MMOG

1997: *Grand Theft Auto*, first sandbox-style game in which players interact and experiment with the entire environment

2003: *EyeToy Play*, first games played with any control via a camera

2006: *Wii Sports*, first game played with a wireless, kinetic remote control

2008: *Spore*, evolutionary-style video game

2008: *Little Big Planet*, game in which players create and submit levels for others to play

game was heavily criticized for exhibiting prolific amounts of gore and violent, senseless action. Congressional hearings on video game violence followed, becoming the impetus for the Entertainment Software Association to create the self-regulated Entertainment Software Ratings Board. Just a few years later, David Walsh, PhD, founded the National Institute on Media and the Family. It produced its first report card on the video game industry in 1998 and continues today to research the positive and harmful effects of media on children and youth.

Game Arcades

Because most computers were housed in the basements of universities, the popular way to play for the first 20 years was in arcades. Teens would congregate in arcades in the same way they congregated in pool halls in the 1950s and 1960s, spending their quarters. According to Education World's *Lesson Plan on the 1980s*, 20 billion quarters were spent in arcade machines in 1981.[18] As recently as 2001, laws concerning youth in arcades have been passed; *Kendrick v American Amusement Machine Association, 01-329* was found to be unconstitutional by the U.S. Supreme Court in March 2001. American computer programmers made the first arcade games. Then, in 1978, Japan invaded the American dream with *Space Invaders,* followed by *Pac-Man,* which became the most popular arcade game in history (see Figure 1.5).

Figure 1.5. *Pac-Man* Arcade Machine

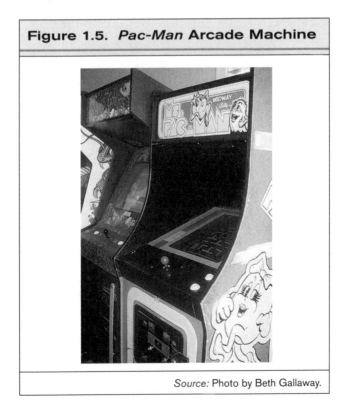

Source: Photo by Beth Gallaway.

Home Consoles

Other breakthroughs were reached in the 1980s, including the increased popularity of the console game. In the early stage of console games, the gamers were not only players but also game makers. Creating console games was a popular hobby. Some of the best-loved gaming characters, such as Sonic the Hedgehog, were created by gamers who today are programmers, designers, or artists.

The first console systems, manufactured by Atari, Nintendo, and Sega, were developed to play smaller versions of arcade classics. In 1966, Ralph Baer began work on what eventually became the Magnavox Odyssey (also known as the "Brown Box" for its earlier noncommercial prototype), the first home video game console.[19] Then, in 1977, Atari (creators of the arcade game *Pong*) released a home console, the VCS, that would play different games on computer chips located in cartridges, and it quickly emerged as the leader of home gaming (see Figure 1.6). Atari, like many other game developers demanding long hours for low pay, experienced many employees leaving the company for the third-party game development market.

Video games were in their golden age when the game *ET*, based on the popular Spielberg film, was released. Most games take 18 months to develop, but *ET*, which cost over $21 million in royalties (to obtain permission to produce the game), had only a six-week development period. Five million copies were produced, but only one million sold, and the unsold copies were dumped in a landfill in New Mexico.[20] Considered to be one of the worst games ever created, it left distaste for games in the

Figure 1.6. The Atari 2600

Many people believe that Atari's *Pong* was the first video game; really, it was the first popular game, and it was little more than an emulation of *Tennis for Two*.

Source: Atari. Wikipedia. Photo by joho345, 2007. Available: http://en.wikipedia.org/wiki/Atari (accessed: April 16, 2009).

mouths of American fans. At this time, critics said every game that could be made with the pixilated graphics had been developed, and the market was saturated with too many poorly designed games.

Across the ocean, video games were still thriving in Japan, and a young Shigeru Miyamoto was developing games for a card company turned video game company called Nintendo. Miyamoto introduced the concept of story to video games with the arcade classic *Donkey Kong* (Nintendo, 1981). In 1985, Nintendo reintroduced video games to America, with the "Nintendo Entertainment System" debuting in New York City during the Christmas season. That year, 50,000 units were sold in the United States,[21] and Nintendo has spent the next 30-plus years bringing video games to homes around the world.

In the 1980s, Nintendo's biggest rival was Sega. Sega's console, developed a few years after the original Nintendo, ran faster than Nintendo's console. Sega invested in advertising and created their own icon, *Sonic the Hedgehog*, who could move as fast as their console could process information. Sega's ad campaign targeted teenagers and implied that to be cool you must own a Sega, resulting in Nintendo gaining a reputation as a kiddy machine. Nintendo, run by Japanese businessmen, invested only in their systems and in the content of their games, slowly losing the console war with Sega and future systems.

> For more on the rich history of video games, check out the Dot Eaters' Web site at www.doteaters.com. The site has archival video and screenshots to round out articles.

Online Games

On-line Systems (which evolved into Sierra On-line) was founded in 1980 as the first national online service dedicated to gaming, incorporating chat with gameplay. With players now able to connect and compete with one another at great distances, Multi-user Dungeons (MUDs; a text-based, multiplayer gaming experience) saw renewed popularity as the integration of modems into home computers made it possible to connect online, across networks.

Doom (id Software, 1993) introduced online gaming via local area networks in the early 1990s. Online gaming quickly became the theme of the late 1990s and is strong in the new millennium. *EverQuest* (Verant Interactive/Sony) and *Lineage* (NCSoft), both sword and sorcery games in the *Dungeons & Dragons* tradition, were released in 1998. *Quake III: Arena* (id Software, 1999) focused on multiplayer action from *Capture the Flag* (Carr Software, 1993) games to player versus player combat via the Internet. *UltimaOnline* (EA, 1997), hailed as the first massively multiplayer online role-playing game (MMORPG), developed a persistent world populated with self-policing characters that created a nonlinear story. In 1997, only 1.5 million people played online games; within five years, that number had reached 3.5 million, and, in 2008, MMOG subscriptions hit 16 million.[23] The numbers continue to climb—Level 6 examines what the future might hold for online gaming.

> Multi-user Dungeons, or MUDs, were popular on academic networks since Roy Trubshaw and Richard Bartle developed one at Essex University in 1977.[22]

With the advent of *The Sims* (Maxis, 1995), players were viewed as co-developers and brought in to test games. This was unique to other industries; it is a good example of the community and social aspects of video games, and it helped create loyal fan bases. When *UltimaOnline*, the first MMOG with a persistent self-policing world, ran out of money in beta stages, 50,000 faithful players sent $2 to fund testing. *Quake* (id Software, 1996) was another milestone: a graphical MUD with clan-based play, encouraging community. Players gathered at QuakeCon in Texas at a convention/LAN party of members of the *Quake* IRC channel. Instigated by Jerry Wolski, the convention became an annual event, and *Quake III* is part of the Cyberathlete Professional League's annual world tour and lineup of competitive events.

Professional Gaming

Imagine making money playing video games! Not so surprising, considering that the spread of games has been likened to a physical sport: baseball. Baseball teams began as recreational in nature; their popularity spread from the rich and leisure class to the poor and working class; there were few rules until standardization; "teams" formed; resources were pooled; and profit and efficiency increased as the game became more orderly.

In the mid to late 1990s, gaming took a professional bent. Angel Munoz founded the Cyberathlete Professional League in 1997, and it ran for nearly ten years. The Cyberathlete Amateur League for online gaming launched in 2001 and grew to 500,000 registered members. It was acquired by United Arab Emirates in 2008; there have not been any events since. The Professional Gaming League (PGL) launched in 1998 and was overhauled in 2008.

An intercollegiate electronic gaming league was formed in 2009, with 27 colleges joining to compete in *Starcraft* (Blizzard, 1998).[24]

Major League Gaming (MLG) was founded in 2002 by Sundance DiGiovanni and Mike Sepso. They host live national and international events broadcast on ESPN. Players are endorsed or sponsored by companies and organizations.

Library video game tournaments may be a way to launch future professional gamers. With the release of Ann Arbor District Library's *GT System* (gaming tournament software) in fall 2008, libraries have the opportunity to participate in a national leaderboard system (a leaderboard is the board that displays the leaders in a competition). In addition to registration, scoring, and standings, *GT System* offers player logos, leaderboards, event promotion and preregistration, career histories, and numerous types of statistics. It's possible that a player with a strong history of wins on the *GT System* could catch the attention of the MLG or PGL and end up with a career in professional gaming. Register for the *GT System* at http://wiki.gtsystem.org/.

Notes

1. Castaldi, Chris. 2009. "Universal Game Model: Starting the Conversation about Games and Education." Thesis. University of Advancing Technology, Phoenix, AZ.
2. Johnson, Steven. 2005. *Everything Bad Is Good for You*. New York: Riverhead Books.
3. Castaldi, "Universal Game Model."

4. Ibid.
5. King, Lucien, ed. 2002. *Game On: The History and Culture of Videogames.* London: Laurence King Publishing.
6. King, Brad and John Borland. 2003. *Dungeons and Dreamers: The Rise of Computer Game Culture from Geek to Chic.* New York: McGraw-Hill Osborne Media.
7. Bellis, Mary. "The History of Computer and Video Games." About.com (December 15, 2008). Available: http://inventors.about.com/library/inventors/blcomputer_videogames .htm (accessed: April 16, 2009).
8. Ibid.
9. Koster, Raph. "MUD Timeline." Raph Koster's Web site (February 20, 2002). Available: www.raphkoster.com/gaming/mudtimeline.shtml (accessed: April 16, 2009).
10. Brand, Stewart, 1972. "Spacewar: Fanatic Life and Symbolic Death among the Computer Bums." *Rolling Stone,* no 123 (December 7).
11. Koster, "MUD TimeLine."
12. Ibid.
13. Ibid.
14. King and Borland, *Dungeons and Dreamers,* 3.
15. McCollum, Greg. "The aMazing History of Maze: It's a Small World After-all." PowerPoint presentation at the Vintage Computer Festival, Mountain View, CA, November 7, 2004.
16. Atari Archives. "Table of Contents: Basic Games." Available: www.atariarchives.org/ basicgames/ (accessed: April 16, 2009).
17. Kushner, David. 2003. *Masters of Doom: How Two Guys Created an Empire and Transformed Pop Culture.* New York: Random House.
18. Hopkins, Gary. "Celebrate the Century: Search the Web for U.S. History of the 1980s." Lesson Planning Channel Education World (2000). Available: www.education-world.com/ a_lesson/lesson215.shtml (accessed: April 16, 2009).
19. Burnham, Van. 2001. *Supercade: A Visual History of the Video Game Age 1971–1984.* Cambridge, MA: MIT Press.
20. The Dot Eaters. 2006. *Player 3 Stage 6: The Great Videogame Crash.* Available: www .thedoteaters.com/p3_stage6.php (accessed: April 16, 2009).
21. Burnham, *Supercade.*
22. Kelly, Kevin, and Howard Rheingold. 1993. "The Dragon Ate My Homework." *Wired.* 1.03 (July/August). Available: www.wired.com/wired/archive/1.03/muds.html (accessed: April 16, 2009).
23. "Active MMOG Subscriptions." MMOG Charts. Available: www.mmogchart.com/ Chart4.html (accessed: April 16, 2009).
24. Cohen, Patricia. 2009. "Video Game Becomes Spectator Sport." *New York Times,* April 11. Available: www.nytimes.com/2009/04/12/sports/othersports/12star.html?_r=2 (accessed: April 16, 2009).

Bonus Round 1:
Gamer Trivia

1. Nintendo Company was founded in the year _____.
   a. 1889
   b. 1929
   c. 1969
   d. 1989

2. _____ is the first popularized video game ever invented.
   a. *Tennis for Two*
   b. *Spacewar!*
   c. *Pong*
   d. *Donkey Kong*

3. _____, one of the first interactive computer games, opens with the line: "You are standing in an open field west of a white house, with a boarded front door. There is a small mailbox here."
   a. *Myst*
   b. *Final Fantasy*
   c. *Zork*
   d. *World of Warcraft*

4. Shigeru Miyamoto, the first member to be inducted into the Academy of Interactive Arts & Sciences Hall of Fame, is credited as creator of what game?
   a. *Pac-Man*
   b. *Civilization*
   c. *Final Fantasy*
   d. *Super Mario Bros.*

5. The cheat code "Up, Up, Down, Down, Left, Right, Left, Right, B, A, Start" allowed the player to get 30 extra lives in the classic game _____.
   a. *Zork*
   b. *Tetris*
   c. *Dance Dance Revolution*
   d. *Contra*

6. _____ is credited with being a landmark first person shooter (FPS) game.
   a. *Halo*
   b. *Quake*
   c. *Doom*
   d. *Counterstrike*

7. _____ is the best-selling PC video game of all time.
   a. *Pac-Man*
   b. *Grand Theft Auto*
   c. *The Sims*
   d. *Myst*

8. Disney's Web site is the most popular one for kids on the Internet; what game site was ranked #2 in 2005?
   a. www.neopets.com
   b. www.shockwave.com
   c. www.runescape.com
   d. www.clubpenguin.com

9. Which of the following legislators is *not* pushing for a law making it illegal to sell games to minors?
   a. Jack Thompson
   b. Edward Kennedy
   c. Joe Lieberman
   d. Hillary Rodham Clinton

10. Which of the following celebrities has endorsed a video game?
   a. Tony Hawk
   b. John Madden
   c. Tiger Woods
   d. All of the above

Sources:

1. Nintendo Company History. Available: www.nintendo.co.jp/corporate/outline/index.html (accessed: April 18, 2009).
2. Chaplin, Heather and Aaron Ruby. 2005. *Smartbomb: The Quest for Art, Entertainment, and Big Bucks in the Video Game Revolution.* New York: Algonquin Books.
3. GameSpy Hall of Fame. Available: http://archive.gamespy.com/legacy/halloffame/zork_a.shtm (accessed: April 18, 2009).
4. Academy of Interactive Arts & Sciences Hall of Fame. Available: www.interactive.org/awards/annual_awards.asp?idAward=1998 (accessed: April 18, 2009).
5. Cheat Code Guides. 2009. IGN. Available: www.cheatcodesguides.com/nes-cheats/contra (accessed: April 18, 2009).
6. Kushner, David. 2003. *Masters of Doom: How Two Guys Created an Empire and Transformed Pop Culture.* New York: Random House.
7. Morris, Chris. "Hello *Sims*, Goodbye *Myst*." *CNN Money*, March 28, 2002.
8. Kushner, David. "The Neopets Addiction." *Wired*, December 2005.
9. *Video Game Law Blog.* Available: www.davis.ca/community/blogs/video_games (accessed: April 18, 2009).
10. Gamestop. Available: www.gamestop.com (accessed: April 18, 2009).

Answers: 1: a, 1889; **2:** b, *Spacewar!* (1962, MIT); **3:** c, *Zork* (1977); **4:** d, *Super Mario Bros.* (Nintendo, 1985); **5:** d, *Contra* (Konami, 1986); **6:** c, *Doom* (id Software, 1993); **7:** c, *The Sims* (Maxis, 2000); **8:** a, www.neopets.com; **9:** b, Edward Kennedy; **10:** d, all of the above!

Chapter 2

Level 2: Video Games at the Library

Embracing Video Games at the Library

Libraries are about stories, and information, and access to stories and information, regardless of format. Video games must be regarded as a new, interactive, multimedia, three-dimensional (3D), digital format for conveying stories and information. Today's patrons are fast becoming format agnostic, as evidenced by the *Harry Potter* series. Eager to read the final volumes of the series, youth devoured print, audio, film, Internet, toy, and game components of the *Harry Potter* franchise (see Figure 2.1), and, when time between versions was too long, they became content creators, writing fan fiction, drawing fan art, and creating fan podcasts.

A sampling of responses by teens to the question, "Gaming at the library was..."

"Very fun. Definitely do it again sometime. I had a lot of fun playing *DDR [Dance Dance Revolution]* with my friend and meeting new people."

"A fun and enjoyable experience. I have never played *DDR* or *Guitar Hero*. I found them very fun and interesting at the same time. I was not very good at *DDR* at first, but I had fun trying to beat my high score. I really liked *Guitar Hero* because it's fun to play with the guitar."

"This is a great way to draw teens into the library. They will see it as a fun gathering place, not just an area to come and do homework. Maybe they will come across a book they like while here!!!"

"It was lots of fun. I think they should have it every week. Although, there should be a section devoted to games like *Soul Calibur.*"

Source: A compilation of responses from Get Your Game On! Videogame Free Play events at public libraries in Massachusetts from 2005–2008. Libraries may include: Agawam, Ashland, Belmont, Billerica, Brewster, Brookline, Cambridge, Carlisle, Chatham, Dedham, Florence, Franklin, Gloucester, Groton, Groveland, Hamilton-Wenham, Haverhill, Lawrence, Lincoln, Manchester, Medford, Melrose, Millis, Nantucket, Needham, Newton, North Attleboro, Norwell, Oxford, Scituate, Seekonk, Sharon, Springfield, Swampscott, Tyngsboro, Wakefield, Wellfleet, Wellsley, Weston, and/or Wilmington.

Figure 2.1. *Harry Potter* Formats

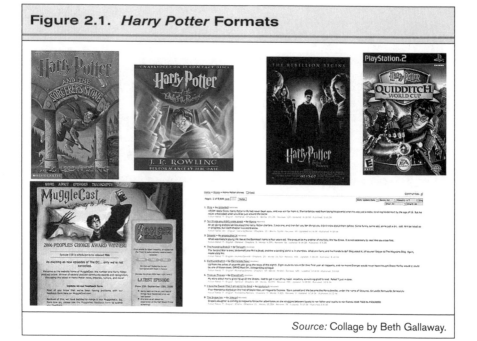

Source: Collage by Beth Gallaway.

Gaming is experiential; one cannot form a valid opinion about gaming without trying it. Parents thank librarians who offer video game programs for providing a social opportunity in a safe setting. Librarians even thank their colleagues for gathering teens in one space, curbing noise and behavioral issues. Teens themselves show their appreciation for their gaming experiences through simple and formal evaluations.

Video Game Ratings

Video games that opt into the Entertainment Software Association's (ESA) rating system carry ratings. Like film ratings, the game ratings process is voluntary. Games are labeled with one of seven icons assigned based on about 40 different criteria by an ESA board. Currently, only PC and console games carry ratings; Internet, cell phone, iPod, and PDA games remain unrated at the time of publication.

The ESA is the only U.S. organization dedicated exclusively to serving the business and public affairs needs of companies that publish computer and video games, defined as "games for videogame consoles, personal computers, and the Internet."[1] The ESA established the Entertainment Software Rating Board (ESRB) as a self-regulatory body in 1994;[2] the ESRB independently applies and enforces ratings, advertising guidelines, and online privacy principles adopted by the industry.

As games evolve, ratings adapt. In 2005, the E+10 rating was added, following a controversy about a pornographic cheat available for *Grand Theft Auto: San Andreas* (Rockstar Games, 2003). Rating criteria continue to evolve as new elements are introduced into gameplay. See Figures 2.2 and 2.3 for the ESRB ratings chart and content descriptors.

Figure 2.2. ESRB Ratings Chart

ESRB Rating Symbols

 EARLY CHILDHOOD
Titles rated **EC (Early Childhood)** have content that may be suitable for ages 3 and older. Contains no material that parents would find inappropriate.

 EVERYONE
Titles rated **E (Everyone)** have content that may be suitable for ages 6 and older. Titles in this category may contain minimal cartoon, fantasy or mild violence and/or infrequent use of mild language.

 EVERYONE 10+
Titles rated **E10+ (Everyone 10 and older)** have content that may be suitable for ages 10 and older. Titles in this category may contain more cartoon, fantasy or mild violence, mild language and/or minimal suggestive themes.

 TEEN
Titles rated **T (Teen)** have content that may be suitable for ages 13 and older. Titles in this category may contain violence, suggestive themes, crude humor, minimal blood, simulated gambling, and/or infrequent use of strong language.

 MATURE
Titles rated **M (Mature)** have content that may be suitable for persons ages 17 and older. Titles in this category may contain intense violence, blood and gore, sexual content and/or strong language.

 ADULTS ONLY
Titles rates **AO (Adults Only)** have content that should only be played by persons 18 years and older. Titles in this category may include prolonged scenes of intense violence and/or graphic sexual content and nudity.

 RATING PENDING
Titles listed as **RP (Rating Pending)** have been submitted to the ESRB and are awaiting final rating. (This symbol appears only in advertising prior to a game's release.)

Source: The ESRB ratings icons are registered trademarks of the Entertainment Software Association. Used with permission.

Figure 2.3. ESRB Content Descriptors

ESRB Content Descriptors

▶ **Alcohol Reference** – Reference to and/or images of alcoholic beverages
▶ **Animated Blood** – Discolored and/or unrealistic depictions of blood
▶ **Blood** – Depictions of blood
▶ **Blood and Gore** – Depictions of blood or the mutation of body parts
▶ **Cartoon Violence** – Violent actions involving cartoon-like situations and characters. May include violence where a character is unharmed after the action has been inflicted
▶ **Comic Mischief** – Depictions or dialogue involving slapstick or suggestive humor
▶ **Crude Humor** – Depictions or dialogue involving vulgar antics, including "bathroom" humor

(Cont'd.)

Figure 2.3. ESRB Content Descriptors *(Continued)*

ESRB Content Descriptors *(Cont'd.)*

▶ **Drug Reference** – Reference to and/or images of illegal drugs

▶ **Fantasy Violence** – Violent actions of a fantasy nature, involving human or non-human characters in situations easily distinguishable from real life

▶ **Intense Violence** – Graphic and realistic-looking depictions of physical conflict. May involve extreme and/or realistic blood, gore, weapons and depictions of human injury and death

▶ **Language** – Mild to moderate use of profanity

▶ **Lyrics** – Mild references to profanity, sexuality, violence, alcohol or drug use in music

▶ **Mature Humor** – Depictions or dialogue involving "adult" humor, including sexual references

▶ **Nudity** – Graphic or prolonged depictions of nudity

▶ **Partial Nudity** – Brief and/or mild depictions of nudity

▶ **Partial Nudity** – Brief and/or mild depictions of nudity

▶ **Real Gambling** – Player can gamble, including betting or wagering real cash or currency

▶ **Sexual Content** – Non-explicit depictions of sexual behavior, possibly including partial nudity

▶ **Sexual Themes** – References to sex or sexuality

▶ **Sexual Violence** – Depictions of rape or other violent sexual acts

▶ **Simulated Gambling** – Player can gamble without betting or wagering real cash or currency

▶ **Strong Language** – Explicit and/or frequent use of profanity

▶ **Strong Lyrics** – Explicit and/or frequent references to profanity, sex, violence, slcohol, or drug use in music

▶ **Strong Sexual Content** – Explicit and/or frequent depictions or sexual behavior, possibly including nudity

▶ **Suggestive Themes** – Mild provocative references or materials

▶ **Tobacco Reference** – Reference to and/or images of tobacco products

▶ **Use of Drugs** – The consumption or use of illegal drugs

▶ **Use of Alcohol** – The consumption of alcoholic beverages

▶ **Use of Tobacco** – The consumption of tobacco products

▶ **Violence** – Scenes involving aggressive conflict. May contain bloodless dismemberment

▶ **Violent References** – References to violent acts

Back to Top

NOTE:

When a content descriptor is preceded by the term **"Mild,"** it is intended to convey low frequency, intensity or severity of the content it modified.

Content descriptors are not intended to be a listing of every type of content one might encounter in the course of playing a game. For more detail about how ESRB assigns content descriptors, click here

Online Rating Notice

Online-enabled games carry the notice **"Online Interactions Not Rated by the ESRB."** This notice warns those who intend to play the game online about possible exposure to chat (text, audio, video) or other types of user-generated content (e.g., maps, skins) that have not been considered in the ESRB rating assignment

Source: The ESRB ratings icons are registered trademarks of the Entertainment Software Association. Used with permission.

The ESRB makes it increasingly easy to learn what games are rated. They publish an excellent poster and brochure titled "OK to Play," designed to explain ratings to vigilant parents, educators, and the concerned public. The search engine on their Web site allows searching by title, platform, and rating. In spring 2008, to facilitate sharing information about ratings, the ESRB created a widget so that anyone (game reviewers, Web site owners, bloggers) could install the ESRB search box on a Web site.

Video Games and Gender

It's a myth that video game play is dominated by men. According the ESA's most recent survey, 40 percent of gamers are female.[3] The girl games movement began in 1994, and, in 1996, the Psycho Men Slayers (PMS), an all-female *Quake* team, joined the annual LAN (local area network) party fray of QuakeCon.[4] The following year saw the launch of the GameGirlz Web site, and Henry Jenkins and Justine Cassell published a collection of essays on gender and video games titled *From Barbie to Mortal Kombat* (MIT Press, 1997). A 2003 survey by massively multiplayer online game (MMOG) player and enthusiast Nick Yee revealed that "Female players play *EverQuest* to build relationships, male players play *EverQuest* for achieving goals."[5]

> "The creation of something new is not accomplished by the intellect but by the play instinct acting from inner necessity. The creative mind plays with the objects it loves."
>
> – Carl Jung, psychologist, in *Psychological Types*

The video game industry may be today where the comics industry was 25 years ago: women portrayed stereotypically or with few girl heroes because, while boys primarily favor male heroes, girls are equally likely to identify with boys or girls. Part of *The Sims'* (EA, 2001) success as the best-selling game of all time is that it was favored by women and had a strong female representation on the game's design team. As more women design games, games will become more female friendly. Libraries of all types can play their part by allowing girls an opportunity to interact with technology in ways that they are comfortable—through expressing themselves, creating, and socializing. A recent *New York Times* article on computer use and gender showed that many cyberpioneers—innovators and entrepreneurs—are young women.[6]

Video Games and Ethnicity

In July 2006, University of British Columbia researcher Robert Parungao analyzed *Kung Fu* (Nintendo, 1985), *Warcraft III* (Blizzard, 2002), *Shadow Warrior* (Atari, 1997), and *Grand Theft Auto III* (Rockstar, 2001) for examples of racism in characters and storylines and came to the conclusion that video games are behind the times in positive portrayal of nonwhite characters, calling negative portrayals "blatant" in the games he played.[7] This is another case in which change has to come from within. As more minorities design games, games will become less racist, prejudiced, and biased.

Look for games with global locations as a setting, such as *Tiger Woods PGA World Tour* (EA Sports, 2008), in which characters and tournaments represent a variety of ethnicities and locations. Seek games in which the player has control over character creation and can create an avatar in one's own image, like *Rock Band* (Activision, 2008), or in which the character is an animal or vehicle that supersedes ethnicity. Finally, consider serious games that address the topic head on, like *Iced* (Breakthrough Productions, 2008; available online at www.icedgame.com).

The Serious Games Initiative is a video game design movement focused on creating games for education and training based on issues such as health, poverty, human rights, public policy, and the environment. Some examples include the following:

Ayiti: The Cost of Life (Gamelab, 2006). Available: www.costoflife.org (accessed: April 16, 2009). Simulation of a Haitian family struggling to make ends meet through making decisions about work, health care, education, and more (see Figure 2.4).

Figure 2.4. *Ayiti* Screenshot

Source: Global Kids. *Ayiti: The Cost of Life* (Gamelab, 2008). Available: www.gamelab.com/game/ayiti (accessed: February 3, 2009).

Darfur Is Dying (USC Interactive Media, 2006). Available: www.darfurisdying.com (accessed: April 16, 2009). Game focused on genocide in Darfur.

Free Rice (Free Rice, 2007). Available: www.free-rice.com (accessed: April 16, 2009). Players answer multiple choice vocabulary lessons to earn grains of rice that are donated to impoverished areas.

Iced: I Can End Deportation (BreakThrough Productions, 2007). Available: www.icedgame.com (accessed: April 16, 2009). Game about immigration and deportation.

Psychological Effects of Video Games

Violence

Fantasy and violence have been strong themes throughout the history of games. "There is an inherent competitive aggressiveness"[8] in any game; one plays to win. Content and effect of media are sources of constant battle as each generation struggles to understand the next. *Dungeons & Dragons* was once criticized for worship of the occult, violent behavior, and suicides, coming under fire like comic books, moving pictures, and pool halls in their times: Atari and Nintendo once had strict policies against violence. Atari's programmers were not allowed to harm a humanoid figure in any game, while Nintendo didn't condone the use of blood: In *Mortal Kombat* (Acclaim, 1992), for example, blood is green instead of red, and in *Perfect Dark* (Rare, 2000) programmers included a paintball mode. The option to tone down levels of violence and obscenity rests in the hands of users today. All the new consoles come with parental controls, and games like *Fallout 3* (Bethesda, 2008) have options for players to turn down the blood and change the dialogue.

> It is interesting to note that Atari, the first home video game system, and *Dungeons & Dragons*, a pencil and dice role-playing game, were born in the same year, 1972.

Penny Arcade is an irreverent Web comic that focuses its dark humor on the videogame playing experience. Creators Jerry Holkin and Mike Krahulik often take potshots at the game industry and media misconceptions of gaming as well. In this cartoon, they take a humorous look at claims that playing video games makes people more inclined to commit violent acts (see Figure 2.5).

The first violent video game was *Death Race* (Exidy, 1976).[9] This arcade game encouraged players to run over pedestrians for sport. The pedestrians were pixilated,

---

Figure 2.5. Video Game Violence

Source: Mike Krahulik and Jerry Holkins, 1998. "Video Violence." *Penny Arcade* (December 9). Available: www.penny-arcade.com/comic/1998/12/9/. Used with permission.

but the violence was present nonetheless. As the use and quality of graphics increased, the realism of the violence increased. *Mortal Kombat* (Acclaim, 1992), a street fighting game, is categorized as one of the most violent games, with moves such as tearing out an opponent's heart or pulling a spinal column out via the skull. In 2002, the arcade version of *Mortal Kombat* was ported to Sega and Nintendo consoles, and the first Congressional hearing about video game violence and its effects on children was held. In response, the software industry decided to moderate itself and created the ESRB.

> "Anti-violence advocates like Groseman and the many anti-gaming 'family-values' organizations are political actors, fighting for their own authority in the court of the media; it's not necessarily in their interest to present all the evidence openly."
>
> – Clive Thompson, quoted in Lucien King's *Game On: The History and Culture of Video Games*

Throughout the history of video games, single titles are used as an example of the content of games. Because games are just another format, librarians should examine them under the same lens as the other media they collect. Professional standards hold us to collecting a breadth and depth of materials appropriate to community interests, which may include books, movies, and music depicting violence, sex, and substance abuse. Like the ratings given to movies, the ESRB ratings can be a guide to finding the games appropriate for your collection and programs. An M rating is very similar to an R rating on a movie and should be treated the same: only recommended for ages 17 and up.

> Marc Prensky says it best in his book *Don't Bother Me, Mom—I'm Learning:* "…one thing is certain: absolutely no one can say, when all the complex factors in a single child's life are taken into account, whether any individual child will be negatively influenced overall."

There are correlations between teens who drive fast and teens who play racing games. Does this mean that the desire to drive fast is gained from the game or that racing games provide a safe environment for many teens to experience driving for the first time without endangering physical objects?

The incident at Columbine in 1999, recognized as the deadliest high school shooting ever, was initially blamed on violent video games, because the teenaged gunmen were players of *Doom* and *Quake*. The media scapegoating of violent video games prompted tech writer Jon Katz to moderate the "Voices From the Hellmouth" series on the Slashdot Web site in 1999. The forums were filled with posts composed by gamers responding to the reality and stigma of playing video games. Many youth said that feelings of wanting to murder classmates didn't stem from wearing a trench coat, from listening to Marilyn Manson's music, or from playing shoot 'em up style games.

It is interesting to note that an estimated 80 percent of the news coverage about video games focus on M rated games. Yet only 15 percent of games sold in 2006 were rated M for mature or higher. An overwhelming majority of titles produced are suitable for ages 16 and under.[10] For more information about some teen-appropriate games, see the Level 5 Strategy Guide: Recommended Gaming Collections.

Some research has demonstrated a correlation between violence and video games. It should be noted that these studies are most often done with college age males.

Researchers Lawrence Kutner, Cheryl Olson, and Eugene Beresin at Harvard Medical School undertook a series of studies with youth and their parents to examine the effects of all types of games, and what they found about *Grand Theft Auto* may surprise you. Their survey of 1,200 middle school students found that the youth were adept at recognizing that the violence was fantasy and that some actions carried out in the game were not actions to be repeated in real life. Only 6 percent of students surveyed reported that they did not play violent video games. Reasons for playing include the lure of the forbidden, but the primary reason was "to get my anger out," followed by "to relieve stress."[11] Students clearly experience, and can articulate, the cathartic effect of such games. Kutner and Olson discuss these findings further in their book *Grand Theft Childhood: The Surprising Truth About Violent Video Games and What Parents Can Do* (Simon and Schuster, 2008), which debunks myths about cause/effect relationships between violent acts and video games.

A brain-imaging study from Indiana University, published in November 2006, suggests that playing violent video games may indeed change the way a person feels and acts. A group of 44 13–17 year olds (two-thirds male) were randomly broken into two groups playing video games for 30 minutes at a time; one group played the first person shooter and WWII simulation *Medal of Honor* (EA, 1999), and the other played *Need for Speed: Underground* (EA, 2003), a nonviolent car chase game. Researchers then used functional magnetic resonance imaging to look at the teens' brains. "Researchers found that teenagers who played a violent videogame exhibited increased activity in a part of the brain that governs emotional arousal. The same teens showed decreased activity in the parts of the brain involved in focus, inhibition and concentration."[12]

For every study that shows a benefit to playing video games, there is another that shows the negative effects of video game violence. Lt. Col. Dave Grossman, founder of the Killology Research Group and author (with Gloria DeGaetano) of *Stop Teaching Our Kids to Kill: A Call to Action Against TV, Movie and Video Game Violence* (1999), links school shootings and, more important, the shooting accuracy of young gunmen, to first person shooter games despite the consensus of many researchers that it is far more likely that youth with violent or destructive tendencies are drawn to violent video games. A video game is a tool, like a knife, that can be used with good or ill intent.

If video games are violent and may make players more aggressive, why then are video games valid materials for libraries to review, purchase, circulate,

> Not sure what to believe about video games and violence? Don't have time to read lengthy articles? Check out PBS's "Culture Shock: You Decide: Video Game Violence" (www.pbs.org/wgbh/cultureshock/provocations/videogames/warning.html) for an interactive introduction to the role and uses of vicarious violence.

and build programming around? The good outweighs the bad. Researchers John Beck, Mitchell Wade,[13] Henry Jenkins III, James Paul Gee,[14] Constance Steinkeuler,[15] and Kurt Squire[16] have found substantial evidence that video games contribute to learning and literacy and have value well beyond improved hand–eye coordination. Even the "worst" video game may incorporate pattern recognition, map reading,

reading and writing, physics, math, history, geography, exercise, social skills, critical thinking, and problem solving. Best of all, the interactivity encourages creativity and thinking. The gameplay experience of collecting, interpreting, evaluating, and applying information has taught useful skills to unsuspecting gamers. Henry Jenkins III,[17] professor of Comparative Media Studies at MIT, argues that video games teach players to explore, create, socialize, bond, strategize, and share information.

> "Play permits the child to resolve in symbolic form unsolved problems of the past and to cope directly or symbolically with present concerns. It is also his more significant tool for preparing himself for the future and its tasks."
>
> – Bruno Bettelheim, child psychologist, in *A Good Enough Parent: A Book on Childrearing*

In *The Uses of Enchantment*, Jungian psychologist Bruno Bettelheim[18] makes a valid case for the use of stories that involve danger and violence to impart lessons and to offer catharsis to even the very young. Similarly, Steven Johnson's[19] *Everything Bad Is Good for You* examines a compelling argument for how today's television and video games make us smarter by making our brains think and process information in new ways.

Addiction

In August 2005, a South Korean man collapsed at a Japanese Internet gaming cafe after playing an MMOG for 50 hours straight. The government of South Korea reacted by enforcing time limits for play based on logins and created over 40 treatment programs to deal with video game and Internet addiction. Like other addictions, excessive play is a problem for only a minority of the population. An MMOG takes time to learn and level up, and spending hours a day at it is not unusual unless food, sleep, work, chores, and/or school are forfeited to play. Like a good book is gripping, some games are more "un-put-down-able" than others.

Playing games in a group setting may encourage breaks and result in less time spent gaming. Gamers who play in libraries may be subjected to more structure, limits, and rules than when they play at home. Most libraries impose time limits on computer use, so playing a game in a library rarely involves unregulated screen time; many players means lots of rotation and turn-taking. As in everything else in life, balance is key.

Pain Relief

In 2006, researchers at the University of Maryland studied pain tolerance in children while they played video games. Sixty children immersed their hands in ice water. Children playing a game with the opposite hand were able to withstand the cold and pain for 400 percent longer than those who did not.[20] Another study examining nondrug pain management found that music, games, and cartoons are effective distractions from health-related discomforts.[21]

Physical Effects of Video Games

Repetitive Strain Injuries

Excessive text messaging, computer mouse use, or video game button mashing can cause repetitive strain injury to the thumb. Tagged "Nintenditis," symptoms include swelling and pain at the base of the thumb. Although the new wireless kinetic controllers can be manipulated with a subtle flick of the wrist, gamers playing *Wii Sports* (Nintendo, 2006) treat the six-inch remote as if it were a full-sized tennis racquet, golf club, or baseball bat. Muscles unaccustomed to such movements may well be sore the next day. Although the Wii prompts the player to take a break by opening a separate window at intervals (as shown in Figure 2.6), some players get very wrapped up in the self-competitive nature of the games and don't cease when they should. Doing any repetitive activity for too long is going to result in discomfort; injury from playing a game is not much different from eye strain from too much continuous screen viewing, sore thumbs from too much texting, damaged eardrums from too much headphone use with loud music, or knee damage from too much stretching. Sometimes damage to the surrounding environment occurs. The debut of the Nintendo Wii led to a number of Web sites (like that in Figure 2.7) and blog posts concerned with Wii injuries and appliance breakage.

Epilepsy-like symptoms caused by on-screen media featuring pulsing flashes of light and color have been documented since 1952 to induce seizures in children. One particular episode of the *Pokémon* television series triggered an epidemic of seizures in 1997, resulting in a mass of emergency room visits.[22]

Video Games and the Obesity Epidemic

Youth gaming is so extensive that physicians are concerned that this generation is the first in history to have a lower life expectancy than their parents due to inactive lifestyles and poor eating habits. Professor Arlette C. Perry, chairwoman of the exercise and sports-sciences department at the University of Miami School of Education,

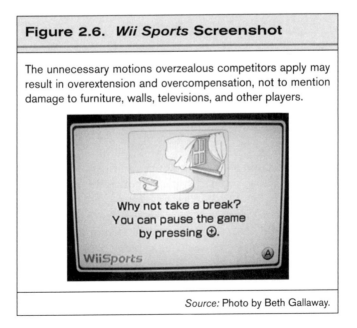

Figure 2.6. *Wii Sports* Screenshot

The unnecessary motions overzealous competitors apply may result in overextension and overcompensation, not to mention damage to furniture, walls, televisions, and other players.

Source: Photo by Beth Gallaway.

Figure 2.7. Wii Have a Problem Screenshot

Source: Wii Have a Problem. Available: www.wiihaveaproblem.com (accessed: April 16, 2009).

conducted a study that found playing video games provides a slight physical workout and is not nearly as sedentary a nonactivity as watching television. *Tekken 3* (Namco, 1998) is "equal to walking about two miles per hour metabolically."[23]

A new generation of video games encourages couch potatoes (and mouse potatoes) to get off their derrières and onto their feet for gameplay that includes physical activity. They range from dancing games performed on floor pads to drumming games. Sony's PlayStation EyeToy uses a camera to read motion and light, eliminating the need for a physical controller and forcing the player to stand up and move, mimicking such actions as skateboarding, chopping vegetables, sawing logs, and playing a variety of sports. A game like *Guitar Hero 3* (RedOctane, 2007) that

Figure 2.8. Guitar Heroes

Source: Photo by Beth Gallaway.

requires the player to stand and play (see Figure 2.8) burns more calories than a sedentary game like *Katamari Damacy* (Namco, 2004).

Dance Dance Revolution (Konami, 1998), or *DDR* as it's known in the vernacular, is a video game in which players dance similar to the old handheld electronic pattern game *Simon* (Milton Bradley, 1978). Distributed for play on Xbox, PlayStation, and Wii consoles, *DDR* gained popularity in Japan in 1998 as a coin-operated arcade game. To play, players stand on a padded mat instead of holding a controller. Music plays while the screen shows a pattern of arrows pointing left, right, up, and/or down. The pad has matching arrows; the goal is to step on the pad's corresponding buttons as the vertically scrolling arrows on screen pass a horizontal row at the top of the display (see Figure 2.9).

With more complicated songs or levels, steps combine, and the player might have to step on more than one arrow at a time or in fast succession. Points are awarded for speed and accuracy and are combined with the number of correct steps in a row to add up to a letter grade of AAA-E. Miss enough steps and the song ends; perfect your timing and earn bonuses and cheers. Each song has four levels of difficulty and six levels of speed. New songs are unlocked as a reward for progressive improvement and higher scores.

A 2005 Penn State University study on the cardiovascular benefits of *DDR* in children aged 12 to 16 recorded heart rates between 100 and160 beats per minute.[24] Hawaii uses *DDR* in at least one school district,[25] and the West Virginia Department

Figure 2.9. *DDR* Screenshot

DDR players follow directional arrows, using their feet to step on a nine-square gridded pad as corresponding arrows scroll on a screen.
Source: Photo by Beth Gallaway.

of Education installed *DDR* in 157 middle schools in 2006,[26] with a plan in place to put DDR in 1,500 schools by the end of 2010 as part of the physical education program. In fact, "perform simple dance sequences using smooth transitions in speed, level, and direction in time to music" is a criteria in the Fifth Grade Physical Education Content Standards and Objectives.[27] Finally, in California, the San Joaquin Valley credits incorporation of DDR and a stationary bicycling racing game with raising the number of students passing the statewide fitness test[28] (see Figure 2.10).

DDR requires visual literacy—the player must "read" the symbols on the screen to figure out where to put his or her feet. *DDR* improves visual and aural pattern recognition skills. Based on the hypothesis that "matching movements to visual and rhythmic auditory cues...may strengthen neural networks involved in reading and attention and thereby improve student outcomes," a 2005 study confirmed a positive relationship between the number of *DDR* sessions completed by sixth graders with attention deficit hyperactivity disorder and the gains made on the West Virginia Receptive Coding and Finger Sense Recognition subtests that are part of the state's reading and writing battery to measure reading impairment.[29]

DDR and other rhythm games like *Rock Band* and *Guitar Hero* appeal to kinetic and musical learners, as defined by Howard Gardner's research on multiple intelligences.[30] Successful gameplay relies on a combination of watching, listening, and moving. Traditionally about books and quiet, libraries may not appear to be the most appealing spaces for hands-on types of games; *DDR* programs can be a way to

Figure 2.10. *DDR* Players

At a glance, even the casual observer can see that *DDR* is a calorie-burning aerobic activity as players become winded, sweaty, and aromatic.

Source: Photo by Beth Gallaway.

diversify services. Songs in the games are from all around the world and include traditional music styles, such as samba, in addition to rock and pop from a range of time periods. Characters featured on screen reflect both genders and a variety of ethnicities. Both of these features increase the players' exposure to music from different cultures and generations.

The PlayStation 2 has a camera accessory in lieu of a controller to encourage players to stand and move; the camera uses light and motion sensors to read kinetic movement. The Nintendo Wii, with its wand controllers, demands an upright position and active use of one's limbs to play a variety of games.

In 2008, Nintendo introduced *Wii Fit*, a series of balance and fitness games with a controller reminiscent of a step aerobic stair tread. Games for the *Wii Fit* Balance Board are more like productivity software with a personal fitness trainer component: yoga, dancing, skiing, and soccer are featured. Other games include *Shaun White Snowboarding* (Ubisoft, 2008) and *Wii Music* (Nintendo, 2008) in which the Balance Board becomes the bass drum kick pedal.

The Benefits of Video Games at the Library

Often, "video games" in the same sentence with "libraries" raises eyebrows. Much of the information we receive about games from the mainstream media is negative, and we have seen that some games are violent, addictive, and stereotypical to women or minorities.

Many public libraries have mission statements with words like "educational," "recreational," "all ages," and "diversity." Gaming service, programs, and collections can fulfill a library's mission to meet the educational and recreational needs of its users of all ages. Teens are perceived as the primary users of video games, with a reported 97 percent of them playing on a regular basis.[31] Take into account that games include not just first person shooters but also word games and online chess and card games, and it is apparent that more middle-aged women than teenaged boys are playing. The average age of the gamer is 35 and rising, and 26 percent of gamers are over age 50, the most famous of the senior crowd being Old Grandma Hardcore, a 70+ year old gaming grandmother whose gaming experiences have been highlighted in her grandson's blog, resulting in an invitation to E3 and a spotlight on MTV.[32]

Eli Neiburger, author of *Gamers... in the Library?! The Why, What, and How of Videogame Tournaments for All Ages* (ALA Editions, 2007), hosts a number of year-round gaming programs and tournaments at the Ann Arbor (MI) District Library, making it the premiere video gaming library in the United States. Neiburger analogizes game programs for teens to storytimes for children. Both are entertaining, educational social activities that bring new users to the library to build community. Libraries shouldn't be concerned that teens may not check out books at library programs any more than they should be concerned that storytime attendees may not check out books; libraries present nonbook-related programs all the time for other age groups.

The Gamer Generation™ Characteristics

A generation is defined by a series of shared experiences that help shape peoples' perceptions of the world. The generations of children born in the 1980s and 1990s have several experiences that are associated with video games. Some gamer characteristics are related to their developmental needs as children, teens, and young adults. However, some things are universal. Technology is one key factor in a generation, and the gamer generation shares a familiarity with personal computers, cell phones, and the Internet. Libraries have helped this generation by providing public computers for research and personal use. Games play an important role in the development of the technology, because it is the game companies that push computers to their maximum capacity and drive money toward the development of faster and better computers and computer systems. Many breakthroughs in artificial intelligence were the result of using game software. In many ways, today's games give us glimpses of the future of everyday technology about ten years down the road.

Playing a game involves a series of choices based on one's environment. Unlike the school experience in which facts are in many cases the main focus, the game places players in real world situations, with the knowledge that there is a way out. This trains gamers to use trial and error to solve problems and incorporates real world strategies to solve problems. In the book *Got Game*, John Beck and Mitchell Wade write about how this impacts the business world: "[Gamers] have a systematically different way of working. They choose systematically different skills to learn and different ways to learn them. They desire systematically different goals in life. The way that members of this generation think about their careers, their companies, and their coworkers is a long way from what boomers have come to expect."[33]

Gamers are risk takers, because video games set up a series of problems and set the player in the world with the knowledge that "you can solve this." When faced with challenges, gamers tend to enjoy solving problems within the big picture. They work best collaboratively: fixing their own problems and creating their own solutions.

The Internet plays a large role in the lives of gamers. Their friend structure is not organized geographically but rather by interest. Online communities play a large role in gamers' social development, and with online games they are able to connect with others who are similar to themselves. As in other social groups, there are basic requirements that must be met to be included in the online group: the abilities to understand the social rules of the environment and to respect fellow players.

One thing that is unique to this generation is that members do not passively consume media. Gamers take the environments they love and re-create them in new forms, adding to the development of literature, art, and technology. Gamers are used to collaborating not just to play the game but to improve the game by creating fan fiction, fan art, machinima and music videos, and new games.

Machinima is the art of creating short films from video game clips. The name comes from "machine" plus "cinema": film created with a machine.

Players film their gameplay with video capture tools provided in the game by the designers, or with third-party screen capture software, and then edit clips to tell a story, adding dialogue, subtitles, music, and special effects as necessary. The most famous machinima is probably *Red vs. Blue*, created with *Halo* (Microsoft, 2001), which involved filming soldiers standing around and adding humorous (and sometimes offensive) voiceover dialogue.

Machinima movies are featured on the following Web sites:

Academy of Machinima Arts & Sciences. Available: www.machinima.org (accessed: April 16, 2009); contains machinima examples and FAQs (the Academy hosts a festival, with entries posted online at http://festival .machinima.org/)

Koinup. Available: www.koinup.com/on-videos (accessed: April 16, 2009); features machinima from games like *The Sims* and virtual worlds like *Second Life*

Red vs. Blue. Available: http://rvb.roosterteeth.com (accessed: April 16, 2009); popular sitcom created from *Halo/Halo 2*

This Spartan Life. Available: www.thisspartanlife.com (accessed: April 16, 2009); machinima talk show created from Halo

Warcraft Movies. Available: www.warcraftmovies.com (accessed: April 16, 2009); features *World of Warcraft* machinima

Gamers are extremely social. They need opportunities to share their knowledge, have their opinions listened to, and contribute to the community. Watching teens assist one another in figuring out how to play *Guitar Hero* and *DDR* in libraries in New England has been very enlightening. They apply social skills and teamwork skills in addition to improving through practice and repeated play.

> "You can discover more about a person in an hour of play than in a year of conversation."
> – Plato, Greek philosopher

Gamers are collaborative. In fact, 51 percent of gamers play with another person, and 25 percent play with someone else online![34] They help their peers improve their gameplay, even in the midst of competition. They share controllers. They play in social groups, physically and online. They impose self-regulation to make sure everyone has a turn to try the game.

Gamers are used to being the heroes and experts of their game worlds. In the real world, they use this to be game experts. All of this helps define the generation but is not characteristic of any specific person. Each gamer is different and experiences games differently. In early childhood, children use play to explore the different roles and responsibilities they will have as adults. Teens use games to try on different personas and escape to a world where they have an equal opportunity to do the things they want. Adults play games for fun, but fun is not the driving force behind why people play. Richard M. Ryan's 2006 survey of 1,000 gamers revealed that the psychological "pull" of games may be due to their capacity to "engender feelings of autonomy, competence, and relatedness." These feelings not only motivate further play but "also can be experienced as enhancing psychological wellness, at least short-term."[35]

Gamers are competitive. While there is some playful competition in the form of teasing or praising friends about their scores, most focus on competing against themselves to better their own scores.

Developmental Needs of Teens

In the past many games were simple, and most of the games adults think of are very simple in nature. However, since the development of complexity in games, today's children, teens, and young adults aren't playing the same games as the average gamer. One thing to know about today's gamers is that they are just normal kids. Just as people have different tastes in reading material and movie genres, gamers do, too. Many game elements meet developmental needs of teens, and libraries can host programs to facilitate those needs being met.

Not every game meets all seven of the key teen developmental needs defined by National Middle School Association,[36] but *DDR* and other dancing games certainly do. The group play and turn-taking in *DDR* encourage positive social interaction with adults and peers. The rules of the game enforce structure and clear limits, as do the library behavioral guidelines enforced during the program. The game itself requires physical activity.

In *DDR*, once the basic steps are mastered, players can select how to press the buttons—using their toe or heel, dropping down to slap a button with a hand, spinning when a series of combination steps appears. They can alter the pace, direction, and appearance of the arrows on the screen. They can elect to play in a choreography mode that allows gamers to set their own moves to a particular song, resulting in creative expression.

Improved gameplay over a short time period results in feelings of competence and achievement. An intergenerational program or one hosted by a school or in lieu of physical education classes results in meaningful participation by families, schools, and communities. Finally, the act of playing allows teens to define themselves in new ways: "gamer," "ddrfreak," "winner" (Figure 2.11), "newbie," "expert," and even "physically fit."

The Developmental Assets

The midwestern applied social science research organization, the Search Institute®, has been dedicated to positive adolescent development that produces healthy, happy

Figure 2.11. *DDR* Winner!

Source: Photo by Beth Gallaway.

contributing members of society since 1958. It has established 40 Developmental Assets® for adolescents[37] that many youth-oriented organizations, including the Young Adult Library Services Association, implement in their work. The assets are divided into two groups, external (created by experiences through outside sources) and internal (reflective of internal growth), of four categories (Support, Boundaries and Expectations, Empowerment, and Positive Values). A variety of games meet the Developmental Assets in a myriad of ways.

The first category is Support. Parents can provide support to their teens by becoming actively involved in helping them succeed in school. Parents can build this asset by limiting the time spent playing games and by monitoring what games their children play. Family support can also come in the form of a parent or guardian signing a permission slip allowing a teen to participate in a game tournament. Showing concern for a child's whereabouts is a show of support. Support comes not just from blood relatives; in fact, the Search Institute's guide states that a teen needs three adult mentors who are not relatives. Playing games together formally, such as in a library program, allows teens to see librarians in a whole new light. Playing games together online allows teens to be experts and mentors to adults new to the game arena. Positive communication is another Support asset that can be cultivated through families playing games together.

Boundaries and Expectations are established and maintained through the rules of a game, including physical constraints and the legal policies players agree to, such as end user license agreements and terms of service. When in a formal game program or tournament, another level of rules is required (tournament style play and turn-taking), in addition to the regular library behavior guidelines.

Empowerment is fostered because the community shows that it values youth. Youth are used as resources. Listening to teens' suggestions for what kinds of gaming magazines to subscribe to, polling gamers to determine what games to buy, and allowing teens to run a gaming tournament are all models of empowering youth by acknowledging their expertise in this area.

Library programming centered on games provides a constructive use of time doing something creative and physical that enforces the idea that the library is a fun place to be. Basing a reader's advisory board on a game, hosting a fan fiction or machinima contest, and supporting players with strategy guides and magazines encourage reading for pleasure.

Games incorporate many skills that demonstrate a commitment to learning, including reading, problem solving, critical thinking, music, math, and employing the scientific method. There is an educational aspect inherent to all games, and gamers learn that practice results in improvement.

Games instill Positive Values, such as responsibility, because they require players to work together in groups known as "guilds" or "clans"; each member has a role to play. MMOGs that bring together people from all over the world foster empathy, caring, equality, and social justice through relationships formed, and playing such games from other countries that feature a multicultural cast or viewpoint provides exposure to other cultures. Abstinence is perhaps the least talked about asset in the

Positive Values category; it is much safer to live vicariously through a game character than to experiment with dangerous activities in real life, and games like *The Sims* provide valuable simulations to safely experiment in.

Games require planning and decision making when turn-taking and selecting, demand conflict resolution skills to accomplish teamwork, and build self-esteem—all social competencies. Identity is defined through simulations, and interpersonal competence can be established through gameplay. Positive communication is yet another asset that can be cultivated through games.

Games and Learning and Literacy

James Paul Gee (in *What Video Games Have to Teach Us About Learning and Literacy*, Palgrave McMillan, 2003) defines 32 learning principles inherent in games, including risk-tasking in a "safe" environment, the rewards practice, use of affinity groups, probing cycles, situated meaning, self-knowledge, and identity formation. Hand–eye coordination is the most common skill connected to video games.

Beth Israel Medical Center in New York City, in conjunction with the National Institute on Media and the Family, studied 303 surgeons participating in a laparoscopic surgical procedure training course that included video games. Researchers found that surgeons who played video games immediately before the training drill completed it an average of 11 seconds faster than those who did not. Any errors committed during the training lengthened the time it took to complete the task—indicating that faster finishers made fewer mistakes.[38] The results supported findings from a small study conducted by Rosser in 2003, which showed that doctors who grew up playing video games tended to be more efficient and less error-prone in laparoscopic training drills.[39] Finally, games like *Super Monkey Ball* (Nintendo, 2008), an iPhone game that forces players to use both hands equally while tilting the screen (see Figure 2.12), can help improve surgeons' skills by strengthening their nondominant-hand dexterity.

Other positive qualities that video games foster include mentoring and leadership skills, critical thinking skills, problem solving skills, creativity, high self-esteem, loyalty, teamwork, and calculated, strategic risk taking. Video games also teach pattern recognition, incorporate reading and writing, are based on real physics, integrate math and economics, provide historical context, require geography and map reading skills, and develop social skills.

Gaming reinforces new forms of literacy.[40] Today's students may no longer be proficient with reading, writing, and arithmetic but must expose knowledge, employ information, express ideas compellingly, and practice ethics on the Internet. How do new literacies relate to the game environment? Let's look at information gathering, which goes beyond just locating information and includes the ability to understand and explain found information regardless of its format, evaluate information, and organize information.

In *Everything Bad Is Good for You*, Steven Johnson maps out the objectives for navigating *Zelda: The Wind Waker* (Nintendo, 2002), one example of a popular game developed for Nintendo's GameCube:

Figure 2.12. *Super Monkey Ball*

Source: Photo by Beth Gallaway.

1. Your ultimate goal is to rescue your sister.
2. To do this, you need to defeat the villain Ganon.
3. To do this, you need to obtain legendary weapons.
4. To locate the weapons, you need the pearl of Din.
5. To get the pearl of Din, you need to cross the ocean.
6. To cross the ocean, you need to find a sailboat.
7. To do all the above, you need to stay alive and healthy.
8. To do all of the above, you need to move the controller.[41]

This process of evaluating the game requires that the player prioritize what actions to take and then behave appropriately for the situation. The game sets up a series of problems for the player to solve, and as time progresses the character gains knowledge, experience, and the things needed to rescue his sister.

Employing information includes not simple math computation and measurement, but analysis and application of numbers. A game like *RollerCoaster Tycoon 3* (Hasbro, 2004), a popular roller coaster building simulation game, is really an economics game about running an amusement park. In this game, crowds, which provide income, depend on everything from attractions to concessions to restrooms (see Figure 2.13).

Expressing ideas compellingly means having the ability to take the information gathered and employed and convey that information to someone else. Mechanics matter, creativity and efficiency are highly rated, and the expression can be in any or multiple formats: text, images, audio, and/or video.

Figure 2.13. *RollerCoaster Tycoon 3* Screenshot

Source: RollerCoaster Tycoon. Available: www.atari.com/rollercoastertycoon/us/gameinfo/coasters (accessed: April 16, 2009).

The popularity, breadth, and depth of Web sites like *World of Warcraft* Movies (www.warcraftmovies.com), YouTube (www.youtube.com), FanFiction (www.fanfiction.net), and *The Sims Resource* (http://thesimsresource.com) demonstrate the prevalence of remixing in video game culture. Remixing comes in several forms. Modding (derived from "modifying") is the alteration of game content to make the game do something is wasn't intended to do by changing data contained in the game. Examples include using the game engine of *Doom* to insert Barney the purple dinosaur in place of the aliens and exporting a red couch from *The Sims* into a graphics program, recoloring it to be blue, and importing it back into the game. Running a code within the game to change the outcome or enhance the experience is a little different, more exploitative, and is considered hacking. An add-on is a piece of user-created software that allows the user to extend and customize the game.

Fan fictions are stories about characters created or owned by someone else. For example, a fiction piece could be created by recording the actions it took to accomplish the Rage Fire Chasm quest of the *World of Warcraft* by guild members in a detailed saga. Another example of a piece of fan fiction is *World of Workcraft* (see Figure 2.14) in which characters from the popular game *World of Warcraft* engage in their own game: a simulation of working in an office.

Machinima is the art of filmmaking through recording video game playing, editing clips together to create a story, and inserting an audio soundtrack. Machinima may be short films, music videos, commercials, or even periodic episodes. More information about serving gamers by harnessing content creation tools is provided in Level 3.

Figure 2.14. *World of Workcraft* **Screenshot**

Source: Available: www.wegame.com/watch/World_of_Workcraft (accessed: December 20, 2008).

Notes

1. Entertainment Software Association. "About the Entertainment Software Association" (2009). Available: www.theesa.com/about/index.asp (accessed: April 16, 2009).
2. Entertainment Software Ratings Board. "About ESRB" (2009). Available: www.esrb.org/about/index.jsp (accessed: April 16, 2009).
3. Entertainment Software Association. "2008 Essential Facts about the Computer and Video Game Industry" (2008). Available: www.theesa.com/facts/pdfs/ESA_EF_2008.pdf (accessed: April 16, 2009).
4. King, Brad, and John Borland. 2003. *Dungeons and Dreamers: The Rise of Computer Game Culture from Geek to Chic.* New York: McGraw Hill Osborne Media.
5. Yee, Nicholas. "The Norrathian Scrolls: A Study of EverQuest" (version 2.5; 2001). Available: www.nickyee.com/eqt/report.html (accessed: April 18, 2009).
6. Rosenbloom, Stephanie. "Sorry Boys, This Is Our Domain." *New York Times,* February 21, 2008. Available: www.nytimes.com/2008/02/21/fashion/21webgirls.htm (accessed: April 16, 2009).
7. Parungoa, Robert. 2006. "Asianness in Video Games." Sociology Department, University of British Columbia.
8. King and Borland, *Dungeons and Dreamers,* p. 5.
9. Wikipedia. "Death Race (1976 game)" (2009). Available: http://en.wikipedia.org/wiki/Death_Race_(1976_game) (accessed: April 16, 2009).
10. Entertainment Software Association. "Essential Facts About the Computer and Game Industry" (2008). Available: http://theesa.com/facts/pdfs/ESA_EF_2008.pdf (accessed: April 16, 2009).
11. Olson, C.K., L.A. Kutner, and E.V. Beresin. 2007. "Children and Video Games: How Much Do We Know?" *Psychiatric Times* (October). Available: www.psychiatrictimes.com/display/article/10168/54191 (accessed: April 16, 2009).

12. Springen, Karen. "This Is Your Brain on Violence." MSNBC (November 28, 2006). Available: www.newsweek.com/id/44720 (accessed: April 16, 2009).

13. Beck, John C. and Mitchell Wade. 2005. *Got Game: How the Gamer Generation Is Reshaping Business Forever.* Cambridge, MA: Harvard Business School Press.

14. Gee, James Paul. 2003. *What Video Games Have to Teach Us About Learning and Literacy.* Hampshire, England: Palgrave McMillan.

15. Steinkuehler, C. 2007. "Massively Multiplayer Online Gaming as a Constellation of Literacy Practices." *eLearning* 4, no. 3: 297–318. Available: website.education.wisc.edu/steinkuehler/mmogresearch.html (accessed: April 16, 2009).

16. Squire, Kurt. *Replaying History: Learning World History Through Playing Civilization III.* Available: www.website.education.wisc.edu/kdsquire/dissertation.html (accessed: April 16, 2009).

17. Jenkins, Henry. "The Video Game Revolution: Reality Bytes: Eight Myths About Video Games Debunked." PBS (2006). Available: www.pbs.org/kcts/videogamerevolution/impact/myths.html (accessed: April 16, 2009).

18. Bettleheim, Bruno. 1976. *The Uses of Enchantment: The Meaning and Importance of Fairy Tales.* New York: Knopf.

19. Johnson, Steven. 2005. *Everything Bad Is Good for You: How Today's Pop Culture Is Actually Making Us Smarter.* New York: Riverhead, p. 50.

20. Jana, Renee. "Harnessing the Power of Video Games." MSNBC (August 22, 2006). Available: www.msnbc.msn.com/id/14468654 (accessed: April 16, 2009).

21. Bauman, B. and J. McManus, Jr. 2005. "Pediatric Pain Management in the Emergency Department." *Emergency Medicine Clinics of North America* 23, no. 2: 393–414.

22. CNN. "Japanese Cartoon Triggers Seizures in Hundreds of Children." CNN (December 1997). Available: www.cnn.com/WORLD/9712/17/video.seizures.update (accessed: April 16, 2009).

23. Perry, Arlette and Xuewen Wang. 2006. "Metabolic and Physiologic Responses to Video Game Play in 7- to 10-Year-Old Boys." *Archives of Pediatric and Adolescent Medicine* 160: 411–415.

24. Yang, S.P. and G. Graham. 2005. "Project GAME (Gaming Activities for More Exercise)." *Research Quarterly for Exercise and Sport* 76 (suppl 1): A-96.

25. Schiesel, Seth. "P.E. Classes Turn to Video Game That Works Legs." *New York Times*, April 30, 2007. Available: www.nytimes.com/2007/04/30/health/30exer.html (accessed: April 16, 2009).

26. Patton, Zach. "Dance Dance Obesity Revolution!" Governing.com (January 26, 2006). Available: http://13thfloor.governing.com/2006/01/dance_dance_obe.html (accessed: April 16, 2009).

27. West Virginia Department of Education. West Virginia Board of Education Policy 2520.6: 21st Century Physical Education 5-12 Content Standards and Objectives for West Virginia Schools (March 19, 2007). Available: wvde.state.wv.us/policies/p2520.6_ne.doc-2007-03-19 (accessed: April 16, 2009).

28. Yi, Matthew. "Playing Games in School / Using Videos Helps Students Love to Learn Their Lessons." *The San Francisco Chronicle*, February 20, 2006. Available: www.sfgate.com/c/a/2006/02/20/BUG86H9SBD1.DTL (accessed: April 16, 2009).

29. Yang and Graham, "Project Game."

30. Gardner, Howard. "Frames of Mind: The Theory of Multiple Intelligences." (1993). Available: www.howardgardner.com/Papers/documents/MI%20at%2025%20%204-15-08%202.doc (accessed: April 16, 2009).

31. Lenhart, Amanda, et al. "Teens, Video Games and Civics." Pew Internet and American Life Project (September 2008). Available: http://pewinternet.org/PPF/r/263/report_display.asp (accessed: April 16, 2009).

32. Stehilaire, T. "Old Grandma Hardcore." Available: http://oghc.blogspot.com (accessed: April 16, 2009).

33. Beck and Wade, *Got Game*.

34. Entertainment Software Association, "Essential Facts About the Computer and Game Industry."

35. Ryan, Richard M. 2006. "The Motivational Pull of Video Games: A Self-Determination Theory Approach." *Motivation and Emotion* 30, no. 4 (December).

36. National Middle School Association Research Summaries. "Young Adolescents Developmental Needs" (1996). Available: www.nmsa.org/Research/ResearchSummaries/Developmental Characteristics/tabid/1414/Default.aspx (accessed: April 16, 2009).

37. Search Institute. Available: www.search-institute.org (accessed: April 16, 2009).

38. Rosser, James C. Jr., et al. 2007. "The Impact of Video Games on Training Surgeons in the 21st Century." *Archives of Surgery* 142, no. 2: 181–186. Available: archsurg.highwire.org/cgi/content/abstract/142/2/181 (accessed: April 16, 2009).

39. Rosser, James C. et al. 2006. "The Use of a "Hybrid" Trainer in an Established Laparoscopic Skills Program." *JSLS, Journal of the Society of Laparoendoscopic Surgeons* 10, no. 1: 4–10. Available: www.ingentaconnect.com/content/sls/jsls/2006/00000010/00000001/art00002 (accessed: April 16, 2009).

40. Warlick, David. 2005. "The New Literacies." *Scholastic Administrator* (March–April). Available: http://content.scholastic.com/browse/article.jsp?id=263 (accessed: April 16, 2009).

41. Johnson, *Everything Bad Is Good for You*, p. 50.

Bonus Round 2:
Exposing Information, Employing Knowledge, and Expressing Ideas in *World of Warcraft*

Figure 2.15. *World of Warcraft* Screenshot

My character Phoibe (see Figure 2.15) is a level 66 human paladin ("specced," or geared and trained for tanking: hitting enemies and causing them harm without taking a lot of damage herself). She is trained in mining and smithing in order to make and sell armor, so her backpack might contain metal ore as well as food, potions, gear, and quest items. In October 2008, there were 70 levels in the game, so level 66 represents nearly a year of gameplay, several hours a day. The number of levels increased in November 2008 with the expansion pack, *Wrath of the Lich King* (Blizzard, 2008). In Figure 2.15, my paladin is seated on her epic mount, a fast-moving unicorn outside of the Scryer's Inn in Shattrath, a location for players level 68 or higher.

Figure 2.16. World of Warcraft Matching Game

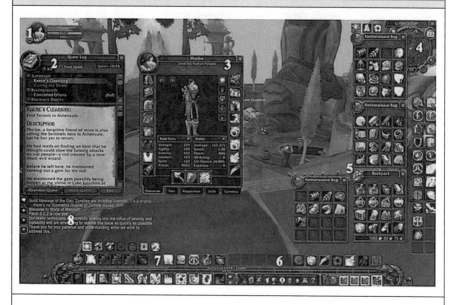

1. Character Status	A. Armor & weapons, skills, reputation
2. Quest Log	B. Inventory of items carried
3. Character Window	C. In-game chat
4. Map	D. Progress of current goals
5. Bags	E. Health and Mana levels
6. Menu	F. Hot keys for frequently used functions
7. Action Bar	G. Information about character, quest log, help
8. Chat	H. Displays current location

The screenshot shown in Figure 2.16 depicts the *World of Warcraft* (Blizzard, 2004) User Interface. In this exercise, can you match the number to the description and function of the windows on the screen? Give it a try, and then read on for the answers.

In Figure 2.16, the top left-hand corner illustrates the character's health and mana (energy). The "Zzzz" indicates the character is currently resting, and both health and mana are at 100 percent.

The window on the left side of the screen is a quest log—a copy of each order received, which may include a location to go to, a character to talk to, monsters to kill, items to collect, or goods to deliver. The quest log updates automatically to show the progress made on a quest, and the quest and its notes disappear when the quest is turned in.

The window in the center side of the screen contains detailed character information:

Character: shows armor and weapons. Every piece of clothing offers a layer of protection against enemies and damage through battle or death. Pointing to any item of clothing reveals the strength and current damage to the item. The window has tabs for overall character ability, broken down into categories such as spirit, stamina, intellect, and agility. Potions, spells, and armor can help boost these numbers, making Phoibe less susceptible to damage when attacked.

Pets: shows mount (horse, etc.) and pets Phoibe might be able to control, such as a remote control-operated robot, or companions that just follow her around, such as an owl or a Siamese cat.

Reputation screen: indicates Phoibe's standing in the eyes of other factions and races in the game. Phoibe is exalted in the dwarven city of Ironforge because of the number of quests completed and turned in, as a service to the city, but in the surrounding areas she is hated by the Bloodsail Buccaneers (pirates).

Skills screen: monitors Phoibe's progress at survival skills such as cooking, fishing, and first aid and professions such as mining and smithing.

Currency: money on hand as well as honor marks earned by high-level quests. These marks can be turned in for advanced weaponry and armor.

The circle at the top right-hand side of the screen is a map of Shattrath, the location where Phoibe is currently resting. The player can zoom in and out on the map or press the M key for an overview of the city. Phoibe can cast a spell so that mining nodes or fishing holes or class trainers will be marked on the map, to increase her skill in those areas.

Shattrath is a trade center where players can barter and trade, accept and turn in quests, hone skills, rest, and store goods. If the current location were outdoors between cities, Phoibe would be monitoring potential attacks from wild animals and other players in the game environment along with other variables.

The inventory windows on the right show equipment, supplies, and trade goods that the character carries. Items can also be stored in bags in bank vaults in major cities. Each bag has a limited number of slots, and some items become irrelevant as the character gains experience and ascends to the next level, so constant shuffling is required. For example, cloth is stored in stacks of twenty pieces. Forty linen swatches take up four squares. They could be woven into one stack of 20 bandages that would take up fewer slots. As the character levels up, items that were useful at lower levels, like a minor healing potion, become less useful, because it takes more (mana, potion, etc.) to heal or re-energize. It's better to trade three or four items for one that is more potent. The character might carry items from kills that can't be used or worn (e.g., Phoibe is restricted to wear only plate and chain mail armor, so leather armor won in battles must be carried in her inventory until she can trade or sell it). Bag icons on the bottom right-hand side of the screen shrink or expand the inventory.

Continuing along the center of the bottom row are action bars containing hot keys (i.e., shortcuts). The center ones launch help screens, a chat box, the quest log, character stats, a spell book, and so forth. The icons on the bottom right side of the screen are action hot keys—actions that can be accomplished with one click, such as eating food to restore mana, drawing a weapon to attack, summoning a shield to hurl at an enemy, or casting a healing spell. Note the yellow up/down arrows next to the buttons: the player can set up many rows of hot keys and scroll through sets of them, keeping many actions at the ready and saving keystrokes. For example, summoning your horse without a hotkey involves opening the spell book, clicking on a tab to find the right page, and clicking the correct spell-making one click instead of three saves time when you are in a hurry to get away!

The chat log at the bottom left contains all the in-game conversation—notes from the game server, guild messages, party chat among players grouped to accomplish the same quest, private messages between players, local chat groups organized by geographic zone, and channels for people looking for groups or to buy/sell/trade goods and services. Behind the chat log is a combat log that details damage dealt and taken.

Hopefully, this gives some sense of the amount of information a typical *World of Warcraft* player is continuously interpreting and evaluating. In a battle, dungeon, or raid scenario, the amount of information increases exponentially; the screenshot doesn't encompass monitoring other players in a group or managing add-ons (plug-ins to enhance the game).

Answer key: 1. E; 2. D; 3. A; 4. B; 5. H; 6. G; 7. F; 8. C

Level 2 Strategy Guide: Gaming Resources

Online Resources

Especially for Libraries

American Library Association. "Gaming." Available: http://www.gaming.ala.org/resources/index.php?title=Main_Page (accessed: April 16, 2009).

> Wiki and news blog dedicated to best gaming practices in all types of libraries.

American Library Association. Game and Gaming Member Interest Group. Available: www.ala.org/ala/mgrps/memberinitiativegroups/index.cfm (accessed: April 16, 2009).

> Designed to engage those interested in all types of games and gaming activities in libraries and to collaborate with ALA units to support gaming initiatives and programs across the Association.

Johnson, Megan and Robert Slater. "Video Game Magazine Breakdown." Animeted .org. Available: www.animeted.org/4librarians/video-games/game-mags.htm (accessed: April 16, 2009).

> Discussion of the pros, cons, and audiences for numerous magazines by two reviewers who are gaming librarians.

Scalzo, John. "The Video Game Librarian." Available: http://video gamelibrarian.com (accessed: April 16, 2009).

> News, reviews, and more.

Schwarzwalder, Jami. "Video Game Collections. The Mario Brothers Memorial Public Library." Available: www.mbmpl.org/vg/hcollect.pdf (accessed: April 16, 2009).

> Recommended books and games for a fictitious library dedicated solely to video games.

Wolfwater, Meredith, et al. "Gaming." Library Successes: A Best Practices Wiki. Available: www.libsuccess.org/index.php?title=Gaming (accessed: April 16, 2009).

> Events, success stories, bibliography, and more.

Young Adult Library Services Association. Teen Gaming Interest Group. Available: http://connect.ala.org/node/70744 (accessed: April 16, 2009).

> Group discusses issues related to teens (aged 12–18) and gaming and develops and disseminates best practices in collections, programming, and related topics for all types of gaming.

Young Adult Library Services Association. "Top 50 Core Recommended Collection." (Summer 2008). Available: http://wikis.ala.org/yalsa/index.php/Gaming_Lists_%26_Activities#Top_50_Core_Recommended_Collection_Titles (accessed: April 16, 2009).

> Annotated list of 50 recommended titles for circulating game collections for teens.

E-mail Discussion Groups

American Library Association. Games and Gaming Member Interest Group Mailing List. Available: http://lists.ala.org/sympa/info/gaminginlibraries (accessed: April 16, 2009).

> For discussion of all types of games and gaming.

Becta Games in Education. Available: http://lists.becta.org.uk/mailman/listinfo/gamesandeducation (accessed: April 16, 2009).

> A practical information-sharing and discussion forum for those interested in examining the potential of computer and video games in education.

Edu Discussion List. Available: http://lists.looneylabs.com/mailman/listinfo/edu (accessed: April 16, 2009).

> A place for educators to discuss various ways that Looney Labs tabletop games can be used in educational settings. Part of the Looney Academy, which offers lesson plans, an index of how Looney Lab games compare to the U.S. National Education Standards, a brochure with overviews of the educational content of popular Looney Lab games, and a virtual meeting space. Hosted by Looney Labs and archived online.

Games-for-Health Discussion Listserv. Available: www.gamesforhealth.org/maillist2.html (accessed: April 16, 2009).

> Support for designers of games with applied purposes in the field of health care, such as patient care, education, training, policy, and management. Run by Digitalmill, Inc., and archived online.

LibGaming Google Group. Available: http://groups.google.com/group/libgaming (accessed: April 16, 2009).

> Six hundred–member e-mail distribution list dedicated to discussing all things gaming.

Serious Games Discussion Listserv. Available: www.seriousgames.org/maillist2.html (accessed: April 16, 2009).

> Support for designers of games for purposes other than entertainment, such as education, training, policy, and management. Run by Digitalmill, Inc., and archived online.

Research and Statistics

Entertainment Software Association. Available: www.theesa.com (accessed: April 16, 2009).

    Provides industry facts, statistics, news, and research.

Game Research. Available: www.game-research.com (accessed: April 16, 2009).

    A Danish site that collects knowledge on computer games from the areas of art, business, and science.

Game Studies. Available: www.gamestudies.org (accessed: April 16, 2009).

    Web site for the *International Journal of Computer Game Research.*

The Lion & Lamb Project. Available: www.lionlamb.org (accessed: April 16, 2009).

    Archival site with links to research supporting the viewpoint that violence is inappropriate for youth. Mission: working to change the tolerance level for violence as a "cool" theme for toys and other entertainment products for children.

Media Research Hub. Available: http://mediaresearchhub.ssrc.org (accessed: April 16, 2009).

    Host site for academic and scholarly research on media, including games.

MMOG Chart. Available: www.mmogchart.com (accessed: April 16, 2009).

    Tracks the growth of subscription-based massively multiplayer online games (MMOGs).

MobyGames. Available: www.mobygames.com (accessed: April 16, 2009).

    Game documentation project that attempts to "catalog" all video games.

National Institute on Media and the Family. Available: www.mediafamily.org/about/index.shtml (accessed: April 16, 2009).

    A research-based organization interested in the positive and harmful effects of media on children and youth. Publishes an annual Video Game Report Card in November.

National Middle School Association. "Young Adolescents Developmental Needs" (1996). Available: www.nmsa.org/Research/ResearchSummaries/Summary5/tabid/257/Default.aspx (accessed: April 16, 2009).

    Article about seven things young adolescents require to navigate successfully to adulthood.

Pew Internet and American Life Project. Available: www.pewinternet.org (accessed: April 16, 2009).

    Pew is a nonprofit "fact tank" that provides information on the issues, attitudes, and trends shaping America and the world. Their *Technology and Internet Evolution* reports are particularly noteworthy for libraries.

Search Institute. *50 Years of Discovering What Kids Need to Succeed.* Available: www.search-institute.org/ (accessed: April 16, 2009).

    Addresses youth development and behavior in terms of assets children and teens need to become happy, healthy contributors to adult society.

VGchartz. Available: www.vgchartz.com (accessed: April 16, 2009).

Reviews, editorials, and sales figures for games and consoles.

Warrior Science Group. 2008. Available: www.warriorsciencegroup.com (accessed: April 16, 2009).

Includes information on training soldiers via interactive media.

Yee, Nick. "The Daedalus Project." Available: www.nickyee.com/index-daedalus.html (accessed: April 16, 2009).

Ongoing studies of massively multiple online role-playing games.

History and Archives

Atari Archives. "Table of Contents: Basic Games." Available: www.atariarchives.org/basicgames (accessed: April 16, 2009).

Archives include books on programming for Atari games.

Bellis, Mary. "The History of Computer and Video Games." About.com. Available: http://inventors.about.com/library/inventors/blcomputer_videogames.htm (accessed: April 16, 2009).

An overview of early arcade machines, the history of home consoles, and the history of the video game.

The Digibarn Computer Museum. Available: www.digibarn.com (accessed: April 16, 2009).

Online museum of milestones in video game history.

Dot Eaters. Available: www.thedoteaters.com (accessed: April 16, 2009).

History of video games site that incorporates video and screenshots.

Hopkins, Gary. "Celebrate the Century: Search the Web for U.S. History of the 1980s." Lesson Planning Channel Education World (2000). Available: www.education-world.com/a_lesson/lesson215.shtml (accessed: April 16, 2009).

Includes video games in the context of 1980s pop culture and history.

Katz, John. "Voices From the Hellmouth. Slashdot." Available: http://slashdot.org/articles/99/04/25/1438249.shtml (accessed: April 16, 2009).

In the wake of the Columbine High School massacre in 1999, students posted about their high school experiences as outsiders (many of them gamers).

Koster, Raph. "Online Worlds Timeline." Available: www.raphkoster.com/gaming/mudtimeline.shtml (accessed: April 16, 2009).

Timeline of online and virtual worlds through 2002.

McCollum, Greg. "The aMazing History of Maze: It's a Small World After-all." PowerPoint presentation at the Vintage Computer Festival, Mountain View, CA, November 7, 2004. Available: http://www.docstoc.com/docs/1046782/The-aMazing-History-of-Maze (accessed: April 16, 2009).

MobyGames. Available: www.mobygames.com (accessed: April 16, 2009).

Online catalog of video games.

Replacement Docs. Available: www.replacementdocs.com/news.php (accessed: April 16, 2009).

A Web archive of game manuals.

Gaming Blogs and News

Entertainment Consumer Association. "Game Politics." Available: www.gamepolitics .com (accessed: April 16, 2009).

Covers political issues related to video games, including legislation and lobbying.

Escapist Magazine. Available: www.escapistmagazine.com (accessed: April 16, 2009).

Weekly online publication of articles about video gaming, each issue focused on a specific topic.

Game Couch. Available: www.gamecouch.com (accessed: April 16, 2009).

Covers video games and related geek culture.

Joystiq. Available: http://joystiq.com (accessed: April 16, 2009).

Independent, unbiased video game news reporting.

Kirriemuir, John. "Silversprite." Available: www.silversprite.com (accessed: April 16, 2009).

Posts cover *Second Life* in education, digital games in libraries and information science, digital libraries, online economy, social networking, and the participatory Internet.

Methenitis, Mark. "Law of the Game." Available: http://lawofthegame.blogspot.com (accessed: April 16, 2009).

Covers video gaming and gambling legal issues.

Peacefire. Available: www.peacefire.org (accessed: April 16, 2009).

Dedicated to free speech and freedom of access to information; includes to disable the different Internet filtering programs.

Stehilaire, T. "Old Grandma Hardcore." Available: http://oghc.blogspot.com (accessed: April 16, 2009).

The continuing adventures of a senior gamer, as told to the reader by her grandson.

Wii Have a Problem. Available: www.wiihaveaproblem.com (accessed: April 16, 2009).

Features damage done to homes and bodies during gameplay.

Gaming Award and Review Sites

1Up. Available: www.1Up.com (accessed: April 16, 2009).

Publisher of *Electronic Gaming Monthly* and other console and computing magazines, 1Up provides blogs, podcasts, reviews, forums, and news.

Academy of Interactive Arts & Sciences. Available: www.interactive.org (accessed: April 16, 2009).

Gives awards for outstanding achievement in various fields of excellence for the games of the past year.

Board Game Geek. Available: www.boardgamegeek.com (accessed: April 16, 2009).

Reviews and forums, as well as resources for finding local board game clubs.

British Association of Film and Television Arts. Available: www.bafta.org (accessed: April 16, 2009).

All nominations judged in each of 13 categories by a jury of industry practitioners, including developers and publishers.

Bub, Andrew. "Gamer Dad." Available: www.gamingwithchildren.com (accessed: April 16, 2009).

Video game advice column for parents.

ELAN. Available: www.theelans.com (accessed: April 16, 2009).

Canadian awards for electronic and animated art, given in 15 categories, including Video Game Hall of Fame.

Game Critics Awards. Available: www.gamecriticsawards.com (accessed: April 16, 2009).

Gives awards in 15 categories. Winners determined by poll of members from over 30 media outlets that cover gaming.

Game FAQs. Available: www.gamefaqs.com (accessed: April 16, 2009).

CNET site for game information.

Game Informer. Available: www.gameinformer.com (accessed: April 16, 2009).

Web site for companion magazine. Focused on new releases and soon-to-be-released titles.

Game Rankings. Available: www.gamerankings.com (accessed: April 16, 2009).

Clearinghouse of reviews. Publishes average score for each game, for each console, with links to reviews.

Game Spy. Available: www.gamespy.com (accessed: April 16, 2009).

Reviews, news, previews, downloads, cheats, and a game of the year award.

Games for Windows. Available: www.gamesforwindows.com (accessed: April 16, 2009).

Reviews, news, previews, downloads, and cheats for PC games.

Gay Gamer. Available: www.gaygamer.net (accessed: April 16, 2009).

Gaming news, reviews, and awards from a gay perspective.

Games Radar. Available: www.gamesradar.com (accessed: April 16, 2009).

News, reviews, strategy guides, and walkthroughs.

Genesee Valley BOCES. "Swift Six Games." Available: http://sls.gvboces.org/gaming (accessed: April 16, 2009).

Advocates for board games in education review games and aligns board games to the national American Association of School Librarians' (2008) *Standards for the 21st-Century Learner.*

IGN. Available: www.ign.com (accessed: April 16, 2009).

Gaming Web site with reviews, previews, and a game of the year award.

Nicholson, Scott. "Board Games with Scott." Available: http://boardgameswithscott .com (accessed: April 16, 2009).

Online video tutorials on how to play board and card games.

PC Gamer. Available: www.pcgamer.com (accessed: April 16, 2009).

Reviews, news, previews, downloads, and cheats for PC games.

Video Game Report Card. Available: www.mediafamily.org (accessed: April 16, 2009).

Guide for selecting appropriate titles for holiday gifts.

What They Play. Available: www.whattheyplay.com (accessed: April 16, 2009).

A parent's guide to video games, featuring news, reviews, information about game ratings, and more.

Cheat Code Sites

Cheat Code Central. Available: http://cheatcc.com (accessed: April 16, 2009).

IGN. Available: http://cheats.ign.com (accessed: April 16, 2009).

Gaming Organizations

Cyberathlete Competitive League (CPL). Available: http://thecpl.com (accessed: April 16, 2009).

Home of the CPL, organizer of international competitive video game tournaments.

Entertainment Software Ratings Board (ESRB). Available: www.esrb.org (accessed: April 16, 2009).

The ESRB is a self-regulating body established by the Entertainment Software Association. ESRB applies and enforces game ratings, advertising, and online privacy principles. They are primarily known for evaluating games for violence, sex, language, and substance abuse.

Game Developer's Association. Available: www.gamechoiceawards.com (accessed: April 16, 2009).

Industry organization for designers, providing support, continuing education, and awards in ten categories; awards to people who further the game industry; and three choice awards, both nominated and voted on by the development community.

International Game Developer's Association. Available: www.igda.org (accessed: April 16, 2009).

Professional organization for game developers, dedicated to improving developers' careers and lives through community, professional development, and advocacy.

Major League Gaming. Available: www.mlgpro.com (accessed: April 16, 2009).

Hosts national and international contests among registered franchise teams made up of professional gamers on salaried teams.

Professional Gaming Circuit. Available: www.pglcircuit.com (accessed: April 16, 2009).

Local area network (LAN) party league.

Serious Games Initiative. Available: www.seriousgames.org (accessed: April 16, 2009).

The Serious Games Initiative promotes using games to explore management and leadership challenges facing the public sector. Part of its overall charter is to help forge productive links between the electronic game industry and projects involving the use of games in education, training, health, and public policy. They founded Games for Health and Games for Change.

Video Game Voters Network. Available: www.videogamevoters.org (accessed: April 16, 2009).

A movement of American gamers of voting age to protect free speech and defend video games from intrusive legislation and regulation.

Gaming Publishers

Wizards of the Coast. Available: www.wizards.com (accessed: April 16, 2009).

Web site for *Dungeons & Dragons, Magic the Gathering,* the *Forgotten Realms,* and *DragonLance* series.

Games to Play

Interactive Fiction Archive. Available: www.ifarchive.org (accessed: April 16, 2009).

Collection of text-based adventure/role-playing games.

PBS. "Culture Shock: You Decide: Video Game Violence." Available: www.pbs .org/wgbh/cultureshock/provocations/VideoGames/warning.html (accessed: April 16, 2009).

Interactive exercise in examining violence in media.

Zork. Available: www.infocom-if.org/downloads/downloads.html (accessed: April 16, 2009).

Text adventure game.

Content Creation Sites for Gamers

Academy of Machinima Arts & Sciences. Available: www.machinima.org (accessed: April 16, 2009).

Resource for filmmaking within a real-time, three-dimensional (3D) virtual environment, often using 3D video game technologies.

Doppleme. Available: www.doppleme.com (accessed: April 16, 2009).

Create a two-dimensional avatar. Free, Java based, registration optional. Download an avatar or take a screenshot.

Face Your Manga. Available: www.faceyourmanga.com (accessed: April 16, 2009).

Create a two-dimensional avatar. Free, Java based, registration optional. E-mail image to yourself or take a screenshot.

Fan Fiction: Games. Available: www.fanfiction.net/game (accessed: April 16, 2009).

Collection of writings based on copyrighted game franchises.

IMVU. Available: www.imvu.com (accessed: April 16, 2009).

Create a three-dimensional avatar. Download required, account required.

LEGO. Available: www.reasonablyclever.com/mini/flash/minifig.swf (accessed: April 16, 2009).

Create a two-dimensional LEGO-style avatar. Free, no registration required.

Meez. Available: www.meez.com (accessed: April 16, 2009).

Create a three-dimensional animated avatar. Free, account optional.

Simpsons. Available: www.ebaumsworld.com/flash/play/3677 (accessed: April 16, 2009).

Create a two-dimensional *Simpsons*-style avatar with a background. Flash based, no registration required.

The Sims on Stage. Available: http://thesimsonstage.ea.com/index.html (accessed: April 16, 2009).

Mashup and machinima creation Web site.

The Sims Resource. Available: http://thesimsresource.com/intro (accessed: April 16, 2009).

Community Web site for *Sims* content creation.

South Park. Available: www.southparkstudios.com/fans/avatar (accessed: April 16, 2009).

Create a two-dimensional *South Park*–style avatar. Free, flash based, no registration required.

Warcraft Movies. Available: www.warcraftmovies.com (accessed: April 16, 2009).

A collection of machinima using Blizzard's *World of Warcraft* game.

Yahoo! Avatars. Available: http://avatar.yahoo.com (accessed: April 16, 2009).

Create a two-dimensional avatar with a background. Free account required. Copy and paste code to embed or take a screenshot.

Game Design

Castaldi, Christopher. "Discovering Game." Available: www.discoveringgame.com (accessed: April 16, 2009).

Web site with forums dedicated to game design instruction.

Kongregate. *Understanding Games: Episode 1* (2008). Available: www.kongregate .com/games/pixelate/understanding-games-episode-1 (accessed: April 16, 2009).

Interactive game about game design; episode 1 covers rules, interactivity, representation, and simulation in games.

Kongregate. *Understanding Games: Episode 2* (2008). Available: www.kongregate .com/games/pixelate/understanding-games-episode-2 (accessed: April 16, 2009).

Interactive game about game design; episode 2 covers player motivation.

Kongregate. *Understanding Games: Episode 3* (2008). Available: www.kongregate .com/games/pixelate/understanding-games-episode-2 (accessed: April 16, 2009).

Interactive game about game design; episode 3 covers learning in video games.

Kongregate. *Understanding Games: Episode 4* (2008). Available: www.kongregate .com/games/pixelate/understanding-games-episode-2 (accessed: April 16, 2009).

Interactive game about game design; episode 4 covers identification in video games.

Podcasts, Lectures, and Conference Presentations

Aldrich, Clark. "Simulations and the Future of Learning: Accelerating Change" (November 6, 2004). Available: www.itc.conversationsnetwork.org/shows/detail372 .html (accessed: April 16, 2009).

Presentation on learning via simulations.

Czarnecki, Kelly, Chuck Thacker, Diane Colletti, Lori Bell, and Matt Gullett. "Thinking Inside the Box: Games, Teens and Librarians." OPAL (July 15, 2005). Available: http://lispodcasts.com/archives/2005/07/22/thinking-inside-the-box-games-teens-and-libraries (accessed: April 16, 2009).

Presentation on the Bloomington (IL) Public Library's GameFest program.

Gunn, Moira. "Dr. Henry Jenkins: Video Games and Education." *Tech Nation* (March 15, 2005). Available: www.itc.conversationsnetwork.org/shows/detail435.html (accessed: April 16, 2009).

Interview with Dr. Henry Jenkins, director of the Comparative Media Studies Program at MIT; 25 minutes.

Gunn, Moira. "When Gamers Enter the Workforce: Interview with John Beck." *Tech Nation* (March 15, 2005). Available: http://itc.conversationsnetwork.org/shows/detail436.html (accessed: April 16, 2009).

> Interview with John Beck, author of *Got Game: How the Gamer Generation Is Reshaping Business Forever* (Harvard Business School Press, 2005); 17 minutes.

Lewis, Andrew. "Exploring Multimedia for Engaging Children with Libraries in Windsor and Maidenhead." Library and Information Services, Royal Borough of Windsor and Maidenhead. LILAC 2005, Imperial College, London (April 5 2005). Available: www.lilacconference.com/dw/resources/2005/lewis.pdf (accessed: April 16, 2009).

MacWorld. "WWDC 2008 Keynote—Live Update" (June 9, 2008). Available: www.macworld.com/article/133798/2008/06/wwdckeynote.html (accessed: April 16, 2009).

McCollum, Greg. "The aMazing History of Maze: It's a Small World After-all." PowerPoint presentation at the Vintage Computer Festival, Mountain View, CA, November 7, 2004. Available: http://www.docstoc.com/docs/1046782/The-aMazing-History-of-Maze (accessed: April 16, 2009).

> History and development of the computer game *Maze War*.

Online Computer Library Center. "OCLC Symposium: Gaming and the Significance for Information Literacy" (January 19, 2005). Available: www.oclc.org/reports/escan/ (accessed: April 16, 2009).

> Panelists included George Needham, Vice President, Members Services, OCLC; Kurt Squire, Assistant Professor, University of Wisconsin-Madison; Constance Steinkuehler, Researcher, University of Wisconsin-Madison; Marilyn Mason, Program Director for WebJunction; Migell Acosta, Principal Librarian for Information Management, Santa Monica Public Library; and John C. Beck, President of North Star Leadership Group.

Sydell, Laura. "All Things Considered: Video Games Setting Musical Trends." National Public Radio (March 26, 2005). Available: www.npr.org/templates/story/story.php?storyId=4562679 (accessed: April 16, 2009).

> Examines the trend of music placement in video game soundtracks; 5 minutes.

Wright, Will. "Sculpting Possibility Space." Accelerating Change, Stanford University (November 7, 2004). Available: www.itc.conversationsnetwork.org/shows/detail376.html (accessed: April 16, 2009).

> Will Wright, creator of *The Sims*, discusses the methods, concepts, and tools that he uses to approach game design; 50 minutes.

Gaming Conventions and Conferences

Anime Boston. Available: www.animeboston.com (accessed: April 16, 2009).

> Largest anime convention in the northeastern United States, located in Boston. Includes gaming and science fiction elements. Held in May.

Comic-Con: Gaming. Available: www.comic-con.org/cci/cci_gaming.shtml (accessed: April 16, 2009).

> Gaming events and panels at the leading comics and popular arts convention. Held in San Diego in July.

Consumer Electronics Showcase. Available: www.cesweb.org (accessed: April 16, 2009).

> Tradeshow for consumer electronics in Las Vegas. Hosted by the Consumer Electronics Association, held in January.

Dragon*Con. Available: www.dragoncon.org (accessed: April 16, 2009).

> The largest multimedia, popular culture convention focusing on science fiction and fantasy, gaming, comics, literature, art, music, and film in the United States. Held in Atlanta over Labor Day weekend.

E3: Electronic Entertainment Expo. Available: www.e3expo.com (accessed: April 16, 2009).

> Press conferences and demos for the media. Hosted by IDG in Los Angeles, held in July.

E for All. Available: www.eforallexpo.com (accessed: April 16, 2009).

> Exhibitor conference to connect developers and publishers with consumers, who can test drive the latest video games and related technologies. Hosted by IDG World Expo in Los Angeles, held in October.

Games, Learning & Libraries Symposium. Available: http://gaming.techsource.ala.org (accessed: April 16, 2009).

> Panel presentations on gaming in libraries, covering services, programs, collections, design, and research for all types of games in all types of libraries. Hosted by ALA Techsource, held in November.

Gen Con. Available: www.gencon.com/2009/indy/default.aspx (accessed: April 16, 2009).

> The original, longest running, best attended gaming convention in the world. Hosted by Gen Con LLC in Indianapolis, held in August.

Independent Games Festival. Available: www.igf.com (accessed: April 16, 2009).

> Annual showcase for independent game developers; similar to Sundance, but with games and located in San Francisco. Features awards and summits. Hosted by Think Services, held in March.

Penny Arcade Expo. Available: www.pennyarcadeexpo.com (accessed: April 16, 2009).

> Annual three-day game festival in Seattle for tabletop, video game, and PC gamers. Hosts tournaments and freeplay area, concerts, panel discussions, and exhibitors. Hosted by Penny Arcade, held in August.

Republic of Gamers Convention. Available: www.rogcon.com/location (accessed: April 16, 2009).

> Old-school local area network (LAN) party fun located in Dallas. Hosted by ASUS and Intel, held in August.

Tokyo Game Show. Available: http://tgs.cesa.or.jp/English (accessed: April 16, 2009).
Annual conference for toys and games located in Tokyo, Japan. Hosted by the Computer Entertainment Supplier's Association, held in October.

Gaming Vendors

How to Find Equipment and Materials

1. Start with your local game shop or hobby store.
2. Then, try direct from retailers, such as RedOctane, Wizards of the Coast, Looney Labs, and Days of Wonder.
3. Next, try retailers that accept purchase orders, such as Best Buy (government and education division), Amazon.com (library accounts), and library jobbers like Crimson Multimedia and Baker & Taylor. More are listed in the next section.
4. Finally, try retailers like Wal-Mart or Toys 'R Us. You may have to use a personal credit card and get reimbursed.

Retailers That Accept Purchase Orders

Amazon.com
Available: www.amazon.com
866-216-1072

Baker & Taylor, Inc.
Available: www.btol.com
2550 West Tyvola Road, Suite 300
Charlotte, NC 28217
P: 800-775-1800
btinfo@btol.com

Best Buy for Government & Education
Available: www.bestbuybusiness.com
P.O. Box 9312
Minneapolis, MN 55440-9312
P: 877-393-1038

Fun Again Games
Available: www.funagain.com/control/rc?p=libraryschool
1662 Ashland Street
Ashland, OR 97520
P: 541-482-1939
F: 541-482-6573

Thomas Klise/Crimson Multimedia
Available: www.crimsoninc.com
P.O. Box 720
Mystic, CT 06355

Tabletop Games Direct

Days of Wonder
Available: www.daysofwonder.com
334 State Street, Suite 203
Los Altos, CA 94022
P: 866-WONDER8 (866-966-3378)
F: 415-480-1314

Looney Labs
Available: www.looneylabs.com
P.O. Box 761
College Park, MD 20741
P: 301-441-1019
F: 301-441-4871
thelab@looneylabs.com

Wizards of the Coast
Available: http://wizards.com
Wizards of the Coast, Inc.
P.O. Box 707
Renton, WA 98057
P: 425-226-6500
corporateinfo@wizards.com

Video Games Direct

RedOctane
Available: www.redoctane.com
444 Castro Street
Mountain View, CA 94041
P: 800-937-0092
F: 860-536-5141
info@crimsoninc.com

Computer Vendors

Alienware
Available: www.alienware.com
14591 SW 120 Street
Miami, FL 33186-8638
P: 1-888-253-4355
F: 786-388-5722
governmentsales@alienware.com
corporatesales@alienware.com

Dell
Available: www.dell.com

One Dell Way
Round Rock, TX 78682
P: 1-800-www-dell

Toy and Game Retailers

Game Stop
Available: www.gamestop.com
GameStop Corporation
625 Westport Parkway
Grapevine, TX 76051
P: 817-424-2000
F: 817-424-2002

Hobby Town USA
Available: www.hobbytown.com
6301 S. 58th Street
Lincoln, NE 68516
P: 866-492-8718
customerservice@hobbytown.com

Toys 'R Us
Available: www.toysrus.com
P: 1-800-ToysRUs

Wal-Mart
Available: www.walmart.com
702 SW 8th Street
Bentonville, AR 72716-8611
P: 1-800-Wal-Mart

Digital Projectors

InFocus
Available: www.infocus.com/
27500 SW Parkway Avenue
Wilsonville, OR 97070-8238
Toll Free: 800-294-6400
P: 503-685-8888
F: 503-685-8887

Optima USA
Available: www.optomausa.com
515 Sycamore Drive
Milipitas, CA 95035
P: 408-383-3700
F: 408-383-3702

Storage, Support, and Supplies

Demco
Available: www.demco.com
P.O. Box 7488
Madison, WI 53707
P: 1-800-279-1586
F: 800-245-1329
custserv@demco.com
orders@demco.com

Naki-World
Available: www.naki-world.com

249 Paseo Tesoro
Walnut, CA 91789
P: 909-594-818
F: 909-594-8208

Pelican Cases
Available: www.pelican.com
23215 Early Avenue
Torrance, CA 90505
Toll Free: 1-800-473-5422
P: 310-326-4700
F: 310-326-3311
sales@pelican.com

CHAPTER 3

Level 3:
Providing Library Services
to Gamers

N ot every library is going to rush out and purchase a PlayStation 3 or invest $1,000 in a circulating video game collection. Every library, however, can provide services of some kind to gamers in their communities.

If you are thinking about programs or collections, start small with other kinds of services that appeal to gamers. Small-scale services let gamers know that the library has gaming on its radar, creates raving fans of the library, and validates gaming as a constructive use of time. Finally, and most important, it allows librarians to build relationships with gamer patrons, who can become valuable assets when developing programs and collections.

Gamer Mentality

It's All About Me

Gamers are used to playing in a first person perspective and strongly identify with the characters they play, thinking of the character as "me." When a game character loses a life, gamers will talk about the character as if they *are* the character, saying, "I died." One theory is that our sense of self extends to our personal space—to our fingertips. Reaching for something, even while holding an object, extends your brain's mapping to reflect the action.[1] Holding a controller in your hands extends the concept of personal space to the controller and, thus, to the character.

Avatars that represent player characters are becoming more and more customizable. The Nintendo Wii features many games in which the character is a "Mii" that the player has created, and Xbox Live allows players to create an avatar in conjunction with their user profiles.

Self-centeredness is not generally perceived as an attractive quality. It can make gamers seem demanding: they want things their way, right now if not sooner. A desire for customization and a heightened self-awareness are characteristics of being self-centered. The Web 2.0 movement, with its emphasis on customized Web applications that require a profile, may well be the result of programmers growing up with games.

In Sanskrit, "avatar" refers to a bodily manifestation of the divine. In computing terms, it's a digital extension of yourself and your personality, represented by an object or an image (some examples are shown in Figure 3.1). If you could make a "perfect" version of yourself, what would you look like? A cat? An alien? A blue, winged creature? A robot? Creating staff avatars and putting them on your library's Web site and offering a workshop on avatar use and creation that includes Internet safety are two ways librarians can reach out to gamers. Web sites with avatar creation applications independent of video games include the following:

Doppleme. Available: www.doppleme.com (accessed: April 16, 2009). Create a two-dimensional (2D) avatar (download avatar or take a screenshot); free, Java based, registration optional

Face Your Manga. Available: www.faceyourmanga.com (accessed: April 16, 2009). Create a 2D avatar (e-mail an image to yourself or take a screenshot); free, Java based, registration optional

IMVU. Available: www.imvu.com (accessed: April 16, 2009). Create a three-dimensional (3D) avatar; download and account required

---

Figure 3.1. Avatar Forms

**Avatars from Face Your Manga (*top*), LEGO (right),
Doppleme (*bottom*), Yahoo! (*center*), and Simpsons (*left*).**
Source: Collage by Beth Gallaway.

LEGO. Available: www.reasonablyclever.com/mini/flash/minifig.swf (accessed: April 16, 2009). Create a 2D LEGO-style avatar; free, no registration required

Meez. Available: www.meez.com (accessed: April 16, 2009). Create a 3D animated avatar; free, account optional

Simpsons. Available: www.ebaumsworld.com/flash/play/3677 (accessed: April 16, 2009). Create a 2D *Simpsons*-style avatar with a background; Flash based, no registration required

South Park. Available: www.southparkstudios.com/fans/avatar (accessed: April 16, 2009). Create a 2D *South Park*–style avatar; free, Flash based, no registration required

Yahoo! Avatars. Available: http://avatar.yahoo.com (accessed: April 16, 2009). Create a 2D avatar with a background (copy and paste code to embed or take a screenshot); free account required

Libraries can appeal to gamers' self-centeredness by treating the library's Web site like a virtual branch, with services like reference, reader's advisory, and downloadable digital materials available 24/7. Pay attention to Web 2.0 characteristics like customization. Library sites that look and work more like Web 2.0 applications (with the ability to log in to a profile with the library card number, change the look of the screen, and contribute content, such as tagging items in the collection or submitting reviews of materials to the catalog) will appeal to gamers. The University of Pennsylvania is one school that allows patrons to tag materials in the library catalog (see Figure 3.2).

Zoom!

In addition to using the first person perspective in which the gamer looks through the character's eyes (see Figure 3.3), many games contain the ability to change perspectives. In some, gamers can zoom out and view the character from behind, in a second person perspective (see Figure 3.4) or zoom out even further to examine the game from a third person omniscient aerial world view (see Figure 3.5) to look at a map or track progress. The process of zooming in and out gives gamers the unique ability to both focus on small details and survey the big picture.

Embrace Change

Gamers are accustomed to a constantly changing environment; the action in video games is often fast moving and constantly evolving. Are gamers comfortable with

Figure 3.2. Tagging at Penn State

Source: Penn Tags. Available: www.tags.library.upenn.edu (accessed: April 16, 2009).

Figure 3.3. *Halo 3* **(Microsoft, 2007) Screenshot**

Halo 3, first person: view down the barrel of a gun.

Source: www.halo3.com

Figure 3.4. *Need for Speed* **(EA, 2008) Screenshot**

Need for Speed, second person: view of car from behind.

Source: www.needforspeed.com/undercover/media.action?id=screenshot-20080903052154
718 &mediaType=photo&pageNum=3

Figure 3.5. *World of Warcraft* (Blizzard, 2004) Screenshot

World of Warcraft, third person: map view.

Source: www.blizzplanet.com/coppermine/albums/wow-burning-crusade/maps/shattrath-city-map.jpg

change because it is a constant, or because it is the kind of change they are in control of? Perhaps it's a combination of both. The end result is that gamers not only anticipate change; they look forward to it.

Libraries can do small things on their Web sites and in their facilities to appeal to gamers. Putting "sticky content" (i.e., content that is frequently updated and easily changed) on your Web site to bring visitors back to see what's new is now easy through the incorporation of RSS feeds. You can add new book reviews, calendar items, photos, a blog, or featured databases, authors, or materials on a regular basis. Apply the concept of sticky content to the library itself by rapidly changing the bulletin boards, materials displays, and furniture arrangements.

A constantly changing environment may also improve gamers' reflexes. In 2007, Dr. James Rosser found that laparoscopic surgeons who played video games like *Super Monkey Ball* (Sega, 2000) at least three hours a week made 37 percent fewer mistakes in laparoscopic surgery and performed surgery 27 percent faster than their colleagues who did not play video games.[2] Rosser now teaches gaming workshops to doctors to improve their hand–eye coordination and to strengthen their nondominant hands. In

October 2008, on the heels of this study, insurance company Allstate sent video games designed to improve mental acuity to 100,000 drivers aged 50 to 75 in Pennsylvania.[3]

Everything Is in Beta

Another hallmark of Web 2.0 is the idea that everything is in beta, which has put an end to the software release cycle. The gaming industry now offers opportunities for gamers to test unfinished video games. Some video game magazines now include CDs of previews of upcoming games, and gaming Web sites now offer exclusive prepublication samples of highly anticipated games. Some companies reward vocal or prolific game critics and fans with a chance to beta test games for bugs. Game companies will at times even hire a critic or a fan to work on programming or content creation.

Imagine that every program or service at your library is in beta—in a trial stage where improvement is expected. Instead of being satisfied with the status quo, you are challenged to make things better, to never get complacent.

The attitude of "it's in beta" is a forgiving one. The soft release of a new service, such as instant messaging (IM) reference or faxing, self check-out, or extended hours, means less pressure to have it perfect on the first try. Beta services allow librarians to hit the "reset" button and streamline after a trial period. Such services also create an opportunity for patron feedback.

Gaming on Library Computers

Scott Nicholson's white paper on the state of gaming in public libraries in 2007 revealed that 82 percent of libraries allow patrons to play games on library computers.[4] The survey didn't require explanations from the 18 percent of libraries that prohibit gaming on library computers. Participants at library workshops, however, cite the following reasons for banning games: not enough computers for research, let alone gaming; not enough bandwidth to run streaming multimedia games; school policy bans all gaming, and Internet filtering software blocks games; IM is banned, and *RuneScape* (Jagex LTD, 2001) is all about IM; behavioral issues associated with gaming may create an unsavory environment for staff and/or patrons; and the information technology department has legitimate security concerns. In addition, some games incorporate code that changes operating system files; and library patrons may not read the fine print of End User License Agreements or Terms of Service documents or know which Web sites are more likely than others to have malicious content such as viruses or spyware embedded into downloadable files.

The "Not Enough Machines" Issue

Public libraries have an average of 12 public access workstations per location.[5] Most libraries will never be able to purchase enough computers to keep up with patron demand—add more machines, and usage increases. Designating specific computers for specific purposes (research only, word-processing only, express e-mail only, gaming only) with the flexibility to switch the function of the machines according to demand and giving preference to information-seeking procedures may be one option. Purchasing additional portable machines may be another solution. If space doesn't allow for more computers, consider laptops or e-machines.

The "Not Enough Bandwidth" Issue

The digital divide is no longer between the Internet haves and have-nots. Instead, it's about access to pipelines for data versus straws for data. Although 98.9 percent of public library branches offer public Internet access,[6] not every library has cable, DSL (digital subscriber line), or broadband access. It seems like a very simple solution would be to purchase more bandwidth, but not every community has the money to do so. In this case, solutions include forming partnerships and consortiums with other local or regional libraries and obtaining grant money.

The "No IM Allowed" Issue

Communication in many multiplayer games—from Yahoo! checkers and chess to *RuneScape*—is via IM. Thus, some games are banned at the library simply because they incorporate a chat feature.

IM may be the death of grammar as we know it. Then again, when the telegraph was invented and people sending telegrams had to pay per character, they rapidly adopted a kind of shorthand for messages, and we don't speak or write in those conventions today. There are formal and informal methods of communication, and they are neither good nor bad—just different. Being able to convey ideas creatively and efficiently is as highly rated as knowing the mechanics of language. Providing access to IM, the preferred method of written communication among teens, is another way libraries can support gamers.

In fact, libraries should go a step further and make reference, reader's advisory, news, and hold notifications available via IM and text messaging. Youth think that "e-mail is for old people,"[7] and libraries that ban IM send a very clear message that they are not interested in youth. One way to begin attracting youth is to provide live chat, which can be done easily. The Luria Library at the Santa Barbara (CA) City College uses meebo me, a live chat widget (a few lines of code generated by the instant messaging aggregator company Meebo [www.meebo.com]), embedded in its Web site to offer live chat capacity (see Figure 3.6).

The "Games Are Banned" Issue

Banning is a distasteful concept to most librarians, who pride themselves on holding thought-provoking, even controversial, materials in library collections. Banning something often makes it more appealing.

Libraries use Internet filtering software to block games. Sometimes every Web site with the word "game" in it gets blocked. One unfortunate result is that users cannot access some legitimate sites, such as a strategy Web site that a gamer wants to consult for research purposes.

Filters fail, and youth are especially adept at disabling filters and blocking software. Gamers' desires to beat any blocks the library throws at them are not necessarily malicious; they just want to play. Remember that hacking began as a way to improve

Figure 3.6. Luria Library Contact Page Screenshot

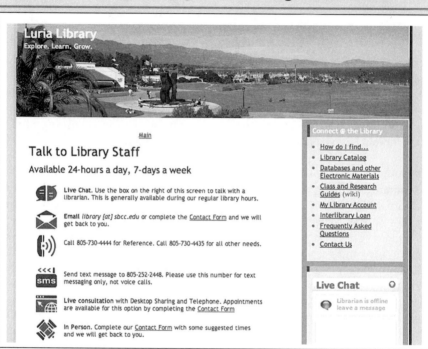

Source: Luria Library at the Santa Barbara (CA) City College. Available: http://library.sbcc .edu/contact.html (accessed: April 16, 2009).

systems, not break them; gamer–hackers may simply be trying to improve their library experience.

Some gamers see bans as a challenge to their own skills, and others, like those who founded Peacefire, see them as a violation of their free speech rights. With the availability of resources like Peacefire's Web site (which provides detailed instructions on using filtering workarounds; see Figure 3.7), library technicians often end up playing a game just trying to keep up with the gamers.

Even if libraries are successful at preventing file downloads and installation and at blocking applications that require Java or Flash, patrons may still be able to find ways to play interactive fiction games or HTML-based games and puzzles. Where is the line going to be drawn? Better to spend our energy on other endeavors—like creating an annotated list of recommended games to play in the library.

The "Curriculum Support" Issue

Certainly a school library's first priority is curriculum support. Although many games involve learning, not every game supports a local, state, or national curriculum. An obvious solution is to find edutainment and serious games that fit with school or

Figure 3.7. Peacefire Screenshot

How to disable your blocking software | Why we do this
You'll understand when you're younger
About Peacefire | Join Peacefire | Blocking Software FAQ | Contact us | Press information

To get around your blocking software: 中文

* 1. First, try a circumvention site like https://www.StupidCensorship.com/. Be sure to type https at the beginning of the URL, not 'http'. Even though this site has been widely known for months, many networks have their blocking software set up incorrectly so that sites beginning with https:// are not blocked, and https://www.StupidCensorship.com/ will still be accessible.

* 2. If that doesn't work, you can join our e-mail list where we mail out new Circumvention sites every 3 or 4 days. Of course, employees of blocking software companies have gotten on this list as well, so they add our sites to their blocked-site database as soon as we mail them out, but in most places it takes 3-4 days for the blocked-site list to be updated. So the latest one that we mail out, should usually still work.

* 3. If you have a computer with an uncensored Internet connection, you can follow these easy steps to set up your own Circumventor site. For example, if you want to get around blocking software at work, and you have a home computer with an uncensored Internet connection, you can install the Circumventor on your home computer. Then it will give you a new URL, and you can take that URL in with you to work and type it into your browser to get around the network blocking software.

* 4. If you're trying to get around blocking software that's installed on the local computer, and not on the network, use these instructions to boot from the Ubuntu Live CD. (These instructions include tips on how to tell the difference between blocking software that's installed "on the local computer" and software that's installed "on the network".)

Install the Circumventor
Is StupidCensorship.com already blocked for you because it's been widely known for so long? This is how you create your own semi-private URL for getting around blocking software.

Source: Peacefire. Available: www.peacefire.org (accessed: April 16, 2009).

college curriculums. Gaming for educational purposes is a growing trend as gamers grow up and move into the teaching profession. Recall the discussion in Level 2 about the Serious Games Initiative: the development of games for education and training in areas such as public policy, the environment, health, and human rights. Such games would be useful in law and health libraries, in particular.

Education Arcade (www.educationarcade.org) is a great resource to find educational video games. It was created by leading scholars of digital games and education, including researchers at MIT. In autumn 2008, the Education Arcade announced the creation of *Caduceus* (see Figure 3.8), an online puzzle game intended to "expose young players (ages 8 to 12) to the concepts of altruism and compassion, while also testing their skills of logic, reason and creativity."[8]

If you truly cannot justify hands-on gaming, develop classroom projects around gaming that don't involve picking up a controller. David Hutchinson's excellent book, *Playing to Learn* (Libraries Unlimited/Teacher Ideas Press, 2007), provides 100 ideas for gaming-related activities with curriculum tie-ins, including writing prompts, studying leaderboards to learn statistics and drill arithmetic, and debating a myriad of controversies surrounding gaming. Public libraries can use the activities as springboards for program ideas, and academic libraries can incorporate them into their curriculum support.

Other alternatives are to limit gaming in schools to recess, lunch, and afterschool hours, when computers are not in demand for homework and curriculum-related projects, and to allow gaming on special occasions within a structured program or environment. See Level 4 for more information on this type of program.

The "Behavior" Issue

I call it the *"RuneScape* effect." Several patrons come in together and sign up for Internet computers. Through the luck of the draw, they are assigned computers that

Figure 3.8. *Caduceus* Screenshot

Source: Education Arcade. Available at www.educationarcade.org (accessed: April 16, 2009).

are not close together. They all log into the same massively multiplayer online game (MMOG) site. They join the same server, wanting to work together or share resources or just show off characters, skills, and loot. Before long, they are talking excitedly across the room and jumping up and down out of their seats or congregating three to a workstation.

Because gaming is such a social activity, it can lead to behaviors such as talking, laughing, and crowding around a computer monitor, all of which is perfectly normal and acceptable until someone nearby is trying to finish a term paper. Today's libraries are not the hallowed quiet study halls of yesterday, but sometimes gaming leads to more noise and larger crowds than can be tolerated in small spaces.

First, make sure you hold users of all ages accountable to the same rules. Librarians cannot shush teens for exclaiming over a game but ignore adults on cell phones or screaming toddlers. Make sure all staff members are on the same page about noise tolerance and are willing to explain and uphold library computer use policies.

If your space allows, configure your workstations to allow for impromptu LAN (local area network) parties or group work (read more about the *RuneScape* clubs in Level 4). The Hartford (CT) Public Library offers tacit approval of social and group computing by the way it configured its workstations (see Figure 3.9). Its configuration also enforces public censorship. Smaller libraries can alternatively designate specific machines for "gaming only" or host the occasional gaming program.

Figure 3.9. Computer Workstations

Facilitating social computing at the Hartford (CT) Public Library.

Source: Photo by Beth Gallaway.

The "Security" Issue

Downloading and installing executable files of any kind carries the potential risk of also installing a virus into the computer, and there is no guarantee that your patrons know how to tell if a download or game sent via e-mail or file transfer is coming from a reputable source. Keeping your virus software up to date and using a program like *Clean Slate 5.0* (FGC, 2008), which wipes content and restores default settings after each reboot, is one solution.

Flash and Java applications have, on occasion, breached security protocols and wreaked havoc on systems. If you must prohibit Java and Flash downloads, consider creating CDs containing library-sanctioned games for in-house use. Some libraries and educational computer labs have been doing this for years.

Guided Access Gaming

If you are ready to embrace gaming, consider bookmarking a list of games for patrons to use in the library. Delicious (www.delicious.com) is an online social bookmarking service anyone can use to create and annotate lists of game site URLs.

The Holdrege (NE) Area Public Library uses Delicious to bookmark games for youth, generating a tag cloud on their Web site (see Figure 3.10, right side of the screen); note that "games" is the largest and boldest tag, indicating that it is the most prolific category. The tag cloud leads to a Delicious page with bookmarked games for youth (see Figure 3.11). Some are annotated.

Alternatively, you can install identical bookmark files on each machine or just make a list and post it on your library's Web site. Keep an eye on the ads for age-appropriateness if you are creating collections for youth, don't link to games that violate your established Internet policy (i.e., don't link to a game that requires a download if patrons cannot download files), and avoid sites with illegal content.

If keeping up with links becomes too much work, download and install a few preselected games. Include content creation tools with gamer appeal, such as game

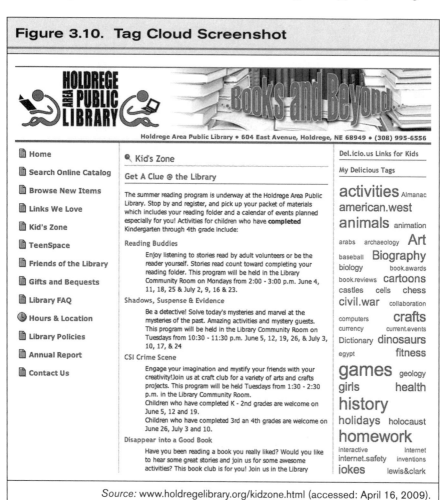

Figure 3.10. Tag Cloud Screenshot

Source: www.holdregelibrary.org/kidzone.html (accessed: April 16, 2009).

Figure 3.11. Delicious Bookmarks Screenshot

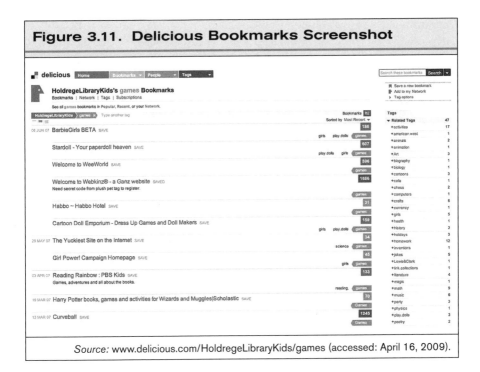

Source: www.delicious.com/HoldregeLibraryKids/games (accessed: April 16, 2009).

design software or video editing for adding captions to machinima. The Level 5 Strategy Guide suggests appropriate downloadable games and games to link to.

The Reader's Advisory Service: Connecting Gamers to Books

The best reader's advisory interactions are really reference interviews. We are used to asking, "What authors do you like to read?" or "What are the last three books you read and enjoyed?" and "What did you like about them?" From there, we try to line readers up with new titles or authors that contain elements similar to the names and titles they mention to us. Instead of asking about books, ask your patrons under the age of 30, "What games do you play?" When they mention a title you are unfamiliar with, simply say "Tell me more!" and "What do you like about it?"

Games, like books, have subjects, and with a short interview you can determine what makes a particular game appealing and offer some read-alike suggestions. For example, some fans of *The Sims 2* (Maxis, 2007) enjoy the drama of relationships and following generations of a family saga; others are interested in architectural and interior design. The Library 2.0 spin would be to invite your gaming patrons to create a booklist, display, or review blog based on these game-related themes.

The rest of this section provides a few examples of themed games and possible book ties. This is by no means an end-all, be-all list! There are many books that can be tied into many types of games, and these examples are just to get librarians thinking about the possibilities. The Level 3 (Gaming Fiction) and Level 4 (Core Collections) Strategy Guides provide many more suggestions.

Sports Games

Madden NFL 05 (EA, 2005) and *Madden NFL 06* (EA, 2006) were the top selling games of 2005[9] and 2006.[10] Other popular sports games include *The Bigs* (2KSports, 2007) and *Tiger Woods PGA World Tour* (EA, 2008). Often, sports game players are fans of spectator sports, so they play because they already enjoy baseball or golf or wrestling.

In some games, players (normally just sports spectators) become managers and build their own dream teams; and an underdog team just could win the World Series in the game environment. Books about sports, adventure, and the lives of athletes may appeal to sports game enthusiasts (see Figure 3.12). Chris Crutcher, Thomas Dygard, Will Hobbs, and Rich Wallace write exciting and engaging play-by-play sports books grounded in teen issues. Matt Christopher has long authored sports fiction for youth and branched out into sports biographies in the late 1990s.

Figure 3.12. Books for Sports Game Fans

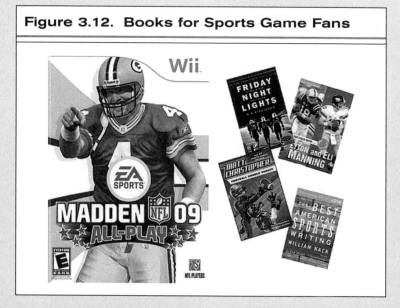

The Best American Sports Writing, edited by Glenn Stout and William Nack (Mariner Books, 2008)
Friday Night Lights by H.G. Bissinger (Da Capo Press, 2000)
Peyton and Eli Manning by Matt Christopher (Little, Brown and Co., 2008)
Football Double Threat by Matt Christopher (Little, Brown and Co., 2008)

Superhero Games

Some superhero games are based on characters in blockbuster films and classic comics. The popularization of graphic novels makes it easy to locate read-alikes for games such as *Spider-Man 3* (Activision, 2007), *LEGO Batman* (Warner, 2008), and *City of Heroes/City of Villains* (NCsoft, 2004). Don't forget titles in comic panel format, including nonfiction and biography, mythologies, novelizations, and fiction and nonfiction about the comic book industry (see Figure 3.13).

Figure 3.13. Books for Superhero Game Fans

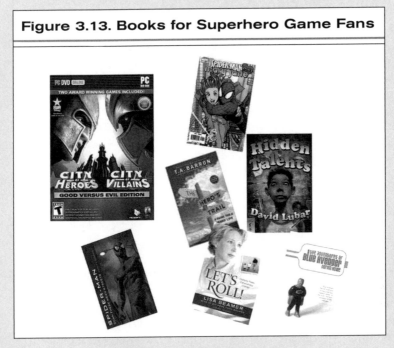

The Hero's Trail by T.A. Barron (Puffin, 2007)
Let's Roll: Ordinary People, Extraordinary Courage by Lisa Beamer and Ken Abraham (Tyndale House, 2006)
Spider-Man Loves Mary Jane by Sean McKeever (Marvel Comics, 2007)
Hidden Talents by David Lubar (Tom Doherty Associates, 1999).
Spider-Man: Down the Mean Streets by Keith R A. DeCandido (Pocket Star Books, 2005).
The Adventures of Blue Avenger by Norma Howe (Holt, 1999).

Massively Multiplayer Online Games

Fans of MMOGs, such as *Runescape* or *Warhammer Online* (Mythic, 2008), might be attracted by their epic fantasy style of character, armor, and setting; the historical component or medieval setting; or the war of good versus evil that creates player-versus-player and clan-versus-clan battles. Players who enjoy MMOGs might be steered to fantasy novels (see Figure 3.14), Arthurian legends, mythologies, and military fiction and to authors such as T.A. Barron, Robert Jordan, C.S. Lewis, Garth Nix, and Philip Pullman, all of whom create rich fantasies with complex issues, complete worlds, great adventures, and strong characters.

Figure 3.14. Books for MMOG Fans

The *Sterkarm Handshake* by Susan Price (HarperCollins, 2000)
The *Annotated Chronicles* (DragonLance: DragonLance Chronicles) by Margaret Weis and
    Tracy Hickman (Wizards of the Coast, 2002)
The *Hunting of the Last Dragon* by Sherryl Jordan (HarperTeen, 2003)
Eragon by Christopher Paolini (Knopf Books for Young Readers, 2003)

Historical Simulation Games

Historical simulation games such as *Civilization IV* (2K Games, 2007), *Age of Empires III* (Microsoft, 2005), and *Prince of Persia* (Ubisoft, 2008) may be popular because of their focus on history, cultures, and societies of ancient civilizations, their economic aspects, and their mythologies or because they offer the ability to control all the action and solve moral dilemmas. Players of historical simulation games often want fiction and nonfiction books (see Figure 3.15) for researching maps and facts that may aid gameplay, experiencing writing set in the time period of a game, accessing biographies of people portrayed in games, or learning about the mythologies and religions of other cultures. Gary Blackwood, Peter Dickinson, Clarence McLaren, Donna Jo Napoli, Julius Lester, and Rosemary Sutcliff write well-researched and minutely detailed historical fiction novels.

Social Simulation Games

Social simulation games such as *The Sims 2* (EA, 2004) and *The Urbz: Sims in the City* (Maxis, 2004) help players form identity by allowing them to make career, family, and social choices in a game environment that they may not try in real life. The appeal may be in manipulating the onscreen characters, building houses, and designing clothing (see Figure 3.16). Gossip magazines and books on architecture, fashion design, and Hollywood scandal are likely to interest social simulation game players.

Figure 3.15. Books for Historical Simulation Game Fans

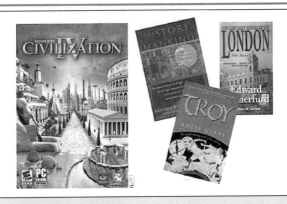

The Story of Mankind by Hendrik Willem Van Loon (Liveright, 1999)
Troy by Adele Geras (Harcourt Children's Books, 2001)
London by Edward Rutherfurd (Fawcett, 1998)

Figure 3.16. Books for Social Simulation Game Fans

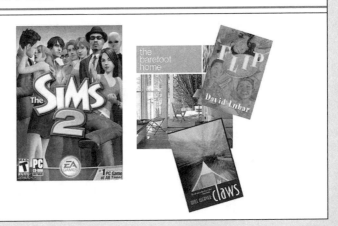

Claws by Will Weaver (HarperCollins, 2003)
Flip by David Lubar (New York: TOR, 2004)
The Barefoot Home: Dressed Down Design for Casual Living by Marc Vassallo and Ken
    Gutmaker (Taunton, 2006)

Authors such as Mel Glenn, M.E. Kerr, Garret Freymann-Weyr, and Cecily von Zeigesar write character-driven books.

Strategy and Puzzle Games

Strategy and puzzle games include titles such as the classic *Myst* (Broderbund, 1993), *Bejeweled* (Pop Cap, 2001), and *Nancy Drew: The Phantom of Venice* (Her Interactive, 2008). People who enjoy solving puzzles in games might like to read mysteries, thrillers, true crimes, puzzle books such as *Where's Waldo* or *I Spy*, and books about magic, the occult, or the unexplained (see Figure 3.17). They may also like games set in exotic places and would therefore like historical or fantasy novels, place biographies, or travel books. Authors E.L. Konigsberg, William E. Coles, Vivian Vande Velde, Dan Brown, and Michael Crichton write stories that blend history, science, and mystery in specific locations.

Figure 3.17. Books for Puzzle Game Fans

Another Kind of Monday by William E. Cole (Atheneum, 1996)
Chasing Vermeer by Blue Balliett (Scholastic Press, 2004)
The Westing Game by Ellen Raskin (Puffin, 1997)
Code Talker: A Novel About the Navajo Marines of World War Two by Joseph Bruhac (Dial Books, 2005)
Nancy Drew #1: Without a Trace by Carolyn Keene (Aladdin Paperbacks, 2004)

First Person Shooter Games

First person shooter (FPS) games such as *Ratchet and Clank: Up Your Arsenal* (SCEA, 2004), *Portal* (Valve, 2007), and *Halo 3* (Microsoft, 2008) get a lot of bad press, but players like elements beyond the aiming and firing! FPS games are competitive, military, suspenseful, horrific, and sometimes historical. Fans of these controversial games may enjoy military fiction, horror stories, apocalyptic fiction, and science fiction (see Figure 3.18). John Marsden, Harry Mazer, James Collier, Tom Clancy, and Robert Westall write military fiction with human interest beyond just battle histories.

Figure 3.18. Books for First Person Shooter Game Fans

Battle Dress by Amy Efaw (HarperCollins, 2000)
Black Horses for the King by Anne McCaffrey (San Diego: Harcourt Brace, 1996)
Soldier Boys by Dean Hughes (New York: Atheneum Books for Young Readers, 2001)

Japanese Games

The appeal of Japanese games is harder to pinpoint. What *do* you give the *Beautiful Katamari* (Namco, 2007) or *Kingdom Hearts II* (Square Enix, 2005) fan? At least *Dragonball Z* and *Pokémon* have anime and now manga tie-ins that make it easy to construct a "play the game/read the book" display. Often, anime/manga fans want books on how to draw, anime guides, and sometimes volumes on Japanese culture (see Figure 3.19). Authors such as Rumiko Takahashi and CLAMP may appeal to Japanese game players. Fans of *Kingdom Hearts* will like Disney fiction based on popular characters featured in the game.

Digital Downloads

For libraries thinking about an in-house, noncirculating collection, digital downloads may be the answer. Playfirst (www.playfirst.com) and IGN's Direct2Drive (www .direct2drive.com) will save you a trip to the store and prevent loss and damage. Another alternative is GameTap (www.gametap.com; see Figure 3.20), owned by

---

Figure 3.19. Books for Japanese Game Fans

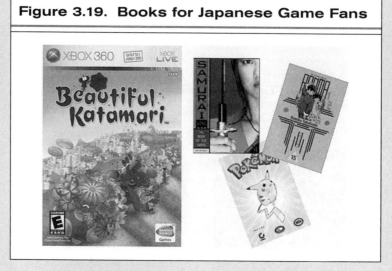

Samurai Girl by Carrie Asai (Simon Pulse, 2003)
Ranma 1/2 #15 by Rumiko Takahashi (San Francisco: VIZ Media, 2005)
Pokémon by Jason Rich (Sybex, 1999)

---

mega media mogul Turner Broadcasting Corporation. GameTap offers arcade classics, console favorites, and PC bestsellers, unique content, and machinima. Instead of scouring the Internet for old favorites illegally hosted online, users log in to a remote server to access an amazing library of over 500 titles (as of this writing) and game-related content, including news and reviews. Some games are free. For $9.95 a month, gamers can play premium games; get an annual subscription and save 50 percent. Games are hosted on a single computer, not circulated; the Terms of Service permits creating one backup copy.

Overdrive (http://overdrive.com) provides online versions of games direct to library patrons at home. Modeled on their successful e-book, e-audio, and e-movie format, the game concept is that patrons download a viewer/player and log in with their library card number. They download an always-available game or productivity software title to their PC, and it expires automatically at the end of the preset lending period. The system eliminates issues of theft and damage. Overdrive promises over 70 program titles in every educational curriculum category for every age group from preschool to adult (see Figure 3.21). A few titles are recognizable by name: *Hallmark Create-a-Card Studio* (Sierra, 2007), *Family Tree Maker* (ancestry.com, 2008), *Mavis Beacon Teaches Typing* (Broderbund, 2008), and *Sudoku Puzzle Addict* (Global Software Publishing, 2006)—no Xbox 360 releases or arcade classics here. Watch for demos at library conferences, and check Overdrive's Web site for more information: www.overdrive.com/products/dlr/mediaformats/games.asp.

Figure 3.20. GameTap Screenshot

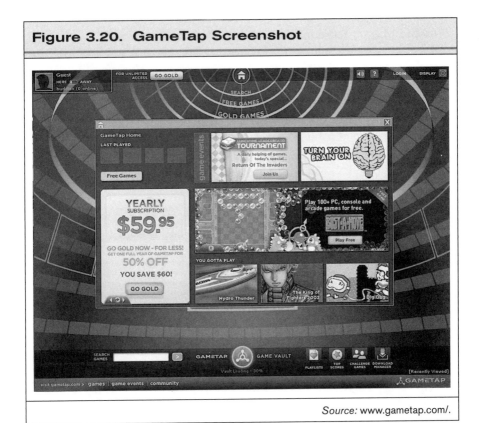

Source: www.gametap.com/.

Reference Services to Gamers

Respecting Gaming Reference Questions

"How do I beat *Final Fantasy XIII*?" (SquareEnix, 2008) is a legitimate reference question and should be treated as such. Serve as a strategy guide to gamer patrons by demonstrating how putting a game title in quotes keeps the words together as a phrase in a search engine, and show them how to specify a platform to limit the results. Show gamers how to employ synonyms ("cheats," "tips," "strategies," "guide") to broaden results. Teaching gamers how to search effectively online for the content they are interested in gives them a skill they can use in other situations.

Strategy Guides, Not Level Bosses

Many video games have levels that become increasingly harder to get through as gameplay progresses. Players learn a new skill, apply it, practice it, and then test it on level bosses: characters with more power, authority, and resources. One consequence of bosses always being the enemy in a game state is engendering a distrust of authority figures. Gamers much prefer helpful mentors who freely share

Figure 3.21. Overdrive Web Site Screenshot

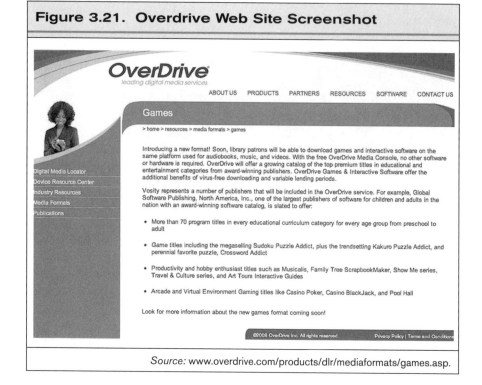

Source: www.overdrive.com/products/dlr/mediaformats/games.asp.

tips than level bosses who withhold information and materials, dispensing them reluctantly.

When providing any kind of bibliographic instruction to gamers, keep their preferences in mind. Make your training sessions hands-on instead of lecture and demo. In one-on-one situations, put your hands behind your back and talk the patron through the searching procedures, asking questions to encourage him or her to read the screen. In group settings, break the group up into teams and issue goals, with very little guidance. Let the groups work together and use the trial and error method they apply to gaming as they search a database. Invite the participants to share what they learned, and then offer suggestions (tips or cheats) to improve the likelihood of retrieving relevant search results.

Notes

1. Blakeslee, Sandra and Matthew Blakeslee. 2007. *Body Has a Mind of Its Own: How Body Maps in Your Brain Help You Do (Almost) Anything Better.* New York: Random House.
2. Rosser, James C. Jr. et al. 2007. "The Impact of Video Games on Training Surgeons in the 21st Century." *Archives of Surgery* 142, no. 2: 181–186.
3. Bland, Eric. "Gaming Makes Grown-ups Safer Drivers." *Discovery News*, October 10, 2008. Available: http://dsc.discovery.com/news/2008/10/10/video-games-drivers.html (accessed: April 16, 2009).

4. Nicholson, Scott. "The Role of Gaming in Libraries: Taking the Pulse" (2007). Available: http://boardgameswithscott.com/pulse2007.pdf (accessed: April 16, 2009).
5. Bertot, John Carlo et al. "Public Libraries and the Internet 2008: Study Results and Findings." Information Institute, Florida State University College of Information (2008). Available: www.ii.fsu.edu/projectFiles/plinternet/2008/Everything.pdf (accessed: April 16, 2009).
6. Bertot, John Carlo et al. "Public Libraries and the Internet 2008: Study Results and Findings." Information Institute, Florida State University College of Information (2008). Available: www.ii.fsu.edu/projectFiles/plinternet/2008/Everything.pdf (accessed: April 16, 2009).
7. Lenhart, Amanda et al. "Teens and Technology." Pew Internet & American Life Project (July 2005). www.pewinternet.org/Reports/2005/Teens-and-Technology.aspx (accessed: April 16, 2009)).
8. Education Arcade. Cambridge, MA: MIT. Available: www.educationarcade.org (accessed: April 16, 2009).
9. Entertainment Software Association. "Essential Facts About the Computer and Game Industry." Washington, DC: Entertainment Software Association (2006). Available: www.theesa.com/www.theesa.com/facts/pdfs/ESA_EF_2006.pdf (accessed: April 16, 2009).
10. Kirdahy, Matthew. "Best Selling Games of 2006." New York: Forbes. Available: www.forbes.com/technology/2006/12/15/video-games-bestsellers-tech-cx_mk_games06_1215sales.html (accessed: April 16, 2009).

Bonus Round 3:
Evaluating Gaming Magazines

Figure 3.22. Gaming Magazine Evaluation

Evaluating Gaming Magazines

Instructions: Preview a video game magazine. Look at the staff list, advertisements, articles, and reviews. Complete this evaluation to assist you in your purchasing decision.

1. Who is this magazine for? How can you tell?

2. Who are the reviewers and editors? Do they reveal age, ethnicity, gender, gaming style, favored platform? What is their expertise? How can you tell their voices are ones you can trust?

3. What is appealing about the magazine?

4. What is unappealing about the magazine?

5. How many reviews does this magazine contain?

6. What is the proportion of reviews?
   ____ % pre-release
   ____ % new releases
   ____ % retrospective

7. What can you learn from the ads?

8. What can you learn from the articles?

9. What information is provided in the review?
   ☐ Publisher
   ☐ Date
   ☐ Summary
   ☐ Critical Evaluation
   ☐ Personal Response
   ☐ Comparison to Similar Titles
   ☐ Game Ranking or Ranking
   ☐ Suggestions for Use
   ☐ ESRB Rating

10. Is this a magazine you'd like to subscribe to for the library? Why or why not?

Level 3 Strategy Guide: Recommended Gaming-related Literature

Gaming Fiction

Bloor, Edward. 1999. *Crusader*. San Diego: Harcourt Brace. 9780152019440.

> Fifteen-year-old Roberta struggles to separate truth from virtual reality when she works in her uncle's failing arcade at the mall in this blend of murder mystery and mall rat culture.

Card, Orson Scott. *Ender's Game* series.

> Set in a future where children are trained for military battle using videogames, Ender rises above his peers to become a commander of a virtual army. Titles include the following:

Card, Orson Scott. 1986. *Speaker for the Dead*. New York: Tor. 9780312937386.
Card, Orson Scott. 1991. *Ender's Game*. New York: Tor. 9780808586166.
Card, Orson Scott. 1991. *Xenocide*. New York: Tor. 9781568652603.
Card, Orson Scott. 1996. *Children of the Mind*. New York: Tor. 9780312853952.
Card, Orson Scott. 1999. *Ender's Shadow*. New York: Tom Doherty Associates Book. 9780312868604.
Card, Orson Scott. 2001. *Shadow of the Hegemon*. New York: Tor. 9780312876517.
Card, Orson Scott. 2002. *Shadowpuppets*. New York: Tor. 9780765304759.
Card, Orson Scott. 2003. *First Meetings in the Enderverse* (short stories). London: Orbit. 9781841493114.
Card, Orson Scott. 2005. *Shadow of the Giant*. New York: Tor. 9780312857585.

The *Diablo* series, based on *Diablo*, a dark fantasy action role-playing game:

Land, Dave. 2001. *Diablo: Tales of Sanctuary*. Milwaukie, OR: Dark Horse Comics. 9781569716823.
Knaak, Richard. 2001. *Diablo: Legacy of Blood*. New York: Pocket Books. 9780671041557.
Odom, Mel. 2002. *Diablo: The Black Road*. New York: Pocket Books. 9780743426916.
Knaak, Richard. 2002. *Diablo: Kingdom of Shadow*. New York: Pocket Books. 9780743426923.
Knaak, Richard. 2006. *Diablo: Moon of the Spider*. New York: Pocket Star Books. 9780743471329.

Fredericks, Mariah. 2004. *Head Games*. New York: Atheneum Books for Young Readers. 9780689855320.

Judith might lack confidence in real life, but her online persona in an online game is intimidating and tough.

Goldman, E.M. 1995. *The Night Room*. New York: Viking. 9780670858385.

Seven teens are selected to participate in "Argus," a virtual reality computer program that sends each to a simulation of their tenth high school reunion.

Gresh, Lois H. 2001. *Chuck Farris and the Tower of Darkness*. Toronto: ECW Press. 9781550224405.

Gresh, Lois H. 2001. *Chuck Farris and the Labyrinth of Doom*. Toronto: ECW Press. 9781550224603.

The Chuck Farris novels are centered around a PlayStation 2.

Horowitz, Anthony. 2004. *Eagle Strike*. New York: Philomel Books. 9780399239793.

After a chance encounter with assassin Yassen Gregorovich, teenage spy Alex Rider investigates a pop star, whose new video game venture involves sinister motives involving Air Force One, nuclear missiles, and the drug trade.

Lubar, David. 2003. *Wizards of the Game*. New York: Philomel Books. 9780399237065.

Role-playing game fan Mercer wants to bring a gaming convention to his middle school. Instead, he attracts four genuine wizards who are trapped on Earth and want his help in returning to their own world.

MacHale, D.J. *Pendragon* series about a time-and-space traveling teen:

MacHale, D.J. 2002. *Pendragon: The Merchant of Death*. New York: Aladdin Paperbacks. 9781416924951.

MacHale, D.J. 2003. *Pendragon: The Lost City of Fa'ar*. New York: Aladdin Paperbacks. 9780743437325.

MacHale, D.J. 2003. *Pendragon: The Never War*. New York: Aladdin Paperbacks. 9780743437332.

MacHale, D.J. 2003. *Pendragon: The Reality Bug*. New York: Aladdin Paperbacks. 9780743437349.

MacHale, D.J. 2004. *Pendragon: Black Water*. New York: Aladdin Paperbacks. 9780689869112.

MacHale, D.J. 2005. *Pendragon: The Quillan Games*. New York: Simon & Schuster, 9781416914235.

MacHale, D.J. 2005. *Pendragon: The Rivers of Zadaa*. New York: Simon & Schuster. 9781416907107.

MacHale, D.J. 2008. *Pendragon: Raven Rise*. New York: Simon & Schuster. 9781416914181.

Miller, Rand. 2004. *The Myst Reader*. New York: Hyperion. 9781401307813.

The volume contains three novels (*The Book of Atru*, *The Book of Ti'ana*, and *The Book of D'ni*) based on the award-winning fantasy puzzle game *Myst*.

Resident Evil series based on the *Resident Evil* game, a horror-themed survival shooter game:

DeCandido, Keith R.A. 2004. *Resident Evil: Genesis*. New York: Pocket Books. 9780743492911.

DeCandido, Keith R.A. 2004. *Resident Evil: Apocalypse*. New York: Pocket Star Books. 9780743493499.

Perry, S.D. 1998. *Resident Evil: The Umbrella Conspiracy*. New York: Pocket Books. 9780671024390.

Perry, S.D. 1998. *Resident Evil: Caliban Cove*. New York: Pocket Books. 9780671024406.

Perry, S.D. 1999. *Resident Evil: City of the Dead*. New York: Pocket Books. 9780671024413.

Perry, S.D. 1999. *Resident Evil: Underworld*. New York: Pocket Books. 9780671024420.

Perry, S.D. 2000. *Resident Evil: Nemesis*. New York: Pocket Books. 9780671784966.

Perry, S.D. 2001. *Resident Evil: Code: Veronica*. New York: Pocket Books. 9780671784980.

Perry, S.D. 2004. *Resident Evil: Zero Hour*. New York: Pocket Books. 9780671785116.

Scott, Michael. 1993. *Gemini Game*. Dublin: O'Brien Press. 9780862783327.

The creators of *Night's Castle* must enter their game to determine why it's causing the players to fall into comas.

Simons, Rikki. *Reality Check!* Los Angeles: Tokyopop, 2003. 9781591822141.

Collin's cat, Catreece, puts on his virtual reality helmet and surfs the Internet, comedic manga style.

Skurzynski, Gloria. 1997. *Virtual War*. New York: Simon & Schuster. 0689813740.

In a future world where global contamination has necessitated limited human contact, three young people with unique genetically engineered abilities team up to wage a war in virtual reality.

Skurzynski, Gloria. 2002. *The Clones*. New York: Atheneum Books for Young Readers. 9780689842634.

This is a sequel to *Virtual War*.

Sleator, William. 1984. *Interstellar Pig*. New York: E.P. Dutton. 9780525440987.

A mysterious and addicting board game is not what it seems.

Sleator, William. 2002. *Parasite Pig*. New York: Dutton Children's Books. 9780525469186.

This sequel to *Interstellar Pig* takes place the following summer.

Stephenson, Neil. 1992. *Snow Crash*. New York: Bantam Books. 9780553351927.

Hiro Protagonist, hacker and pizza delivery guy, gets caught up in helping thwart an attempt to take control of civilization via a drug spread virally over the Internet.

Tangherlini, Arne. 1999. *Leo@fergusrules.com*. Wellfleet, MA: Leapfrog Press. 9780965457873.

Leonora, a teenager of mixed ancestry, begins to spend most of her time in a virtual reality program but is lured into computer-generated danger when a boy she likes disappears.

Valentine, James. 2004. *JumpMan Rule #1: Don't Touch Anything*. New York: Simon & Schuster Books for Young Readers. 9780689868726.

A futuristic series featuring time jumping.

Vande Velde, Vivian. 1991. *User Unfriendly*. San Diego: Harcourt Brace Jovanovich. 9780152009601.

Arvin Rizalli, his mother, and six of his friends pirate a computer-generated, interactive video game that plugs right into the players' brains.

Vande Velde, Vivian. 2002. *Heir Apparent*. San Diego: Harcourt. 9780152045609.

Giannine is trapped in a flawed virtual reality game that will kill her if she doesn't beat it soon.

World of Warcraft Series. This series is focused on events that take place after *Warcraft II*:

Knaak, Richard. *Warcraft # 1: Day of the Dragon*. New York: Pocket Books, 2001. 978-0671041526

Golden, Christie. *Warcraft #2: Lord of the Clans*. New York: Pocket Books, 2001. 978-0743426909

Grubb, Jeff. *Warcraft # 3: The Last Guardian*. New York: Pocket Books, 2002. 978-0671041519

Golden, Christie. *Warcraft # 4: Rise of the Horde*. New York: Pocket Star Books, 2007. 978-0743471381.

The *Sunwell Chronicles* are a *World of Warcraft* back story focused on the resurgence of the Sunwell power source:

Knaak, Richard and Jae-Hwan Kim. *The Sunwell Chronicles #1*. Dragon Hunt. Tokyopop, 2007. 978-1595327126

Knaak, Richard and Jae-Hwan Kim. *The Sunwell Chronicles #2*. Shadows of Ice. Tokyopop, 2007. 978-1595327134

Knaak, Richard and Jae-Hwan Kim. *The Sunwell Chronicles #3*. Ghostlands. Tokyopop, 2007. 978-1595327147.

The *War of the Ancients Trilogy* is a *World of Warcraft* back story that takes place ten millennia before the first *Warcraft* games, during the Burning Legion's first invasion of Azeroth.

Knaak, Richard. 2004. *War of the Ancients #1: The Well of Eternity*. New York: Pocket Books. 0743471199.

Knaak, Richard. 2004. *War of the Ancients #2: The Demon Soul*. New York: Pocket Books. 0743471202.

Knaak, Richard. 2005. *War of the Ancients #3: The Sundering*. New York: Pocket Books, 0743471210.

Weis, Margaret and Tracy Hickman. 1988. *DragonLance Legends*. Renton, WA: TSR. 9780880386531.

The three books in this series focus on a pair of brothers, one with dark leanings, the other with light. The volume includes *Time of the Twins*, *War of the Twins*, and *Test of the Twins*.

Weis, Margaret and Tracy Hickman. 1999. *The Annotated DragonLance Chronicles.* Renton, WA: TSR. 9780786915262.

Set in the magical world of Krynn, a band of friends set out on an adventure and become unexpected heroes. The volume includes *Dragons of Autumn Twilight, Dragons of Winter Night,* and *Dragons of a Spring Dawning.*

Werlin, Nancy. 2000. *Locked Inside.* New York: Delacorte Press. 9780385327008.

When Marnie is kidnapped by a crazed fan of her late mother's, an Internet gaming friend comes to the rescue in this mystery/thriller.

Wieler, Diana. The *RanVan* series:

RhanVan uses his success at video games under the name "RanVan" to see himself as a modern knight and to cope with life with his grandmother and as an outsider at his Vancouver high school, with his anger, and with girls.

Wieler, Diana. 1993. *RanVan the Defender.* Emeryville, CA: Publishers Group West. 9780888992703.

Wieler, Diana. 1995. *RanVan: Magic Nation.* Emeryville, CA: Publishers Group West. 9780888993175.

Wieler, Diana. 1997. *RanVan: Worthy Opponent.* Emeryville, CA: Publishers Group West. 9780613899710.

Gaming Magazines

Online Magazines

Dragon
Wizards of the Coast

Available: www.wizards.com/default.asp?x=dnd/dragon
$54.90/yr
Coverage: August 2007–present

Dungeon
Wizards of the Coast

Available: www.wizards.com/default.asp?x=dnd/dungeon
$54.90/yr
Coverage: August 2007–present

The Escapist

Available: www.escapistmagazine.com
Free
Coverage: July 2005–Present

Print Magazines

Beckett Massive Online Gamer
Beckett Media LP, 4635 McEwen Road, Dallas, TX 75244

Available: www.beckett.com/beckettMOG
$16.99/yr
Coverage: Massively multiple online games

Game Informer Magazine
Game Informer, 724 North First Street 3rd Floor, Minneapolis, MN 55401
> Available: www.gameinformer.com
> $19.95/yr
> Coverage: All consoles and handhelds, PCs, digital downloads; articles, news, interviews, previews, reviews of "geek gear," games, as well as retro game reviews, sales charts, and a cheat code page

Game Pro
IDG Communications, P.O. Box 37579, Boone, IN 50037-7579
> Available: www.gamepro.com
> $17.97/yr
> Coverage: All consoles and handhelds, PCs; news, interviews, previews, reviews, cheat codes, Editor's Choice Awards and Reader's Choice Award

Nintendo Power
Future US Inc., 4000 Shoreline Court Suite 400, South San Francisco, CA 94080
> Available: www.nintendopower.com/home
> $24.95/yr
> Coverage: Nintendo, Wii, DS; news, articles, previews, reviews

PC Gamer
Future US Inc., 4000 Shoreline Court Suite 400, South San Francisco, CA 94080
> Available: www.gamesradar.com/pc
> $14.95/yr; additional $5.00 for CD demos
> Coverage: PC games; news, previews and reviews, cheats

PlayStation: The Official Magazine
Future Publishing , 4000 Shoreline Court, Suite 400, South San Francisco, CA 94080
650-872-1642
> Available: http://www.futureus-inc.com/products/index.php?magazine=playstation_mag
> $18/yr
> Coverage: PlayStation 2 and 3, PlayStation Portable

Tips & Tricks
LFP Publishing Group, 8484 Wilshire Blvd Suite 900, Beverly Hills, CA 90211
> Available: www.tipstricks.com
> $10/issue.
> Coverage: All consoles and handhelds; previews, detailed walkthroughs, cheat codes, tips, articles, comics

Xbox: Official Xbox Magazine
Future US Inc., 4000 Shoreline Court Suite 400, South San Francisco, CA 94080
> Available: www.oxmonline.com
> $24.95/yr
> Coverage: Xbox 360; news, previews, reviews, interviews, articles

CHAPTER 4

Level 4:
Games and Programs

Programming Nuts and Bolts

Research

To carry off a successful gaming event at your library, start with research. Do your homework! Don't assume that just because *Dance Dance Revolution* (*DDR*; Konami, 1998) works at other libraries, it will work in yours. If *DDR* is part of the local grades 4–6 physical education classes, the teens may not think it's so cool. If the Council on Aging has acquired a Wii, the library won't be cutting edge for sponsoring a Wii Bowling League for seniors. Find out what kind of gaming is already going on in your community. Collaborate, if possible, to share equipment, from gaming consoles to digital projectors.

Poll your community to learn what kind of gaming events the library should host. You can do this informally by talking with your library users or formally with a written survey distributed in your local schools. Alternatively, use a free online poll service like Survey Monkey (www.surveymonkey.com) to create a list of options for potential attendees. Put the link on your blog or Web site, and post the results. The Level 4 Strategy Guide includes two sample polls (see Figures 4SG.4 and 4SG.5), one to determine console preference for programs or library collections and the other to determine which consoles and games to use in a gaming program.

Get an idea about what kinds of games your community members are playing at home. If everyone in town has a Wii, you may not be able to draw them in with the novelty factor alone. What is going to elevate your program beyond the dorm room (or living room) experience?

Complete the majority of your program planning before taking your idea to your administrators. You should be able to answer all of their questions about scheduling, budget, marketing, equipment needs, space needs, and a way to measure success before you ask if you can host a gaming event. Be prepared to articulate what the program is going to do for *them*. Possible returns on the investment might be happy parents, new users in the library, and the opportunity to establish a group of gamers to tap for evaluation of library services or input into a circulating collection of games.

Attendance

How many people should you let into a gaming program? It depends on several variables: staff, space, number of consoles/game setups, and the type of gaming experience the library wants to create. Plan around your local fire regulations. Most rooms have a person-limit posted. Don't register 100 participants if your room limit is 65 persons. Keep in mind that your room limit may be based on chair setup, not on standing room or space to move around and play video games.

Staff

Plan on one adult staff member for every 10–12 participants *or* per console for programs for children. Teen volunteers can take the names of the children and call their names to rotate through turns. They can also demonstrate the games, if needed.

Teens are good at self-regulating gameplay. In a tournament, keeping the competition moving might be a job for an announcer or teen volunteer. For adult programs, a minimum of two staff members is recommended, simply for safety reasons.

Space

What kind of space do you need to host a gaming program? It depends on the program! The best space for gaming has flexible furniture options, like stools or cubes for seating that can be stacked to create a space for kinetic games, or tables on wheels that can be easily rolled out of a storage closet for tabletop gaming.

Room size may dictate the kind of gaming experience you deliver. A space with portable furniture, electrical outlets, and a variety of lighting options (ability to dim lights near screens and brighten them for tabletop gaming) is recommended.

Rock Band (MTV Games, 2007), an active game with many pieces of equipment (see Figure 4.1), may require a lot more room than *Super Smash Bros. Brawl* (Nintendo, 2008), which can be played while seated. Don't forget to leave additional space for spectators and background singers and dancers—chairs should be at a distance to encourage waiting in a line for a turn and participatory watching. Keep seating on hand for those who just come to watch or hang out; in almost every program at least one person will sit in the corner and read or text a friend.

Gaming on handheld devices might be a good solution for smaller libraries—participants can spread out in the library after hours, flop on beanbag chairs in the teen area, sit together in a meeting room or classroom, or sit on cushions or rug squares in the storytime room. With a Nintendo DS, players within 30 feet of one another can connect and share games without any Internet connection.

If you are feeling that your library is just too small, consider holding an afterhours program. You can host multiple board or video games spread out in different areas of the library. Staffing may be an issue; offering a multigenerational program hosted by staff from different departments may be a solution.

Think outside the box. The session doesn't have to be held at your location to be branded a library program. Consider bringing your video games to a senior center or nursing home, city hall auditorium, school cafeteria, YMCA, girls or boys club,

Figure 4.1. Rock Band Setup

Rock Band setup for Videogame Night at the American Library Association's annual meeting in July 2008.

Source: Photo by Beth Gallaway.

church basement, local college, or other space in the community. Having your program outside the library allows for cross-marketing and may be a partnership opportunity.

Meeting Biological Needs

Access to restrooms or the kitchen is always a bonus. Have a broom or vacuum on hand, provide plenty of napkins, sink access, and antibacterial soap. Have hand sanitizer as well as wet wipes at gaming stations (especially during cold season). Use Clorox wipes or a bleach solution to sanitize equipment after each program.

At the very least, serve water at your program. A bucket filled with ice and water bottles works, but a water fountain or a water cooler in the meeting room saves on ice and plastic waste. Consider asking gamers to bring their own water bottles to refill, or offer some as prizes. Customizing, labeling, or tagging a bottle or plastic cup with permanent markers can be part of the program; ink from fine-tipped Sharpie pens survives multiple dishwasher exposures.

If you are thinking about food, you may want to limit it to a separate area. If this isn't possible, consider offering food before or after the program. If you are determined to have food during the session, think about the best type of food to provide (everyone may love to eat pizza, but do you want greasy controllers or stained cards?). Dry, crumbly snacks are easier to clean up than wet, sticky, or greasy snacks. Pretzels, cookies, and pixie sticks are favorites for during the program; chips and pizza are best for after the program. If your refreshments can fit the theme of the program, wonderful! Fruits and veggies at a *Wii Sports* (Nintendo, 2006) program are a healthy choice; ghost-shaped cookies or cupcakes decorated like a Mario Mushroom are very clever. Snack or Die (www.snackordie.com) is a Web site featuring tasty concoctions for gamers, like cookies that pay homage to *Pac-Man* (see Figure 4.2). If you are concerned about stains on a new carpet and you haven't accepted the fact that it's better for a space to be well-used than pristine from nonuse, consider allowing clear beverages only: water, ginger ale, lemon-lime drinks, or apple or white grape juice.

Equipment

Have power strips and extension cords on hand so you don't need to go running all over the building unplugging staff computers on the day of your event. Purchase multiple power strips, and choose the flexible-armed ones (see Figure 4.3) over the traditional bar style.

Board, card, and dice games require tables and are better suited to a meeting room, children's program or craft room, or even study tables near the Reference Desk. A seat for every player is a must. Tables should be well lit and equipped with pencils and scrap paper for scorekeeping. If you are teaching games, have two copies on hand.

If you are thinking about a local area network (LAN) party, you need to consider the structure of your library's networks. A school or college library with a large computer lab may accommodate 30 or more participants. A speedy Internet connection and computers with fast processors, plenty of RAM, and good video cards are a must. If

Figure 4.2. Snack or Die Cookies

Source: Photo by Jocelyn Anderson. Used with permission.

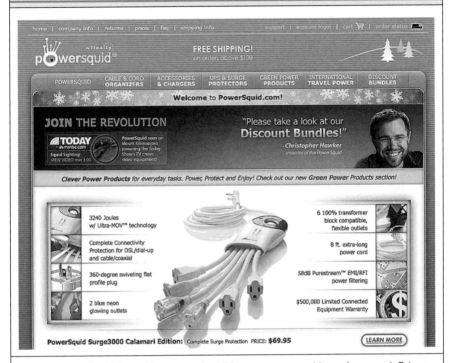

Figure 4.3. "Squid" Power Strip

Source: Power Squid Surge Protectors. Available: www.powersquid.com (accessed: February 8, 2009).

you are concerned that your facility's computers are not up to par for role-playing, shooting, or racing games online, you can invite patrons to bring in their own laptops or PCs and hook up (wired or wireless) to a LAN. These programs can be structured—formal game design workshops, questing in *RuneScape* (Jagex LTD, 1999) or *World of Warcraft* (Blizzard, 2004) on specific servers, *Halo* (Microsoft, 2007) tournaments on others—or unstructured—provide a list of recommended games, go at your own pace game design, or free play.

Games

Game rounds may be three to ten minutes long, depending on the type of game offered. Time is needed between rounds for handing controllers to the next player, vacating seats, choosing a new song, announcing the score, and/or tracking points, so build in a few extra minutes for these activities. A three-minute round of *Beautiful Katamari* (Namco, 2007) or a three-minute song may require five minutes; plan on 20 players an hour, not 24. For two-player games, plan to rotate anywhere from 10 to 24 players per hour. For four-player games, plan to rotate 20 to 40 players per hour.

Consider alternating between games with short rounds and games with longer rounds, and create a sign-up sheet for the games with longer rounds. For music games with long songs, eliminate songs that are more than ten minutes long. At the Glendale (AZ) Public Library, teen services staff write acceptable song titles on slips of paper, put them in a coffee can (bags and hats work just as well), and have players draw titles from the "Coffee Can of Rock."

Time Estimates for Popular Games:

Dance Dance Revolution (Konami, 1998)/*Karaoke Revolution* (Konami, 2003):
2/3/4-player: ~10 songs, 5 min each = 20/30/40 players/hr

Guitar Hero: 2-player: ~7 songs, 7 min each = 14 players/hr

Katamari Damacy (Namco, 2004):
   2-player: ~15 rounds, 3 min each = 30 players/hr
   2-player: ~10 rounds, 5 min each = 20 players/hr
   2-player: ~5 rounds, 10 min each= 10 players/hr

Mario Kart (Nintendo, 2008):
   2/3/4-player race: ~6 races, 8 min each = 16/24/36 players/hr
   2/3/4-player battle: ~5 rounds, 10 min each = 20/30/40 players/hr

Rock Band (MTV Games, 2007): 4-player: ~6 songs, 10 min each = 24 players/hr

Wii Sports (Nintendo, 2006):
   2-player *Baseball*: ~5 10-min, 9-inning game = 10 players/hr
   2-player *Boxing*: ~5 10-min rounds = 10 players/hr
   2-player *Golf*: ~3 20–min, 9-hole courses = 6 players/hr
   4-player *Bowling*: ~3 20-min strings = 12 players/hr
   2/3/4-player *Tennis*: ~5 10-min rounds = 10/15/20 players/hr

---

The Game Experience

A successful gaming program doesn't mean that every participant plays for the entire duration of the program. Consider how long you want players to wait between turns. Attention span is two minutes plus one minute for each additional year of age. Certainly, there is a social element and spectator element to all types of gaming programs. Each participant should get a chance to play multiple times; one round every 20 minutes is ideal. Double-elimination tournaments ensure that even the losers get to play twice.

Video Game Setups

Equipment Needs

Plan your program to be bigger and better than the home gameplay experience. Many games will require a TV with three input jacks rimmed in red, white, and yellow (see Figure 4.4). If your library's TV is small, consider borrowing a larger screened one.

Use a projector with a large screen for at least one game—the game you anticipate to be the most popular. Check the screens you intend to use at least one week in advance. The projector will also need three input jacks rimmed in red, white, and yellow for RCA input (see Figure 4.5). If there are no input jacks, you may need to hit your favorite local electronics store for an adapter. Plug your console directly into the projector.

If the input holes are yellow, light blue, and light green, you need a Y-shaped RCA female to 1/8 inch stereo audio adapter (see Figure 4.6). Connect the yellow-rimmed plug from the console to the projector to transfer the video; connect the red-rimmed and white-rimmed plugs to the adapter, and plug the adapter into the green-rimmed jack to transfer the audio.

If you can get your hands on a projector but not on a screen, there are several creative screen alternatives: project onto a white wall; onto butcher paper, a white sheet, or a white tablecloth hung over a dark wall or over bookcases; onto a large window covered by thick paper; or onto a window shade.

If you are running multiple rhythm games, use the built-in speakers for the digital projector, or plug in auxiliary speakers—the type you use for your computers may work just fine. (Note: this works *only* if your projector has an input *and* output for audio.)

For handheld device programs, you need seating for participants and possibly one console or projector for display. For LAN parties, you need tables and chairs, cables, and lots of power strips.

Figure 4.4. Input Configuration for an HD TV

Source: Photo by Beth Gallaway.

Figure 4.5. Input Configuration for an LCD Projector

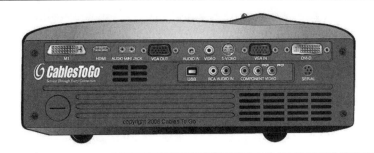

Source: Cables To Go. Available: http://www.cablestogo.com/av_config/projector.asp. Used with permission.

Figure 4.6. Y-Shaped RCA Adapter

Source: Photo by Beth Gallaway.

Creating a Successful Gaming Facility

If you are fortunate enough to be undergoing renovation or new construction, here are some things to keep in mind as you develop a space for gaming. Ideally, the library will host at least two games at the same time, in any combination of console, board, tabletop, computer, or handheld games. Flexible seating and sufficient space for spectators are required.

Provide many access points for power. In addition to wall plugs, ask for floor plugs or drops in the middle of the room to minimize trailing extension cords. The circuitry should be powerful enough to support at least four plugs, one each for the projector, audio, console, and battery charger. Users are going to want to plug in to power their laptops and recharge their handhelds and cell phones. Blowing a fuse in the middle of the program certainly adds some excitement but not necessarily the good kind; have a flashlight (with charged batteries) on hand in case you need to go find the fuse box. Installing a floor channel to cover wires eliminates tripping, but rug remnants and small throw rugs work well too to cover exposed wires. Avoid tape; it makes everything sticky and doesn't hold very well.

If the room has windows, use heavy shades (which can double as a projection screen) or wooden interior shutters to block out daylight. Lights with a dimmer capability set up in banks with separate controls are preferable, so you can have lights off near projection screens and televisions and on in other parts of the room for tabletop, card, and board gaming.

Playing physically exerting games makes one, well, gamey! Ideally, the room will have windows that open to bring in fresh air and a separate HVAC control so the librarian can adjust the room temperature accordingly. Additional ceiling or wall fans for quick cool-downs, or floor fans within easy reach, keep gamers comfortable and the air circulating.

Chances are you can't leave your equipment out all the time. Rolling carts that lock work well for consoles and projectors; handheld controllers may also fit. Roll the entire cart into a lockable storage closet that has enough space to store the carts, *DDR* pads, and folding tables and chairs. Inside cabinets and shelving for games, pieces, and controllers is a bonus. In addition to storage for library-owned equipment, consider storage for participants' belongings. They may need a place to hang their coats, drop their bags, or stick their shoes. Open cubbies or a wheeled bookshelf or laundry bin may suit this purpose.

Most gamers are accustomed to being constantly connected to the Internet. WiFi available at the library allows those who bring their own computers or handheld devices to play games on their own machines or show their games to their friends. Designating WiFi hot spots as gaming spaces provides an opportunity to reach gamers at the library. A WiFi connection or an Internet drop connected to a library-owned "next generation" game console gives the library the ability to download new content and games or, in the case of the Wii, to create a Mii to mingle with library patrons' Miis. Libraries that set up accounts with Xbox Live or PSOnline can participate in nationwide gaming tournaments via GT System (www.gtsystem.org). Finally, publicizing the library's screen name presents an opportunity to befriend local gamers over the network, much like collecting friends on MySpace or Facebook.

Built-in surround sound is nice, but it can be overpowering. An ideal setup would be two separate sound systems at either end of the room, each with easily adjustable speakers. Add to that, sound baffling! Games are noisy. The more soft items you have in the room, the greater the chance of muffling the sound. Consider insulation or sound-deadening material in the walls, floor, and ceiling; fabric or carpet as a wall covering; sound buffer panels hanging from the ceiling; upholstered sofas and chairs; fabric- or carpet-covered seating; and industrial carpeting on the majority of the floor space.

Provide a variety of seating options to accommodate a variety of game experiences. Typical auditorium seating is not that comfortable. Library companies make chairs that recline slightly, Pottery Barn sells rocker chairs and beanbag chairs, and you may find stackable cube, cushion, or stool-style seating everywhere from Target to Wal-Mart to Macy's.

Proximity to kitchens and washrooms is a must for activity rooms of any kind. Ideally, bathrooms will be adjacent to gaming spaces to facilitate afterhours programs locked off from the rest of the library.

Room Setups for Specific Games

Different types of games will require different floor plans. Many rhythm and action games will require a projector and screen and plenty of space to move around in (see Figure 4.7). *DDR* controllers are three-foot-square dance pads—flailing arms and legs may require an additional 6 to 12 inches of space around the pad. Leave a minimum of 16 square feet (a four by four space) for each spectator/dancer you expect to stand behind the players and dance along.

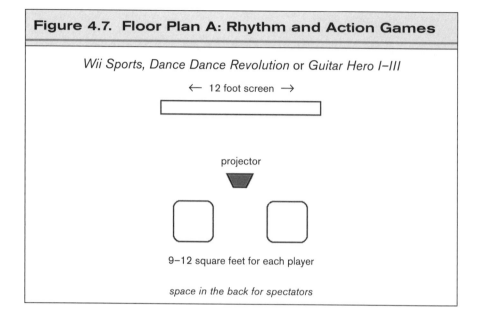

Figure 4.7. Floor Plan A: Rhythm and Action Games

Wii Sports, Dance Dance Revolution or *Guitar Hero I–III*

← 12 foot screen →

projector

9–12 square feet for each player

space in the back for spectators

Many Wii games encourage the players to stand up and move around, swinging their arms as if holding a racket, club, or bat. For Wii games, provide the same amount of space that you would for *DDR*, with seating for spectators on the sides or behind the players.

Band games will also require a screen and projector (see Figure 4.8). For *Rock Band*, you need a chair for the drummer. The bassist and guitarist may want to sit as well. The singer will probably stand.

For games like *Katamari Damacy, Super Smash Bros. Brawl,* and *Mario Kart* (multiplayer console games), expect players to want to sit (see Figure 4.9). Position two to four chairs around the screen, with additional chairs or a table to place the controllers—having a place for participants to put the controllers when they get up means less dropping.

Guitar Hero players may sit or stand. Teens will often lounge, sitting in one chair and propping their feet on another. Gamers using handheld devices will want to sit down (see Figure 4.10).

Board, card, and tabletop games require more direct lighting than the video games, and the way lighting works in your program space, meeting room, or auditorium may determine the room setup. Some rooms have spotlighting around the perimeter; others have only two banks of lights.

Board game programs require one table per game and chairs for each player (see Figure 4.11). Some card games can fit two game setups per table if there are fewer than five players. A staff member can sit in the middle of one side and assist both groups with their gameplay. Role-playing games require tables and chairs, pencils with erasers, and space to lay out paper, reference materials, maps and miniatures,

Figure 4.8. Floor Plan B: Band Games

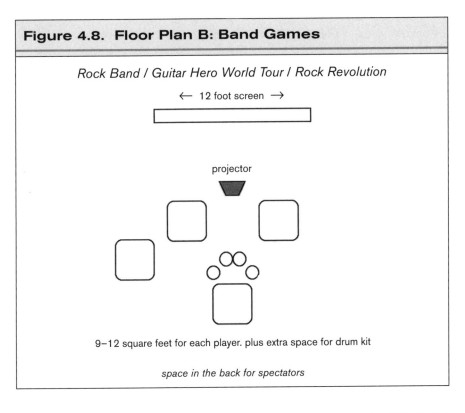

Rock Band / Guitar Hero World Tour / Rock Revolution

← 12 foot screen →

projector

9–12 square feet for each player. plus extra space for drum kit

space in the back for spectators

Figure 4.9. Floor Plan C: 2–4-Player Console Games

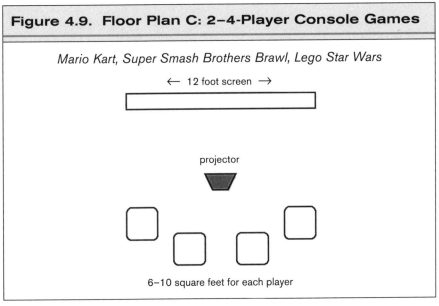

Mario Kart, Super Smash Brothers Brawl, Lego Star Wars

← 12 foot screen →

projector

6–10 square feet for each player

Figure 4.10. Floor Plan D: Handheld Games

DS, PSP & Cell Phone Gaming

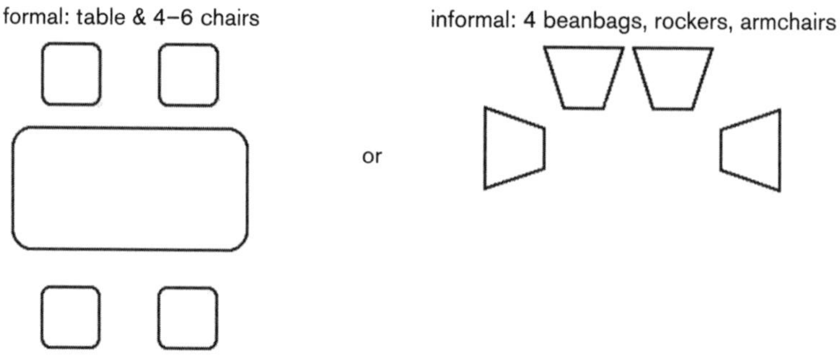

formal: table & 4–6 chairs

informal: 4 beanbags, rockers, armchairs

or

Create as many seating arrangements as you need; a less formal setup allows participants to form their own groups by dragging lighter furniture around.

Figure 4.11. Floor Plan E: Tabletop Games

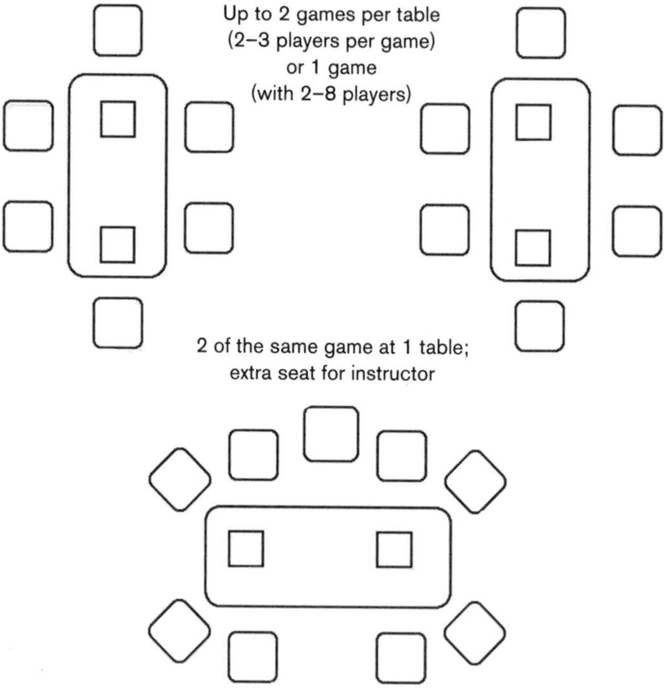

Up to 2 games per table
(2–3 players per game)
or 1 game
(with 2–8 players)

2 of the same game at 1 table;
extra seat for instructor

Figure 4.12. Floor Plan F: Multiple Game Types

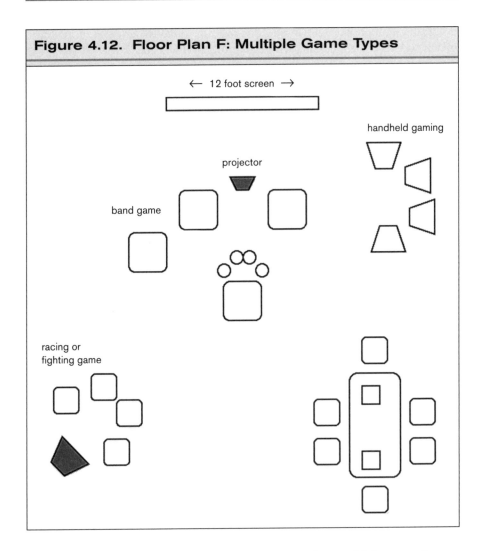

and role dice. You may need to be creative to accommodate multiple types of games in one space (see Figure 4.12).

Scheduling

As with other kinds of library programming, it pays to be aware of other events going on in the community. You may need to work around finals, the football schedule, school dances, holiday weekends, and more. One great way to ensure no-conflict events is to partner with other community institutions and organizations. Not sure what's going on in your community? Host a community calendar on your library's Web site. It's a great service that connects local clubs, creates good PR for the library, and keeps you in the know.

Gaming equipment might be a big deal to set up and break down: securing cords, moving televisions and folding screens, putting together drum kits and dance pads. Plan on 10 to 15 minutes per system for your initial setup and at least 30 minutes for troubleshooting. Consider running a series of programs for different age groups over a weekend or school break to get the best use of your space and time.

Legalities

Software is protected by copyright. Librarians must read the End User License Agreement (EULA) and Terms of Service (ToS) documents for *each* individual game to determine if public performance of a game title is allowed. Some games have a message on the intro or splash screen that reads "for personal use only." This type of "use" is undefined and could include bringing a game to a library to play with others.

> In the case of *Allen v. Academic Games League of America* (AGLOA) 89 F.3d 614 (9th Cir.1996) the court ruled in favor of the AGLOA, declaring that playing video games does not constitute public performance as defined under copyright law. Additionally, "Whether privately in one's home or publicly in a park, it is understood that games are meant to be "played."[1] Read the full case online at http://bulk.resource.org/courts .gov/c/F3/ 89/89.F3d.614.html (accessed: April 16, 2009).

Nintendo has embraced libraries and has given verbal approval for use of Nintendo games in libraries. *Guitar Hero*'s publisher, RedOctane, wants libraries to use their product for tournaments and public performances—you can even charge admission or tournament entry fees. What a nifty idea for a fundraiser! For many *DDR* games, the first splash screen is a copyright notice that says public performance is not allowed; Konami has ignored repeated contacts in an attempt to gain permission. For more about legal issues surrounding gaming, check out the Law of the Game blog at http://lawofthegame .blogspot.com (see Figure 4.13).

Theft

Games and controllers are small and easily pocketed, but even *Rock Band* microphones and cords can get stolen, and several libraries have lost consoles. Replacement parts can be hard to come by when items are sold in a kit. One library recommends scheduling a volunteer who has a checklist of all cords and equipment to run through the list every 15 minutes quietly by each setup to make sure everything is present. All the kids see this, so it's a theft deterrent, too.

Marketing

As for any other program, don't just hang your posters in the library or put information on the library's Web site. Target places gamers go: the pizza joint with one arcade game, the bowling alley, the comic book shop. Get gamers to create your publicity. Game covers are like book covers—designed to be marketing material. You can use a game cover, but write to ask the publisher or rights holder permission if you are going to use a logo or other intellectual property, like a character from a game.

Figure 4.13. Law of the Game Screenshot

LAW OF THE GAME

VIDEO GAMES, GAMBLING, AND OTHER LEGAL DISCUSSIONS
YOUR SOURCE FOR VIDEO GAME LAW

MONDAY, FEBRUARY 2, 2009

LGJ: FTC could target EULAs

This week's *LGJ* focuses on the FTC potentially targeting the EULA.

Read on!

EMAIL THIS • SAVE TO DEL.ICIO.US • DIGG THIS! • DISCUSS ON NEWSVINE • STUMBLE IT! • SUBMIT TO PROPELLER

POSTED BY MARK METHENITIS AT 10:35 AM   0 COMMENTS   LINKS TO THIS POST

LABELS: CONSUMER PROTECTION, EULA, FTC, JOYSTIQ, LAW OF THE GAME ON JOYSTIQ, LGJ

FRIDAY, JANUARY 23, 2009

LGJ: Virtual Taxation

This week's *LGJ* revisits the always popular topic of taxing virtual worlds.

Read on!

EMAIL THIS • SAVE TO DEL.ICIO.US • DIGG THIS! • DISCUSS ON NEWSVINE • STUMBLE IT! • SPHERE: RELATED CONTENT • SUBMIT TO PROPELLER

POSTED BY MARK METHENITIS AT 4:01 PM   0 COMMENTS   LINKS TO THIS POST

AMERICAN BAR ASSOCIATION

Honoree 2007

BLOG ARCHIVE

▼ 2009 (5)
  ▼ February (1)
    LGJ: FTC could target EULAs
  ► January (4)
► 2008 (64)
► 2007 (98)

ABOUT ME

MARK METHENITIS

Mark Methenitis is an attorney with The Vernon Law Group, PLLC, in Dallas Texas. Mark received his Juris Doctorate and his Master of Business

Source: http://lawofthegame.blogspot.com/ (accessed: April 16, 2009).

Create a gaming club or "street team" to help market your gaming events. Members can hang flyers in local businesses (most grocery stores, churches, and some casual dining restaurants host community bulletin boards). Consider postcard, business card, or bookmark style publicity pieces that patrons can take away; alternatively, add tear sheets to your poster, so interested users can rip off a piece of paper containing the event information.

Consider multimedia marketing. Keep in mind that parents are more likely than youth to check out the local paper's press releases, and radio and cable television may be ways to spread the word. A marketing class may be able to create public service events to air on college radio. A public library's teen advisory board might be willing to make a short commercial to post on YouTube and embed into the library's Web site or blog.

Library events on gaming Web sites or community-oriented social networking sites like Meetup.com are likely posted by overzealous patrons, not enthusiastic librarians. Take advantage of online spaces. Market where your users are! Join a gaming group on MySpace. Post your *Guitar Hero* Tournament on RedOctane's Web site. Make social networks part of your strategic and marketing plans.

Posting photos and video clips online after the event will generate interest in future events. Use a generic photo/video release to obtain permission to photograph and film your event. If you are concerned about youth under the age of 18, you can opt to take pictures from behind or use programs like Adobe Photoshop Elements to silhouette figures. Don't label the photos with real names, grades, or schools for additional safety measures.

The Hennepin County (MN) Library uses an online photo release form (see Figure 4.14). It also allows users to submit library photos. Part of the submission form is a disclaimer and agreement for ways the photo may be used.

Some libraries set up blogs to promote and recap gaming activities. Ann Arbor (MI) District Library (AADL) is the model for this. Teens chime in on the AADL GT Web site (www.aadl.org/aadlgt) on a regular basis.

Figure 4.14. Online Photo Release Form

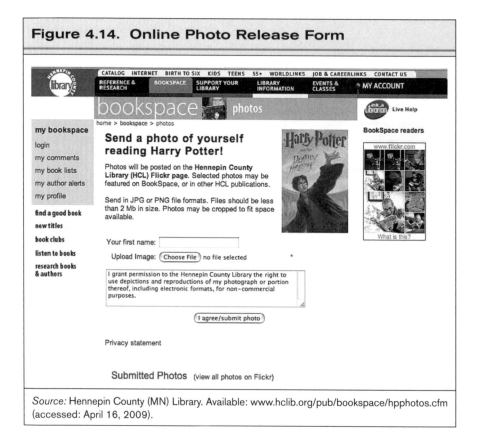

Source: Hennepin County (MN) Library. Available: www.hclib.org/pub/bookspace/hpphotos.cfm (accessed: April 16, 2009).

Record participant contact information at every event. This is a great opportunity to find out how participants prefer to be contacted; so don't rule out Facebook, IM (instant messaging), or SMS (short message service). Use the preferred method of contact to send reminders about your gaming events. If you do go with e-mail, don't forget to use the blind carbon copy (BCC) feature, so the recipients don't get one another's addresses.

Free Play or Tournament

There are pros and cons to each approach—free play and tournament. Free play is a great starter event. There is low pressure to participate, the librarian doesn't have to understand all the nuances of a game or solicit prizes, and everyone leaves happy.

Tournament Prizes

Just as the punishment should fit the crime, so should the prize fit the competition. Keep prizes for game tournaments as game related as possible. An alternative is to give a gift certificate from a retailer (such as Amazon.com or iTunes) known to sell games. Other ideas include the following:

- Make a trophy! Librarians in the LibGaming Google Group report spray painting old controllers gold or silver and attaching them to a base.
- Trinket prizes are good to hand out to the participants at each round—anime or conference freebies, library-card holder, pens/pencils, glow sticks, water bottles, key chains, pins, flash drives, memory cards, stickers, and so forth. If you have a little more to spend ($6–$20), consider gaming-related prizes, such as novelty flash drives or console memory cards.
- Plug-and-play gaming devices—these plug right into a TV and contain old-school arcade games.
- Gift certificates to game stores are probably the best choice—the winner can get a game for the platform she or he owns.
- Donations from local businesses usually go over well—who doesn't love winning movie passes or free pizza?
- A *RuneScape* subscription is perfect for a *RuneScape* program.
- A GameTap subscription is great if the recipient has his or her own computer.
- A gaming magazine subscription requires that you get the address of the winner, and the prize can take weeks to arrive. Purchase at Barnes & Noble or Borders Books and allow the winner to choose his or her prize.
- T-shirts—Try game publishers like RedOctane or companies like Think Geek (www.thinkgeek.com) or J!nx (www.jinx.com).
- Fiction or nonfiction about games—allow winners to choose their own adventure books, comics based on video games, strategy guides, etc.
- Console carrying cases—they cost $20–$40 and are padded, with storage compartments.
- CD wallets—used to store and carry games, they can be imprinted with the library's logo or event information.

Tournaments require a deeper understanding of the game, add drama and excitement, and appeal to expert gamers. With free play the rules are to relinquish your controller at the end of the round and have a good time. With tournaments, the rules are that the better players have more play time, so you would need to have additional play opportunities available. Alternatively, you could create an event in which spectating is a big part of the action, with running commentary, live blogging, and video capture. Tournaments also require playoffs and a winner (see Figure 4.15).

For the younger gamer who may be shy or reluctant to "make a fool of himself," it helps to have the librarian demonstrate the game. The same seems to be true for older participants, too. Once you are willing to be brave and be first, others will try the game.

Teens, on the other hand, generally fall all over each other to be first in line. It's great for them to see librarians from other departments willing to try games. It demonstrates an interest in gamer culture. From a behavioral standpoint, it's strategic for librarians, staff, and teachers to observe the gaming programs. They get to know the teens by name and may see a whole new side to a problem patron who, in a gaming program, exercises good sportsmanship, is polite and respectful, and shows other teens how to play. Conversely, it's good for teens to see librarians as someone other than the people who shushed them last week.

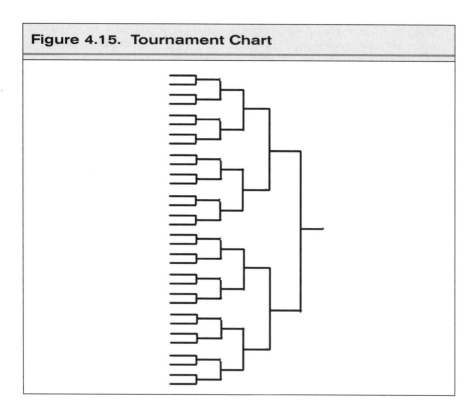

Figure 4.15. Tournament Chart

Best Games for Programs

Buzz: The Big Quiz (Relentless/Sony 2007). PlayStation (PS) 2, PS3. This puzzle game has over 5,000 general interest questions. It is rated E10+ for Everyone age 10 and up. Up to eight players can participate in this animated game show hosted by a Guy Smiley type. *Buzz* received the British Academy of Film and Television Art's Best Casual/Social Game award in 2006. Available: www.us.PlayStation.com/Buzz.

EyeToy: Play series (Sony, 2003). PS2. This innovative collection of minigames features a range of activities, from window washing to boxing to plate spinning to dancing. The quirk? The controller is a camera that sits on your television, reading the movements of your body. Expand your collection with titles that feature minigames, such as *EyeToy: Play 2* (Sony, 2004) and *EyeToy: Play 3* (Sony, 2005) or the sports-related *EyeToy: Antigrav* (Sony, 2004). Available: www.eyetoy.com.

Scene It? Lights, Camera, Action (Microsoft, 2007). Xbox 360. This puzzle game is rated T for Teen for Blood, Language, Suggestive Themes, Use of Alcohol and Tobacco, and Violence. Movie trivia is presented in more than 20 minigame formats—players sequence films by date, attribute quotes, answer questions based on film clips, match actors to their yearbook pictures, recognize films by their posters, and more. Circulate it with the four buzzer controllers, or keep it in your teen area for in-house use. Available: www.Xbox.com/en-US/games/s/sceneitlightscameraaction.

Dance Dance Revolution (Konami, 1998). *DDR* meets all seven teen developmental needs, gets the heart pumping at 140 beats per minute, and exposes users to a broad variety of Japanese pop and club remixes. There is a version of the game for every age group. *DDR* is a franchised game. There are multiple versions for every console. *Dance Dance Revolution: Hottest Dance Party* (Konami, 2007) for the Wii and *DDR Revolution Universe 3* (Xbox 360) and *Dance Dance Revolution: Supernova 2* for PS2, which will play on a PS3 if you purchase PS3-compatible dance mats.

Guitar Hero I, II, III, World Tour (RedOctane, 2005, 2007, 2008). PS2; PS2 and Xbox 360; PS2, PS3, Xbox 360, et al. The *Guitar Hero (GH)* franchise allows any gamer to become a rocker. The game can be played with a traditional controller, but it frequently is bundled with a guitar-shaped controller with a whammy bar, strum bar, and a row of five-colored buttons in place of frets. The game isn't about learning to read music or how to play guitar; it's a rhythm game where success hinges on the ability to hit the colored button on the controller and strum, just as the same-colored "note" slides past the target displayed on the screen.

Guitar Hero III: Legends of Rock outsold *Rock Band* in 2007, and this trend of *GH* dominance has continued with the most recent version. *Rock Band 2* (MTV Games, 2007) has sold only 2.48 million, while *Guitar Hero: World Tour* sold almost that many copies on the Wii alone, totaling 6.13 million copies as of February 8, 2009.[2]

(Cont'd.)

Best Games for Programs *(Continued)*

Each new version of *Guitar Hero* is more than just an expanded playlist; for example, *Guitar Hero II* added two-player modes for bass and harmony, not just rhythm, *Guitar Hero III* added an online component, and *Guitar Hero: World Tour* added a drum kit and microphone to transition from a two-player guitar game to a four-player band game.

Both *Guitar Hero* and *Rock Band* games may be purchased online; visit the Rock Band Store at www.rockbandstore.com/. Beth Gallaway is RedOctane affiliate, and purchasing through her Yahoo! store earns her a 5 percent commission on the sale to help her cover Web site costs. Available: www.store.yahoo.com/cgi-bin/clink?adux+WpPqCG+index.html.

Rock Band 2 (Harmonix, 2008). Xbox 360, PS2, PS3, Wii.
The instruments and gameplay were revamped for *Rock Band 2*, the sequel to *Rock Band*. Up to four players compete or collaborate to play through a variety of current and classic punk, rock, and pop songs. One library keeps *Rock Band* permanently set up. At the Pima County Library (Tucson, AZ), a tournament was held across the system in December 2008, with practice sessions scheduled for specific dates and times at the branches prior to qualifying tournaments. The championship was held Saturday, January 17, 2009, at the Joel D. Valdez Main Library. Available: www.rockband.com/contact.

Wii Sports (Nintendo, 2006). Wii.
Wii Sports is a sports game rated E for Everyone. *Wii Sports* comes with the Nintendo Wii. Games are for two to eight players. Controllers can be traded off, so no extra accessories are needed; just pass around one or two Wii-motes. Tennis and bowling are particularly well suited to group games; golf and baseball, less so. Boxing is the most physically challenging and the longest, running at around ten minutes for three three-minute rounds. Available: www.nintendo.com/wii.

Mario Kart (Nintendo, 2008). DS, GameCube, Wii.
Mario Kart is a racing game rated E for Everyone. It is a great choice! It's a game for two to eight players. Because it has so many options (3 speeds, 8 characters, 16 tracks), it has an amazing depth of play. A discussion of using *Mario Kart* for library programming could fill an entire book. It fact, it does! Eli Neiburger's *Gamers at the Library?!* (ALA Editions, 2007) is an excellent resource of best practices in game tournaments, many with Nintendo platform games. Available: www.mariokart.com.

Halo 2 (Microsoft, 2004). XBox and Windows.
Halo 2 is an exceptional first person shooter game with several gameplay modes. It is rated M for Mature for Blood and Gore, Language, and Violence. Some libraries are starting to offer first person shooter games in teen programming. Permission slips are recommended for teen participation, as *Halo 2* is a Mature rated game. The premise of the game is to hunt down alien or human opponents and slay them with guns, missiles, grenades, tanks, and more. Consoles are networked to create a LAN, or two players play in timed rounds. Available: www.microsoft.com/games/halo2.

Soul Calibur II (Namco, 2008). Gamecube, Xbox, and PS2.
Soul Calibur II is a fighting game. It is rated T for Teen for Animated Blood, Mild Language, Suggestive Themes, and Violence. Multiple characters play in multiple battle venues. Available: www.soulcalibur.com.

Evaluations

What are the criteria for determining the success of your program? Number of attendees? Positive reviews from participants? Enthusiastic comments from parents? Connecting with just a few participants after the event and building relationships with them? Seeing video game program participants come into the library for reader's advisory or homework help?

Informal Evaluations

Cover tables in the program room with butcher paper or newsprint or white paper tablecloths. Put markers on the tables. Invite teens to comment on the program by writing on the tablecloth. Ask a teen volunteer to transcribe the comments for inclusion in your program report or your end of the year report.

Put a flipchart and markers in the room. At the top of the page, write, "Gaming at the library was…" and ask participants to complete the sentence. Let them know constructive criticism is appreciated, but negative comments should be accompanied with a suggestion on how to improve the program.

Formal Evaluations

Create a one-page questionnaire to rate the style of the program, the timing of the program, and the games played. This is a good opportunity to also survey event participants about the kinds of board, card, and video games they like to play, what kinds of consoles they own at home, and what kinds of services and programs the library can offer to gamers. Consider putting the survey online for easier data collection. Adapt the formal, outcome-based Program Survey form (see Figure 4SG.1) in the Level 4 Strategy Guide to fit your needs.

Best Practices

This section describes model programs offered at specific public, special, academic, and school libraries. Programs range from clubs to tournaments to educational programs to drop-in programs.

Gaming Clubs

Description

Gaming clubs may or may not meet on a regular basis. Often participants have some input into gaming program events and services targeted at gamers.

Gaming Club at Carvers Bay (SC) Branch Library

The Gaming Club at the Carvers Bay Branch (in Hemingway, SC) of the Georgetown (SC) County Library System runs weekdays until 8 p.m. Out of a potential pool of 550 high school teens, 40 youth joined the Gaming Club in May 2005. A month later, the number was up to 60, with 30 percent of them checking out books to fulfill their commitments. Approximately 90 percent of the members of the Gaming Club currently are African-American male teenagers, a very important demographic group to engage in using public library services in rural Georgetown County (which has a 30 percent illiteracy rate, a 15 percent unemployment rate, a poverty level exceeding 30 percent, and up to 90 percent of school kids eligible for free or reduced-rate lunches). A meager 2 percent of the population of 7,000 has a library card.

Any individual can use the games for two hours per week. Extra gaming time is earned by joining the Gaming Club. Joining requires:

- a current library card,
- good standing (no serious misbehavior), and
- a commitment to checking out four items per month, two of which must be books.

Once in the club, members accumulate points to become eligible for additional gaming time, group gaming parties, special prizes (headphones, memory units, gift certificates), or use of the conference room with the 46-inch TV. Points are earned by doing at least one of the following:

- Writing a book report
- Attending an after-school program
- Participating in a youth service organization
- Embracing other positive, self-improvement activities

The library owns ten Xbox 360s. One Xbox 360 is in the conference room, connected to a 46-inch LCD television and 5.1 surround sound audio system. Another unit is in the auditorium, connected to the overhead LCD projector with a 120-inch screen and 7.1 surround sound audio system. The remaining eight units have high definition (HD) video and audio signals, two wireless controllers, a Dolby headphone stereo adapter, a four-port headphone distribution amplifier, and two headphones.

The library also owns eight Dell Dimension 9150s gaming computers with 2G memory, a high-end graphics card, and a 20-inch wide aspect flat panel display. Each station has a Dolby headphone stereo adapter, a four-port headphone distribution amplifier, and two headphones for each unit. The library is outfitted with 120 data ports, including strategically located CAT-5 cabling and allowance for future WiFi ports, intended to provide maximum flexibility for regrouping of systems for LAN gaming parties.

The Gaming Club partners with the Frances P. Bunnelle Foundation (www .bunnelle.org), the local school district, and the youth services organization Service Over Self (www.sosvolunteers.org). The school uses part of the grant to offer enrichment classes on some unconventional topics like photography and music as well as provide courses in test preparation. Service Over Self helps coordinate everything, thereby offering students the opportunity to do community service with the possibility of earning scholarships for college. Contact Dwight McInvaill at dmcinvaill@georgetowncountysc.org for more information.

LAN Parties

Description

LAN stands for "local area network." Basically, a LAN party involves linking computers and installing the same games on the linked computers. This creates a shared space for participants to play together. Of course, the library may already have a computer lab with machines on a shared network. LAN parties can be low impact for a library; ask patrons to bring in their own machines, and the library provides cables and snacks.

Games for LAN Parties

Real-time strategy, first person shooter, and role-playing games lend themselves well to multiplayer action. Bear in mind that you need one copy of the software for each computer. Not sure how to set up a LAN? Check out *LAN Parties: Hosting the Ultimate Frag Fest* by William Steinmetz (Wiley, 2004). Appropriate games include the following (most have spawned numerous sequels to the original games):

- Real-time strategy games
  - *Age of Empires* (Microsoft 1997)
  - *Age of Mythology* (Microsoft, 2002)
  - *Civilization* (MicroProse, 1991)
  - *StarCraft* (Blizzard Entertainment, 1998)
  - *Ur-Quan Masters* (Accolade, 1992)
- First person shooter games
  - *BZFlag* (Open source development, many versions)
  - *Counter-Strike* (freeware, requires purchase and installation of *Half-Life* first)
  - *Doom* (id Software, 1993)
  - *Quake* (id Software, 1996)
  - *Unreal Tournament* (GT Interactive, 1999)
  - *Vampire: The Masquerade–Redemption* (Activision, 2000)
  - *Wolfenstein* (id Software, 1992)
- Role-playing games
  - *Neverwinter Nights* (BioWare, 2002)

Some game demos come with LAN features. Neal Starkey, a member of the LibGaming Google Group, recommends checking CNET (www.download.com/3120-20_4-0.html?sort=totalDL&qt=lan+demo+game&tag=srt.td) to see what's available.

Counter-Strike LAN Party at the Santa Monica (CA) Public Library

When this afterhours program debuted at 6 p.m. one Friday night, 60 teens lined up around the block to play. So many teens came that the library had to find alternate activities for those beyond the first 30. Having anime to show and board games on hand helped. The library networked 30 computers and installed the same software so that teens could play *Counter-Strike*, a weapons-based "capture the flag" sort of game, against one another. Teens had to sign in and show a student ID to enter, and they were signed out if they left.

A LAN party requires multiple PCs with good video cards. Don't forget to test the game first! The information technology department may need to reduce security settings in order to install the game and allow gameplay. Although *Counter-Strike* is a free download, you have to first purchase and install a PC version of *Half-Life* (Sierra Studios, 1998). Half-Life costs $35 new; used, it runs between $10 and $15.

Gamers who attended the program joined the Teen Advisory Council. They suggested other programs, and teen programming expanded to include poetry slams, anime, and *Yu-Gi-Oh!* tournaments. Teens came to view the library as a cool and comfortable place to be.

PC LAN Party, Grayslake Area (IL) Public Library

An afterhours teen LAN party is held at Grayslake Area (IL) Public Library about four times a year, from 6 p.m. to 12 a.m. Participants are invited to bring their own computers and game copies for PC gaming. Setup begins at 5:00 p.m., with gaming at 6:00. A pizza order is called in around 6:30 p.m., and the program finishes up at midnight.

Registration is required; interested gamers can sign up in person, contact the Adult Reference Desk in person or by phone (847-223-5313, ext. 200), or register online through the library's Event Keeper Calendar. A minimum of ten registrants are needed to hold the program. Additionally, the program is publicized on LAN Party (www.lanparty.com) to reach nonlibrary users. The site has an article titled "Hosting 101" that is a primer on LAN parties.

Initially, the library tried a more structured approach, listing the games that would be played. This hindered the party, however, as some would have the games and some wouldn't. In its current incarnation, the LAN Party is essentially a free for all as far as which games are being played, with three or four different games going on at once. Participants have also brought Xbox and PlayStation consoles along with their computers, allowing a free-flowing system of "any game goes."

Play has worked out quite well. The teens share different systems, swap machines for a while, compare hardware, and socialize. The library doesn't use any kind of waivers or permission slips; librarians simply set up the meeting room and keep the rest of the library closed off. To date, theft and breakage are nonissues.

Automated Systems Manager Sean Draegert, who implements the programs as scheduled by YA Librarian Dawn Miller, says, "In the beginning, the socialization was the grail for me. I have two teenage children, both who play online games, but the real key to what was missing in my opinion was a face-to-face interaction, which the LAN parties achieve."

All of the gaming equipment is patron owned. All the library needs to provide is some network switches, cables, a DHCP server (of some sort), and Internet access. According to Sean, it is really quite simple: network the guests, have something online to dish out IP addresses, and provide a hole out to the Internet to ensure that software patches can be retrieved. In addition to the cost of the network cables and the server, the library spends roughly $100 per party for refreshments: pizza, chips, and drinks.

The free-for-all approach works well at Grayslake. "Don't be dismayed if they're not all playing the same game at the same time," says Sean. "My goal was to get them face to face to some extent and away from some of the isolation of purely Internet play." For more details, contact Dawn Miller at dmiller@grayslake.info or Sean Draegert at sdraegert@grayslake.info.

RuneScape Programs

In some libraries, *RuneScape* (Jagex LTD, 1999) is the bane of the reference staff's existence, because kids who get excited about the game often exhibit undesirable library behavior: jumping out of their chairs, yelling across the room, grouping around one machine, arguing when their computer time limit is up. Banning of *RuneScape* or *all* streaming media or video game sites happens because of these behavioral issues, or sometimes because the software "hogs too much bandwidth." Beware of eliminating access to sites favored by specific demographics; it smacks of ageism! Certainly, librarians shouldn't be in the position of putting value judgments on how patrons use the Internet or deciding if it's more important to check out materials or offer free Internet access. One solution to the *RuneScape* problem is to dedicate a library program to it.

If bandwidth is an issue, consider holding an afterhours *RuneScape* session so you don't slow down the circulation computers. Another option is to limit the times and days when *RuneScape* is allowed. Maybe it's not allowed during the school day in the media center, but after school it's okay to play. Maybe it's banned Monday through Thursday during the school year but encouraged on Friday afternoons.

If you need to ban games, ban *all* games, not just the ones the teens like. No more *Reader Rabbit* in the Children's room or *Yahoo! Chess* in the adult area, either. Many people consider games to be "sticky content" for Web sites—a frequently changing type of content that both keeps users on a Web site longer and attracts users to the Web site more frequently. Your patrons may want to surf to perfectly legitimate sites for some games that are thinly veiled as product placement. Banning software programs that some games run on, such as Java, is not a viable option because today's Web is increasingly multimedia.

If behavior is an issue, try after hours when the noise and roaming around won't disturb those who need quiet to work. Playing together in a formal library program curbs many of the behavior issues, which are, for the most part, normal teen behaviors that meet a developmental need to interact socially with their peers.

If you don't have enough computers to accommodate the number of players who want to participate, consider laptops! Many libraries have wireless connections now, and inviting youth to bring their own computers is a viable option.

RuneScape Team in the Central Kansas Library System

Chris Rippel, of the Central Kansas Library System, Great Bend, created Library *RuneScape* Teams as an experiment to enable librarians to help *RuneScape* players in libraries have more fun. One goal of the program was to increase the value of libraries in the eyes of young people. Simply taking an interest in what young people are doing is an easy and no-cost way to make the library a comfortable and relevant place for youth to be.

At each participating library, one of the library's Web pages is devoted to its Library *RuneScape* Team. *RuneScape*, like many other massively multiplayer online games, encourages players to band together in groups called "clans"; clans are welcomed as library teams, but it's not required for all game players to be in a clan. Characters are grouped by ranges of combat levels rather than by individual combat level, simply to reduce the amount of time spent to update team information.

To hold participants to a deadline and to create some tension, Josh Parsons, a volunteer at the Wired for Youth Center @ Windsor Park Branch in Austin, Texas, created a roster-type template for participating libraries to put on their Web sites (available online at www.ckls.org/~crippel/runescape/teamform.html). To keep the library involved and credited with any success of this project, Chris Rippel recommends that library staff (rather than the teams) update these pages once a month. The pages should not simply be a list of all the *RuneScape* players in a library, but a list of those players eager to participate in events as a team. The concept is to provide contact information so that players in libraries can find other library players and challenge those teams to contests. "Kids from around the world play *RuneScape*," says Chris. "My dream is that public libraries around the world will have *RuneScape*

To register a Library *RuneScape* Team Web page, create a separate page on your library's Web site that includes the following information:

Team name:
Total number of *RuneScape* members = #
Total number of nonmembers = #
Maximum number of players the team can have on the field at one time = #
Combat levels 1–29 = # members, # nonmembers
Combat levels 30–49 = # members, # nonmembers
Combat levels 50–69 = # members, # nonmembers
Combat levels 70–89 = # members, # nonmembers
Combat levels 90+ = # members, # nonmembers
Any other information the team wants to add:
Team e-mail address:
Character name of team contact:
Library:
City, State/Province, Country:
Library staff contact:
Librarian's e-mail address:
Telephone number:

teams. I hope that someday kids in my Kansas will be playing against kids in Australia and Europe."

Players, not librarians, will decide the place, time, and rules of the contest. The teams and the librarians decide the librarians' roles in these contests; they might be, in addition to Web masters and program hosts, umpires and keepers of antes until contests are over. Librarians *don't* need to play to manage a *RuneScape* team. Chris suggests that if a team wants library staff in the game (on the field) during contests, then the teams should be responsible for creating a *RuneScape* character and leveling up that character for the librarian. After teams turn the characters over to librarians, librarians should change passwords to prevent mischief.

If you sent up a library *RuneScape* Team, don't forget to e-mail the URL of the team's Web page to Chris Ripple at crippel@ckls.org. She asks that you please send questions, suggestions, problems, and criticisms to the same address. Visit http://delicious.com/chrisrippel/RunescapeTeams for a list of Library *RuneScape* Teams.

For more details, contact Chris Rippel at cripple@ckls.org or in *RuneScape* at crippel2.

RuneScape Discussion Group at the Lackman (KS) Branch Library

Chris Koppenhaver, Youth Services Librarian at the Lackman Branch Library (Johnson County, KS), gathered *RuneScape* players together to exchange information, swap stories, and brag. The session was held after hours and drew a crowd of 14 teen boys. Discussion focused on character levels, quests completed, items obtained, play style, and enemies defeated. The group was more excited about individual challenges than tournament or competitive play. The program concluded with playing *RuneScape*. Chris describes the event in his own words at www.ckls.org/gaming/runelackman.html. One conclusion he draws is that it would have been fun to have a computer and projector set up so that teens could log in to their own accounts and show off their characters. The Lansing (IL) Public Library did this for a *RuneScape* tournament in summer 2006.

RuneScape Tournament at the Lansing (IL) Public Library

During its Summer Reading program in 2006, the Lansing (IL) Public Library offered a low-key *RuneScape* Tournament. The program utilized library computers with Internet access; for the finale, gameplay was broadcast via a laptop and projector. Prizes cost less than $60.

The program kicked off at the end of June, with interested teens creating new characters on *RuneScape*. The teen librarian recorded the character names. Kids were able to play anywhere for five weeks. Teens were not told what factors would be used to determine winners but were told to build a well-rounded character. For the finale, teens took turns at the library logging in to *RuneScape* on a PC hooked to a projector screen. They all got to see each other's characters, points, and so forth. At this point they were informed that the number of quests completed would determine the winners. Some players had focused on gathering money or weapons yet hadn't completed any quests. Prizes were third place, a $5 one-month subscription to *RuneScape*; second place, a $15 three-month subscription; and first place, a $30 six-month subscription.

There was also a wildcard winner who won a one-month subscription. "We expected a much larger enrollment in the tournament based on the number of *RuneScape* players we see in the library," said Gail Guzman, librarian. Five teens registered, and four teens attended the finale. Noted Gail, "Our Internet terminals require patrons to log in with an "Internet use" card, and parents have to sign permission for their under-age-18 children. Teens that didn't have Internet access cards couldn't log on to set up a character in our controlled environment. We should have publicized the necessity of the Internet access card a few weeks prior to the sign-up date, so they could have their parents sign the card." For more details, contact Gail Guzman at gguzman@lansing.lib.il.us or Kelli Staley at kstaley@lansing.lib.il.us.

Tournaments

Tournament programs are very successful. The focus on winning builds drama and excitement. Be clear about the rules at the beginning, and double check your math. Consider door prizes via drawing so that everyone has a chance to win something.

DDR Dance Party at Sellers Memorial Free Public Library

Gretchen S. Ipock, librarian at Sellers Memorial Free Public Library (Sellers Library for short; located in Upper Darby Township [PA]), put together a *Dance Dance Revolution* (*DDR*) program for 15 teens in grades 6 to 12. Equipment required was one sixth-generation console (an Xbox), two *DDR* games, four *DDR* dance pads, speakers, projector, and cables to connect everything. The teens played *DDR Ultramix* and *Ultramix 2* for Xbox.

> "*DDR* turned out fabulous! I was ready to do it over and over again. I liked the battle mode, when you got to make the opponent's arrows move down. It was fun!"
> —Tyria, grade 7

Why *DDR*? Teens are familiar with the arcade version of the game. It is available in different formats for the Xbox, PlayStation, and Nintendo platforms, so it has broad appeal among system owners. Dance pad options range from cheap to expensive, flimsy to heavy duty. A middle of the road option is fine for most libraries. Always purchase new pads, not used (see Figure 4.16).

DDR has three easy steps (single arrow, double arrow, and hold step) and just four buttons (left, right, forward, back). It is a challenging game to master, however, with its extensive playlist, multiple modes of play, four levels of difficulty, and abilities to increase speed, play arrows backward, and make arrows. *DDR* is among the number one games played by girls, who prefer titles without story.

The event at Sellers Library lasted for two hours on a Friday night, which gave everyone ample dance time through the evening. Gretchen reports, "Before each song, teens selected the level they wanted to play (Beginner, Light, Standard, Heavy), and collectively agreed on the music. Each disk contains several variations of the *DDR* game, so we switched modes a few times to mix it up a little. We also held a voluntary single-elimination tournament with a game store gift card as a prize. While one group was dancing, other teens watched, practiced the steps alongside the dance pads, talked, or played cards at nearby tables. There was also a table of fiction and

Figure 4.16. DDR Pad Options

Dance Dance Revolution Solutions

Level 1 (Cheap)	Level 2 (Good)	Level 3 (Better)	Level 4 (Best)	Level 5 (Top of the Line)
• TV Dance Pad Plug N Play pad ($40) • No console or game required.	• PlayStation 2 console ($129) • DDR game (~$40) • 2 soft flexible Konami pads ($30 each) • Plastic or vinyl construction • Slowest response rate • Slippery • High failure rate • PlayStation/XBox compatible	• PlayStation 2 console ($129) • DDR game (~$40) • 2 Red Octane Ignition pads ($100 each) • Foam padding lends support – • Vinyl and foam construction • Fairly responsive • Playstation/XBox/ PC compatible	• PlayStation 2 console ($129) • DDR game (~$40) • 2 Red Octane Afterburner pads ($250 each) • Metal construction • Sensitive and accurate response • PlayStation/XBox/ PC compatible	• PlayStation 2 console ($129) • DDR game (~$40) • 2 Cobalt Flux dance pads ($234.50 each) • Plastic and steel construction • Sensitive and accurate response • PlayStation compatible
Note: slippery pads are best for home use or as prizes, not for library programs	Note: pads will wear out over time; socks or barefoot play only.	Note: superior and lightweight; socks or barefoot play only.	Note: durable but heavy. Play best with shoes on	Note: durable, professional grade
www.ddrgame.com/ dadareddrtvp.html	www.ddrgame.com /konami.html	www.redoctane.com*	www.redoctane.com*	www.cobaltflux.com

*thanks for purchasing Red Octane products through www.libgaming.blogspot.com!

Source: Chart created by Beth Gallaway.

graphic novels for them to browse." This was a very low-budget program. The librarian's personal Xbox, games, dance pads, and speakers were used with the library's projector, so there was no equipment cost. "I did spend money on the tournament prize ($10), water ($5), and healthy snacks ($15)," says Gretchen. "The session is so successful (and so cheap!) it's repeated two to four times a year." The permission slip and program flyer Gretchen used for a Game Boy SP event are reproduced in the Level 4 Strategy Guide (see Figures 4SG.7 and 4SG.8).

What advice would Gretchen give to other librarians who might want to replicate this program?

"Go for it! This is a great, low-budget program that can be repeated often. It works well in various time slots, including after school, in the evenings, on Saturday afternoons, and during vacations. If you do not personally own a gaming console, ask teens who attend your programs what they have. Often, they are willing to bring in their own equipment for a gaming program. And don't be afraid to get out there and do it yourself! Shy or inexperienced dancers will welcome this icebreaker, and you will find out that *DDR* is a lot of fun! For more information, please contact me at grrllibrarian@yahoo.com."

—Gretchen S. Ipock

Community Gaming Event, Lake City (FL) Community College

Seventy gamers, including high school and community college students, parents, the local newspaper editor, business people from gaming stores, and faculty, attended a six-hour gaming extravaganza of *Madden*, *Crimson Skies*, *Halo*, *DDR*, and *Project Gotham* Xbox tournaments at the Lake City (FL) Community College. Fourteen games ran on two 52-inch monitors plus 12 other monitors connected to Xbox consoles. In addition, people checked out the new collection of 35 PC games that were purchased through the community college's foundation grant and played them on newly acquired gaming computers. The Anime Club brought their own games. Event collaborators included the audiovisual department, who hired a DJ, and Student Activities, who offered free food. The library hired Ken Schirrmacher from the Technology Department, who is also a *Halo* champ, to run several of the tournaments.

> "We discovered that our old academic library facility is perfectly designed for gaming events, and we are already planning our next event."
> —Vickie Lepore, Reference Librarian

Library director Jim Morris met another librarian, Patricia Hay from Orange Park, Florida, at the July 7th gaming event and they were married in the library in May 2008. To view write-up and photos from the events, visit http://lcccpopculture .blogspot.com; for more details, contact Vickie Lepore at leporev@lakecitycc.edu.

How Can I Pay for Gaming Equipment?

Budget: Purchase equipment out of your program budget. The equipment depreciates with time, but you can extend your initial investment for years to come.

Donors: Keep a wish list of equipment and materials on your library's Web site. Potential givers are more likely to donate when they know exactly where their money is going.

Friends: Ask the Friends of the Library to purchase consoles, games, and controllers.

Grants: Try local banks, national chains, and foundations of all kinds; even library vendors and divisions offer grants! Alternatively, apply for an Institute of Museum and Library Services grant to cover hardware and software costs and licensing fees.

Regional services: Put pressure on your regional library system or consortium to circulate gaming kits; they can write grants to put the kits together.

> "A materials list was presented to the local Sam's Club. Sam's Club has been a contributor to the library in the past. They made a generous decision to contribute a $1000.00 grant to offset the start-up costs for our gaming program. The new equipment made it possible to implement the program concepts and bring gaming to the Youth Services Department in the McCracken Public Library."
> —Iris Garrott, Youth Services Manager, McCracken County Public Library, Paducah, KY

With the Sam's Club donation and numerous others, Iris Garrott helped establish the Young Adult Media (YAM) bar in her library (see Figure 4.17). It opened in June 2003. See Iris's full post about the YAM Bar at http://circulating.wordpress .com/2006/07/02/yam-bar-not-sweet-potatoes-but-no-small-potatoes-either.

Figure 4.17. YAM Bar

Source: Photo by Iris Garrott. Available: http://farm1.static.flickr.com/48/180337146_587a
59016a.jpg?v=0 (accessed: April 16, 2009).

Prizes for the tournaments were generously provided by sponsors, who sent trinkets for tournament winners and drawings: NVidia, Bawls (energy drinks), Alienware, CaseAce, FunCom, and Aspyr. "We attribute the success to the team of seven students and three adults who worked the event," says coordinator Vickie Lepore, Reference Librarian, adding, "The success of a program is not limited to planning and coordinating."

Soul Calibur II Tournament, ImaginOn

The Public Library of Charlotte and Mecklenburg County Library (Charlotte, NC) hosted a system-wide *Soul Calibur II* Tournament from June 13, 2006, to August 2, 2006. It was held in the ImaginOn and coordinated by Kelly Czarnecki, Jesse Vieau, and Matt Roach. *Soul Calibur II* (Namco, 2003) is an adventure fighting game for Nintendo, Xbox, and PlayStation consoles. *Soul Calibur IV* (Namco) was released in 2008 and features characters from the previous titles in the series, as well as special guest appearances. Titles in the series have been rated T for Teen for Animated Blood, Mild Language, Suggestive Themes, and Violence. For more about *Soul Calibur*, please visit www.soulcalibur.com.

> "This works well as a summer-long program."
> —Kelly Czarnecki, Technology Librarian

The program attracted mostly male teens between 12 and 18 years of age and their parents, who came to see the championship round. Teens participated in a warm-up round for about 30 minutes and then competed in double-elimination rounds. Two qualifying winners from each of the eight participating branches then competed in the championship round at ImaginOn in August. The qualifying winners were given $10 gift certificates for EB Games. In the championship, the runner-up received another $10 gift certificate and the winner a $50 gift certificate plus a necklace made out of a controller and chain. GameLAN'd (www.gamelandonline .com) donated all-day passes to their facility to the qualifying winners of the branch tournaments. Prizes totaled $230. Other expenses were the gaming consoles and games (three Xboxes, projectors, and screens), but the library system owned them already.

Kelly Czarnecki advises, "If you want to run a systemwide tournament, have a training for librarians to feel comfortable in participating. Involve teens in promoting the event (one teen produced a video we kept on our Web site during the tournament)." For details, visit the library's Web site at www.libraryloft.org or contact Kelly Czarnecki at kczarnecki@plcmc.org; Jesse Vieau at jesse.vieau@gmail.com; or Matt Roach at mroach@plcmc.org.

The ImaginOn Library Loft hosted a *Super Smash Bros. Brawl* (Nintendo, 2008) tournament in summer 2008, kicking off one branch at a time for single/double-elimination qualifying rounds and a championship at the Main Branch on August 13. A Gaming Zone Forum was set up at http://thegamingzone.wordpress.com.

Tournament Rules:

Competition is limited to teens aged 12–18.
Competition is one player vs. one player.
The hosting library will decide if the session will be double or single elimination.
The top two players from each qualifying round will move on to the championship at ImaginOn.
Those who *do* place first or second at a qualifying round may not compete at another branch until the championship at ImaginOn on August 13th.
Those who *do not* place first or second at a qualifying round may enter more qualifying rounds throughout the summer.

Tournament Game Settings:

Stock 3
5-minute time limit (if tie, go to sudden death)
Random stages
"Medium" items set at random
All characters available

Equipment:

Game will be played on a Nintendo Wii.
All players will use the library's GameCube controllers (no personal controllers).

Super Mario Brothers Melee Tournament at the Escondido (CA) Public Library

Jeff Wyner, YA Librarian at the Escondido (CA) Public Library, insists his method of organizing a tournament will work if you follow his to-do list of instructions slowly and deliberately. He designed an Excel spreadsheet that automatically seeds players for competitive play and notes that the program is designed for any game (not just *Super Smash Bros.*) that allows four people to compete in a head-to-head-to-head-to-head competition. The spreadsheet can be adapted to teams for any game that has two teams or two individual players competing head to head.

Marketing always comes first. Produce flyers and distribute them to schools and libraries. Don't forget to post copies in other places where your intended audience will see them. Next, send an announcement to the media. Confirm the assistance of any sponsors (also send *them* a copy of the PR!). Get your graphics department or a local Kinko's to produce poster-sized tournament charts, at least four copies, each approximately 36 inches high by 48 inches wide.

Produce intake forms for each participant. Jeff created a short form that can fit two players on one sheet (don't forget to cut the double forms in halves!). Entreat volunteers armed with forms and pencils to assist in the sign-in and registration processes. Registration should begin about 30–60 minutes before the start of the tournament, as it will take at least that long to get everyone registered and the tournament charts established. One strategy that worked was to "officially" start the tournaments at 10:00 a.m. when the library opened but to start registration at 9:00 a.m. outside the library near the entrance. Otherwise, there may be a horde of teens roaming the library until start time, and the Reference staff will be less than thrilled over this scenario.

Designate at least one volunteer to be a runner, who will periodically bring forms to the main tournament table. Additional volunteers are needed:

- One to announce which game is to be played at which station
- One (or two) to write results on the wall charts
- One for each game table
- One to assist the librarian at the tournament table (optional)

At the tournament table, set up a laptop computer with a flash drive loaded with game-day programs, a printer with cable and paper, scissors, pens, a microphone, and a copy of the Official Tournament Rules. Post copies of the rules on the walls, near the standings charts, and at each competition station. Print copies of the Tournament Chart with game numbers (the number of players determines the number of games played). Keep one at the tournament table, and post one or more near tournament wall charts.

At the start of the program, explain how a double-elimination tournament works—everyone plays twice—as most players may not understand this concept. Break the competitors into groups, using the intake forms. Write their names and grades onto the sign-up seeding form (school name is optional for statistical reasons only—hide this column), highlight all entrants, and then sort by grade level (descending); this will allow 12th graders to be seeded ahead of 11th graders, and so on. Then split into divisions by grades: upper division, grades 10–12; middle division, grades 8 and 9; lower division, grades 6 and 7. Only 32 (or less) names can be entered into any given division (16 for Team play). If less than 32 names are placed into a division, the remaining spaces should have the word "bye" placed into the "empty" slots; a "bye" automatically loses. Try to balance the number in each split division rather than have one with 32 and the other with what could be substantially less than 32. For example, if you have 42 competitors, create two divisions of 21 each rather than one of 32 and the other of 10.

To "seed" someone, place his or her name at the top of the division list (e.g., someone who won a previous tournament can be seeded in the #1 spot). If you have more than 32 players per division, create two divisions, one with 32 and one with the remaining players or teams.

Jeff's Excel form (see Figure 4SG.22 in the Level 4 Strategy Guide) uses drag and drop to create an automatic seating chart. As play progresses, the chart can be printed at the end of each division (or every eight games for four-player games), and a runner can post the results on the walls. Jeff notes that games should *always* be played in numerical order (Game 1 followed by Game 2 followed by Game 3, etc.), that it's okay to have a different competition table for each division, and that older kids should get to go first (with age comes privilege!).

Set up the room so that each division will play at its own table. For the championship round, Jeff suggests playing this round in reverse order, that is, the upper (oldest) division will play last. If possible, project this last round on a large screen for the audience. Make sure to explain to the audience how the last game(s) are to be played. As many as four games may need to be played in the championship round to determine the champion. Those coming in from the last round already have one loss each. All first and second place players are still considered as having won until there are only two players remaining; then and only then is second place considered to be a loss. With only two players left, the first to acquire two losses will be the division's second place winner; the other player will be the division champion.

Leave time to present trophies or prizes at the end of the competition and to take pictures (in front of wall posters!); give the wall posters to the champions. Copies of the files Jeff uses are online at www.informationgoddess.info/go. For more details, contact Jeff Wyner at jpwyner@yahoo.com.

Gaming Night at the North Hunterdon High School (Annandale, NJ)

> "The tournament is a good chance to meet other students with the same interests as you."
> –TSC Member

Gaming nights at the North Hunterdon High School (Annandale, NJ) are student-run events hosted by the school's Gaming Club. Teens bring their own equipment—Xboxes, Game Boys, PlayStations—and games. The school provides the room, projectors, and extension cords. No limits are placed on game titles. In the past, teens have brought *Halo 2*, *DDR*, *EverQuest*, *Harbinger* (DreamCatcher Interactive Inc., 2003), and others. "The students have been the movers and shakers getting the prizes, the food, the drinks, the setup, and cleanup," says librarian Ginny Konefal. Prizes are donated by online game distributors and the local gaming store. The program costs nothing; an attendance fee turns the event into a fundraiser for computers for Habitat for Humanity. For details, contact Ginny Konefal at gkonefal@nhvweb.net.

Winter Break Pokémania at the Ann Arbor (MI) District Library

Winter Break Pokémania was a week-long *Pokémon* tournament in which kids brought their own Game Boys and copies of compatible *Pokémon* games (*Fire Red*, *LeafGreen, Ruby, Emerald,* or *Sapphire*) and their own *Pokémon* that they've captured and trained. They competed in daily single-elimination tournaments, battling their *Pokémon* against each other on the big screen. Organizer Eli Neiburger said, "It's a real thrill for them, a high-energy event, and *Pokémon* is a highly social affair; still a very big deal for older elementary/early middle schoolers!"

The library got a lot of mileage out of the event, hosting an open tournament on Tuesday, a level 50-plus tournament on Wednesday, an under-50 level tournament on Thursday, and an under-25 level tournament on Friday. Each event ran about four hours. Participation was around 50 elementary/middle school kids and their parents. Many players attended all four tournaments, but each day had different finalists and a different winner due to the strengths and weaknesses of their *Pokémon.*

This was a low-cost event. The library owns a projector, a GameCube with a controller, two Game Boy Advance-to-GameCube cables, a copy of *Pokémon XD* for GameCube, a voice amplification system for play by play, and a laptop for scoring. A house Game Boy with a set of house *Pokémon* was available for new players, but only two kids used them all week. Prizes were one $10 gift card each day for the winner; other costs were about $20 for food each day (pretzels, cookies, crackers, water). A box of trinket prizes (library highlighters, flashlights, plus giveaways that the Youth Department had lying around) was on hand so that every kid got to pick a prize upon elimination.

The event was run by one staff member, with assistance from a youth services librarian who stopped by periodically to restock food, put out materials, visit with parents, and so forth. These are fantastic events to reach that older elementary audience, and it gives these kids an opportunity to put their *Pokémon* skills, knowledge, and experience to use in a "real" battle situation. The technical setup is very easy, although sometimes it can take four to five tries to make a successful Game Boy Advance-to-GameCube connection.

The biggest challenge is knowing how to structure and run the tournament. Eli advises, "Find some Pokéfreaks in your community and get the basics and some guidance before your first event. We used double battle with three *Pokémon*, with a 30-second command limit and ten-minute match limit." Most matches lasted three minutes, and only one went the full ten minutes. Try a *Pokémon* event and embrace the Pokéfans in your community! For more details, contact Eli Neiburger at eli@aadl.org.

Quotes from Participants:

"This has been a great week for all of us!"
—Parents of a 13-year-old girl and an 8-year-old boy who attended all four tournaments

"I thought you were a *Pokémon* expert!"
—Ten-year-old girl, upset that Eli couldn't answer her technical question

"You get paid to do this?"
—Appreciative parent

"Next time, four days in a row is a little much."
—Not quite as appreciative, but still good-natured parent

"We made him take a shower today."
—Parent (who I appreciated) in reference to his smelly son

"Thanks for doing this, it means so much to them."
—Parent of two elementary school boys

"She's going to trade me my Wurmple for her Lugia!"
—My 4-year-old son, talking about the 14-year-old girl he befriended

"Groudon weathers a fierce attack from gy-RAR-dos."
—Eli, on the mic

"That's pronounced GY-rar-dos!"
—Every kid in the room

"I hope you don't know this stuff off the top of your head."
—One of the dads, in reference to Eli's play by play

"No, no, I've got Bulbapedia."
—Eli, in reference to the Wikipedia of the *Pokémon* world
(http://bulbapedia.bulbagarden.net/wiki/Main_Page)

Free Play

Informal, low-key, and inexpensive, free play options range from participant-provided programs to programs with library-owned consoles—available during all library hours or during specific program times. Best practices are described.

Teen GameFest, Tigard (OR) Public Library

The 2007 summer programs for teens at the Tigard (OR) Public Library included a free play gaming event. The library purchased a PlayStation 2 system, two dance pads for *DDR*, and a Nintendo GameCube with two extra controllers so that at least three people could play at once. About 27 teens in grades 6 through 12 came to play *DDR Extreme 2* on a big movie screen and alternate between *Mario Kart Double Dash* and *Super Smash Bros.* on a smaller television screen.

> "Several moms thanked me repeatedly for having a program like this for their teens."
> —Jessica R. Marie, YA Librarian

"Everyone had a *blast* at this event, and many of the teens were asking to do it again very soon. When I told them the next one was scheduled for October (which was two months away), they thought that wasn't soon enough!" says YA Librarian Jessica R. Marie. "*DDR* was the biggest hit, especially with two dance pads. The teens could easily compete with each other if they wanted, and spectator attention was not on just one person at any time. The other teens would often practice their moves while players were on the dance pads." She adds, "All of the participants were well behaved and took their turns in a very civilized fashion."

Playing board games is a great activity for teens who are waiting their turn for *DDR* or other video games. Organizers of this event set up several tables for board games, such as *Life, Clue, Monopoly, Fact or Crap*, checkers, chess, and cards, with two or three games to choose from on each table. Scratch paper and pencils were provided. This was a great way for teens to socialize—often with others they hadn't met before.

Incidentally, Tigard Public Library supports many forms of gaming. Other programs have included improv, or theater games, a trivia night, as well as additional free play video games. On the library's teen blog, the librarian posts about opportunities like music camp that includes *Guitar Hero* and online games to try. She never misses an opportunity to connect books to teens but has absolutely recognized that games and gaming is a huge part of their lives. For details, contact Jessica R. Marie, YA Librarian at Jessica@tigard-or.gov.

Budget Breakdown

This program cost approximately $450, but the amount will be spread over an extended time period because everything can be used again in future programs. The library already owned a television and the board games, so those cost nothing. Purchases included:

two game systems (PS2 and GameCube): $230 combined	three extra controllers: $50
	three video games: $100
two dance pads: $40	snacks and drinks: $20

Teen Library Night Game Night, Corvallis-Benton County (OR) Public Library System

Corvallis-Benton County (OR) Public Library System began hosting a monthly free play event, Teen Library Night Game Night, in 2006, which ran during the second week of every month in four locations. At the main library, the event was held during normal business hours; at the branch libraries, the teens used the entire library after hours. Two years later Game Night is running not once a month but *eight* times a month—the second and fourth week, Monday through Thursday. Librarians set up four systems (two Xbox systems and two PS2 systems on two projectors and two televisions) to play *Halo 2, NBA Street, NFL Street,*

"It has been my experience that the teens are more than willing to help out in terms of providing equipment. It is amazing how much support we have received from teens (in terms of equipment, setup, cleanup, etc.), who are appreciative that we are trying new things at the library."
–Andrew Cherbas, Librarian

Soul Calibur 2, Time Splitters 2, Tony Hawk, DDR, and games in the *Need for Speed* series and the *Burnout* series. As the program grew in popularity, the library upgraded the equipment and games, adding Wiis, Xbox 360s, *Halo 3,* and *Rock Band.* A third projector has been added to run multiple games simultaneously.

Initial startup costs were around $800. Hollywood Video was an original program partner, providing free game rentals for program purposes. Now that the library has incorporated a circulating game collection, there is usually a good selection of games to choose from in the Technical Services Department waiting to be cataloged.

"Be prepared to explain the worth of playing video games at the library, to not only patrons, but other staff members and management. I would also try to include the teens as much as possible," suggests librarian Andrew Cherbas. One small way the library serves gamers is by posting a booklist of titles with gamer appeal online at www.thebestlibrary.net/joomla/content/view/161/113/. For more details, contact Andrew Cherbas at Andrew.cherbas@ci.corvallis.or.us or Heidi Weisel at heidi.weisel@ci.corvallis.or.us.

After-School Zone, Benicia (CA) Public Library

Every Monday through Thursday from 3:15 to 4:45 p.m. when school is in session, between 25 and 45 kids attend the After-School Zone to snack, socialize, do homework, and play games—as long they wash their hands after their snack and read over the Video Game User Policy first! A quiz on the rules precedes picking up a controller.

About half of the patrons take advantage of the Teen Zone's three TVs, an Xbox 360, GameCube, and PS2. The department assistant who supervises the After-School Zone occasionally brings in his Wii so the kids can play *Smash Bros. Brawl,* which is very popular. An upgrade to PS3 was considered, but staff decided that the games the teens like to play on a PS2 (*Guitar Hero,* mostly) wouldn't be materially different with a PS3, and they couldn't justify the cost. On the GameCube, *Mario Kart* and *Super Smash Bros. Melee* are popular. The PS2 is used almost exclusively for *Guitar Hero.* One unique element to the After-School Zone is that kids and teens with signed parental consent forms on file can play M-rated games like *Halo 3* on the Xbox 360. The TV is situated so that the back of it faces the room. Only the players using the Xbox 360 can see the content, preventing those without signed permission slips from glimpsing the content of the M-rated games.

The cost for setting up the gaming at the After-School Zone was about $1,000; the library already had one TV and a power strip. Two additional TVs cost about $180, and an Xbox 360 cost $400. The GameCube came in a bundle with a controller or two—that, and the extra games and controllers, took up the rest of the money. This year, several hundred dollars from the Youth Services' budget were devoted to games; they bought a charger for batteries and new games for the Wii.

Organizer Allison Angell urges librarians to try gaming on a near-daily basis, noting that even an occasional game event would be fun. "It's been great for those kids whose parents expect them to hang out at the library every day (in lieu of a daycare program or babysitter)." The library also has standalone gaming events, such as *Halo 3* and *Guitar Hero III* tournaments, monthly *Scrabble* and chess afternoons, and Old School Game events focused on board games.

After running the program for over a year, Allison noticed that gaming was a way to decrease the digital divide. "[Gaming at the library] is also a chance to level the pop-culture playing field. Kids who don't have the games at home can try them here. Everyone can be a *Guitar Hero*, thanks to the Library." Allison's video game brochure is reproduced in the Level 4 Strategy Guide (see Figure 4SG.9). For more details, contact Allison Angell at aangell@ci.benicia.ca.us.

Tournament Thursdays, Peabody Institute Library (Danvers, MA)

Once a week, the meeting room at the Peabody Institute Library (Danvers, MA) is set up with game stations that teens can jump between: tabletop ping pong sets, various board games, and a television with a DVD player. This is a drop-in program for kids aged 12–18, although the group is mostly made up of middle school students, thanks to support and promotion by the middle school.

> "This is some of the best money I've spent on programming."
> —Michelle Deschene-Warren, YA Librarian

Games include *Ping Pong, Checkers, Scene It!* (The Movie Edition), *Monopoly, Scrabble, Jenga,* and traditional playing cards (see Figure 4.18). The program is scheduled to last an hour but usually ends up going over so kids can finish up games in progress. The star of

---

Figure 4.18. Tabletop Ping Pong Setup

Setup for Tournament Thursdays, Peabody Institute Library, Danvers, MA.

Source: Photo by Michelle Deschene-Warren.

the Tournament Thursdays is *Ping Pong*. At one program over 30 teens vied for time on the four tables. Some of the teens want to start a league; they've even suggested competing against other local libraries (they've begun to think about team names and a design for a T-shirt).

The total cost of the games was around $70. The sets can be found really cheaply. Michelle advises, "If you have an active teen advisory board, get input on what games they enjoy playing. While the group takes advantage of just about every game I put out, they definitely have their favorites, and I would have been better off getting, say, more checker boards than purchasing *Monopoly*." The teen advisory board is currently brainstorming ideas for one big Tournament Thursday in which prizes would be awarded; to date, competition has been informal. They are still working on the specifics, but several teens have expressed interest in playing for prizes. For more details, contact Michelle Deschene-Warren at deschene@noblenet.org.

GameFest, Bloomington (IL) Public Library

The first video game free play event at the Bloomington (IL) Public Library drew 60 teens, aged 12–17 from the Bloomington/Normal area; the library now partners with Bloomington Parks and Recreation, Normal Public Library, and Normal Parks and Recreation to host three events a year. Attendance is around 50 participants each time. Collectively, Bloomington Public Library and Bloomington Normal Education Association own Nintendo GameCube setups, an Xbox 360, Xbox, PS2, dance pads for *DDR*, guitars for *Guitar Hero I, II,* and *III, Rock Band* controllers, monitors, projectors, wires, and controllers. (Normal hosts a quarterly event.)

Activities range from video games like *Rock Band, DDR, Guitar Hero,* and *Mario Kart*; to retro games, board games, and puzzles; to LAN *Unreal Tournament* with 16 players. Staff work normal hours and trade shifts to cover the evenings. A promotional Web site at http:/B/ngamefest.org keeps the community apprised of current events, and photos are posted from previous events are posted on Flickr (www.flickr.com). The librarians note that the teens socialize, not just with their peers, but also with librarians and technical staff. For more information, contact John Fischer at johnf@bloomingtonlibrary.org or Chuck Thacker at chuckt@ bloomingtonlibrary.org.

Advice from John Fischer:

- Have a great tech staff willing to not only help, but play along with you and the teens.
- Make the public aware of what you are doing.
- Promote, promote, promote.
- Be willing to learn the games, play the games, and challenge the other gamers.
- Be willing to be very tired by the end of the night.
- Flickr is a great way to document and promote. See our Flickr site at www.flickr.com/photos/bloomingtonlibrary/sets/.

Game Design

Game Studio, Minneapolis Public Library

A dozen teens aged 12–19 attended each Saturday session offered from July to September 2006 by the Minneapolis Public Library (MPL) on how to create a video game. The kids used *Scratch*, a free beta game program from MIT, to create their own video games. Each Saturday the kids either worked on their established project or created a new one. Each session let them learn a little more. The library provided a PC with *Scratch* loaded onto it and access to the Internet for images. Learning Technologies from the Science Museum of Minnesota (SMM) picked up the cost of the initial sessions through a grant. SMM has staff well versed in the software program and teach classes at the museum using *Scratch*.

Demand was high! YA Librarian Jennifer Nelson advises librarians to plan multiple events because the draw is high; MPL couldn't accommodate everyone who wanted to participate in the space available, even with five sessions. So, they added more sessions. Since 2006, the MPL (now Hennepin County Library) has continued to work with the SMM to bring innovative technology programming to area youth.

Monthly workshops were designed to allow youth to learn and hone new skill sets. The larger focus of the programming effort has been to support youth in creating rich media projects by developing their 21st-century literacy skills. The resources needed for the programs are a set of computers, perhaps a projector, and staff to teach.

"We've been fortunate to have funding from the Best Buy Children's Foundation to engage the highly trained staff from the Science Museum, but any staff with an interest in rich media creation could host the programs," says Jennifer. She notes that costs are cut by using software that is freely available on the Web (like *Picasa* [http://picasa.google.com] for artists, *Audacity* [http:/audacity.sourceforge.net] for musicians, and *Gimp* [www.gimp.com] for digital photographers), with some project Web hosting provided by the software publishers (e.g., games can be posted to the *Scratch* Web site for display and continued development).

Workshops run for three hours, which is generous; kids can get an excellent start on a *Scratch* project/game within that time. Additionally, MPL hosts and staffs open lab times when youth can come in and work on projects. "All in all, at our funded location we offer one class per week most weeks of the year," reports Jennifer. "A second location offers two sessions per month and is staffed by the Teen Tech Squad."

The Teen Tech Squad is a youth development program that began out of the first set of Game Studio workshops. Staff quickly became aware of the high level of knowledge of some workshop participants and their desire to share what they knew with their peers. MPL was able to leverage the funds from Best Buy to offer a group of teens, aged 15–18 (grades 8–12), about $8 per hour to conduct the sessions. The teens teach in teams of two and decide on the curriculum, who will do what, and how to work together. Library teen services staff members Christy Mulligan and Aaron Lundholm mentor the teens, who are also provided extensive training from the Science Museum staff. ("We are so lucky to be able to work with them!" says

Jennifer). The teens typically teach other teens but have also taught classes to adults and younger youth. For many it is a first job experience, and they learn basic job skills. The sessions they run attract five to eight youth participants, depending on the location. The programs could be easily adapted for libraries with smaller budgets by using youth volunteers; Jennifer points out, "We've certainly had interest from other youth who are willing to do it for free."

In 2008, MPL created a Game Studio Literacy Evaluation Project to look at what they were teaching and how to evaluate the 21st-century skills that youth are getting from participating in the workshops. The application for another Institute of Museum Library Services grant to bring the Teen Tech Squad to national partners and evaluate its success in developing youth developmental assets as identified by the Search Institute is in the works. For more details, contact Jennifer Nelson at jrnelson@mplib.org.

Video Game Design, Bloomington (IL) Public Library

In 2006, several teens in the Bloomington (IL) Public Library's after-school technology club learned to make their own games on the library's Dell PCs, using professional game design software from MultiMedia Fusion. The students followed the Youth Digital Arts CyberSchool's (YDACS) curriculum for a month, which taught them the basics of game and multimedia design. The software and curriculum were purchased with grant money from the Illinois State Library's Project Next Generation After-School Program. Each course curriculum fee was $40, and the software was $100 per license, so the initial startup cost for three students was $420. Bloomington continues to make the software available to anyone that wants to develop games with it, utilizing the software purchase to its full extent.

> "The beauty of using the [Youth Digital Arts CyberSchool] service is that you don't have to know how to use the software to offer it."
> —Matt Gullett

Says Matt, "We've had a lot of success in using this curriculum in our after-school activities. In fact, I just received a nice thank you note from a parent that praised us for how we have engaged her son in games, game design, etc." One other aspect of this program is that it is self-led; therefore, library staff members who want to lead such a class do not have to know how to use the software or create the game. They can learn and this would probably be recommended, but it is not a must to offer it to youth as an educational service. The cost of $40 per student may seem prohibitive to many libraries. Matt acknowledges, "It is a bit more than one might expect, but I believe that giving youth this opportunity is more than an experience for them. Besides, how many book titles sit on our shelves that barely circulate that are truly a waste of resources in acquiring, processing and maintaining?" He cites the National Middle School Association's list of developmental needs of teenagers for justification, arguing that game design provides teens opportunities to experience structure and limits, the creative process, socialization, competence and achievement, and self-definition.[3] For details, contact Matt Gullett at mgullett@ gmail.com.

Free Video Game Design Software

Other sites and programs on the Internet that a library or organization can use in teen programs include the following:

Alice. Available: www.alice.org. *Alice* is a free scripting and prototyping environment program for 3D object behavior that runs on Windows 95/98/NT. It has a drag-and-drop graphical interface that translates to Java, C++, and other "production" programming languages, so it also reads many common 3D file formats. It was developed at Carnegie Mellon. The Web site provides tutorials and other instructional materials.

Ben 10 Alien Force Game Creator. Available: http://gamecreator.cartoonnetwork.com. *Ben 10* is a drag-and-drop game creation software program with preset characters and settings. Build your game, test it, and upload it to the Cartoon Network's Web site for others to try!

Game Maker 7.0. Available: www.yoyogames.com/make. *Game Maker* is a free drag-and-drop style game design program. The Web site offers tutorials, support, an online community, games to beta test, and effects to download, such as backgrounds, graphics, and sound effects.

Scratch. Available: http://scratch.mit.edu. *Scratch* is a free scripting and prototyping environment program for 3D object behavior that runs on Windows 95/98/NT. It has a drag-and-drop graphical interface that translates to Java, C++, and other "production" programming languages, so it also reads many common 3D file formats. It was developed at MIT. The Web site provides tutorials and other instructional materials.

Licensed Software for Game Design

Adrift. Available: www.adrift.org.uk/cgi/new/Adrift.cgi. *Adrift* is a text adventure game for Windows 95/98/NT/2K/ME/XP that uses forms and pull-down menus and lists to structure the game.

Click Team. Available: www.clickteam.com/eng. *Click Team* has several Windows software applications at different levels of expertise (and cost): *Games Factory 2*, a simple program for 2D games and screen savers ($59.00); *Multimedia Fusion 2*, more advanced, for creating games and applications ($119.00); and *Multimedia Fusion Developer*, with even more features and options ($369.00).

Educational and Training Opportunities

The serious games movement and the games in education movement are both gaining momentum, though designing an appealing game that is educational, fun, and compelling is a challenge. Three ways that academic libraries are incorporating games are described.

Library Arcade, Carnegie Mellon University

The game design program *Alice* was created at Carnegie Mellon (Pittsburgh, PA), so it's no surprise that the school also offers other training tools. In 2007, graduate students in the university's Entertainment Technology Center designed two library games that are now in Final Testing Stage. You can access them and play them on the university library's Web Site (www.library.cmu.edu/Libraries/etc/index.html; accessed April 28, 2008). The goal of *Within Range* is to organize books in Library of Congress shelf order. The goal of *I'll Get It!* is to deliver the right resources for reference questions.

Government Information Training for Reference Staff, University of Waterloo

At the Dana Porter Library (University of Waterloo, Waterloo, Ontario), library restructuring included retraining reference staff in the government documents area. Innovative reference librarian Christy Branson developed a game-like tutorial as a training mechanism. She devised online tutorials and created Web pages using *Dreamweaver*. Tutorial topics were Understanding Government, Statistics, Legal System, and Best GovInfo Practices. For each topic, Christy wrote a one-page overview with resource links, followed by a challenge—short quizzes and tasks to test learning. Answers to challenges were sent directly to her e-mail box. Humor and Easter eggs were added throughout the lessons as a test to make sure players read thoroughly and a nod to a game design practice. Usability testing with students helped to improve the story line and gameplay.

Staff were divided into teams and were required to work through online material. Reference questions were asked based on the material; points were awarded for individual answers, and team totals were tallied. Small prizes were given to the winning players, and team standings were publicized. Various strategies were employed during gameplay—some staff worked together to come up with correct responses, while others chose to play solo. When a player admitted to "cheating," Christy called it strategizing.

Costs mainly included staff time. Christy reports that the material took roughly one month to prepare prior to the launch. A Master of Library and Information Science co-op student, Kevin Manuel, assisted in the program development.

Prizes were small and consisted of items already owned by the library as well as some donations. To improve the program, Christy wants to include instant feedback. Participants had to wait for staff to review their answers; automation may be possible, using courseware programs. Extending the time line is a future goal; short deadlines were difficult for some to meet. Each of the four lessons could take one to two months to complete, and the training took place over just three weeks.

The training program is archived online at www.lib.uwaterloo.ca/staff/isr/gp2/index.html. For more details, contact Christy Branson at cbransto@uwaterloo.ca.

The Clicker Personal Response System, LaChance Library, Mt. Wachusett Community College

Heidi McCann, the Reference and Instructional Services Librarian at LaChance Library, Mt. Wachusett Community College (Gardner, MA), learned about clicker technology in articles and documentaries and thought it seemed promising for the college's library instruction program. She obtained a set of clickers (Personal Response Systems) for a trial period during a fall semester. "Faculty were intrigued with the clickers," says Heidi, "and by December I was able to convince the Academic

Affairs to buy a set of 24 for the college to use." The library actually didn't purchase the first set or the second; the Office of Academic Affairs (the library and all academic departments fall under this) did.

What is a Personal Response System (PRS)? A PSR consists of battery-powered remote control–like devices called "clickers" that work on an infrared or radio frequency to report to a receiver. Students are able to respond with answers to questions posed by an instructor by clicking buttons that correspond with yes, no, or multiple-choice answers. The response is wirelessly transmitted. The same PowerPoint-compatible software that displays the presentation slides and questions collects all of the answers and provides feedback, such as a graph to show how many respondents picked A, B, or C. Infrared systems require respondents to be in a line of sight with the receiver and can host 40 students/clickers; the radio frequency model does not require line of sight to the receiver and can host ~2,000 students/clickers. Clickers help to maintain students' attention during a lecture, allow instructors to check for understanding, engage students during the class, offer an opportunity for introverted students to participate, and promote discussion.

> "All instructors should be using these."
>
> −Student in bibliographic instruction session

The library invested $2,500 for a set of 32 Q4s made by Qwizdom. They live in the library and are bar coded for circulation to faculty, librarians—any college staff. Between English (ENG 101) and Computer Technologies (CIS 127), the library provides 5 hours of instruction time, so these are always candidates for classes to use clickers in. A core group of 5–10 faculty members use the clickers at least once a semester. The popularity of interactive sessions utilizing the PRS has resulted in more staff hours spent delivering library instruction sessions, as Figure 4.19 shows.

For library instruction, for example, quiz questions like "what is a keyword?" or "what is an abstract?" allow the librarian to expand student vocabularies in terms of academic research, explain searching techniques, and introduce the library and its resources. One participant in the study asked if the class could take all the quizzes using clickers. In fact, yes: some PRSs allow instructors to save results of Q&A to a grade book. "It's worth the money to invest in a PRS," says Heidi. "It's also worth taking the time to learn how to use the technology. It helps you reach out to multiple learning styles, and fosters discussion." For more details, contact Heidi McCann at hmccann@mwcc.mass.edu.

Summer Reading Programs

Teen Loft: "Get Your Game On" Summer Reading Program

> "I admit it, I planned my gaming-themed summer reading program around my teen raffle grand prize: a PSP."
>
> −Sarah Sogigian, YA Librarian

The "Get Your Game On" summer reading program was held from June 20 to August 17, 2006, at the Shrewsbury (MA) Public Library for teens entering grades 5–12 in the fall. The library put a PS2 console in the newly decorated Teen Loft. This room, which was set aside by the Library Board of Trustees for teens to use after school, includes a television with VCR and furniture and

Figure 4.19. Quizdom Usage Statistics

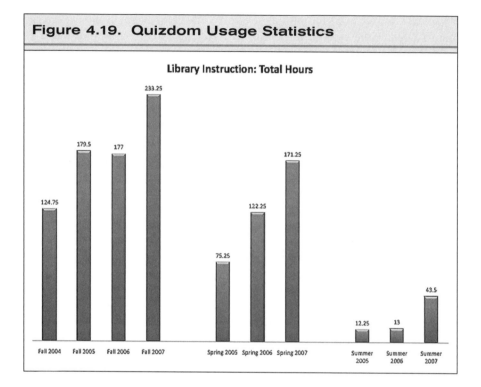

Library Instruction: Total Hours

decorations purchased with funds raised by the teen advisory board through a semiannual basket raffle. The librarian purchased a used PS2 console and, with the help of the custodian, secured it to the cart that houses the television. The console stays on the cart, hooked up to the television, for teens to use whenever they're in the library.

Teen Loft PS2 Rules:

1. Only library-owned games can be played.
2. Games must be checked out and returned to the circulation desk.
3. Players must share the console with others.

Librarian Sarah Sogigian reports, "So far, all rules have been followed, and the PS2 is consistently in use. Plus, the teens have the added bonus of a DVD player in the loft (the PS2 also doubles as a DVD player)!"

Gaming was an effective theme to use to promote the library's gaming collection, the PS2 in the Teen Loft, and the summer reading program. Sogigian created the program's logo, made posters, promoted the program on a blog, and wrote newspaper articles. To complement the gaming theme, the program logo was put on Frisbees that were handed out to teens. The program was very basic: for every reading level–appropriate book participants read between June 20 and August 17, they filled out a raffle entry and were able to pick from a selection of prizes to try to win. The grand prize was a handheld gaming machine, a Sony PSP. The following year, in 2007, the grand prize was a Nintendo Wii.

An end-of-summer concert on Shrewsbury Common featured student bands from Shrewsbury High School, Intermission, and Midway schools. At the concert, the teen advisory group drew the winning raffle tickets and announced the winners. Some prizes were donated by local businesses, including Newbury Comics, Border's Bookstore, and Commerce Bank, while others were purchased. The total cost for the program was $500 for prizes and $220 for sound equipment for the bands. For more details, contact Sarah Sogigian at sarah@mmrls.org.

Tex Teens Read! '08: Game On! Texas

Texas Teens Read! is the annual statewide summer reading program offered by the Texas State Library for teens aged 12–18. The 2008 theme was Game On! An online manual details eight exciting programs focused on electronic gaming, role-playing games, board games, trivia games, extreme sports, and more.

Each program description includes a list of developmental assets that the program could meet, related reading materials, marketing ideas, refreshment suggestions, and multiple specific games and activities. In fact, a library could run an entire six- to eight-week program using only one of the components. The entire manual is online at www.tsl.state.tx.us/ld/projects/ttr/2008/manual. For more details, contact Christine McNew, Youth Services Consultant, at cmcnew@tsl.state.tx.us.

Notes

1. *Allen v. Academic Games League of America*. 89 F.3d 614 (9th Cir.1996): Available: http://bulk.resource.org/courts.gov/c/F3/89/89.F3d.614.html (accessed: April 16, 2009).
2. VGChartz.com. Available: www.vgchartz.com (accessed: April 16, 2009).
3. National Middle School Association. 2007. *Young Adolescents' Developmental Characteristics*. Available: www.nmsa.org/Research/ResearchSummaries/DevelopmentalCharacteristics/tabid/1414/Default.aspx (accessed: April 16, 2009).

Bonus Round 4:
Word Search

Figure 4.20. Word Search

```
s f a a s n p a n u m w r p p m n
n o l o a a r l w n i u a i r i o
o e a u c a u w i i n o e c k e m
g p m m x s m z t e r a f t a w e
a l a r n x z n s o c b e u t a k
r n e s o u l c a l i b u r a a o
d b i g b r a i n a c a d e m y p
d e b n u p e g d e b d u k a d e
n a d h e s l h w e l b b a r c s
a p p l e s t o a p p l e s i d t
s o a r n a b u g l i k r e d r e
n g u i t a r h e r o e a a a o k
o s l w d l a h r m l d w k m c o
e t i - e n e c s b b r o r a k a
g o x i a s t r o p s i i w c b r
n a d n e i o s a s r a r a y a a
u b u r r p n n b a b c a n r n k
d o i m x o l b m o o b w t s d r
```

APPLES TO APPLES	BIG BRAIN ACADEMY
BOOM BLOX	BUZZ
DDR	DUNGEONS AND DRAGONS
FLUXX	GUITAR HERO
HALO	KARAOKE
KATAMARI DAMACY	MARIO KART
PAC MAN	PICTUREKA
POKEMON	ROCK BAND
RUNESCAPE	SCENE-IT
SCRABBLE	SOUL CALIBUR
SSBB	WARIO WARE
WII SPORTS	WITS AND WAGERS

Figure 4.21. Word Search Solution

```
s f a a s n p a n u m w r p p m n
n o l o a a r l w n i u a i r i o
o e a u c a u w i i n o e c k e m
g p m m x s m z t e r a f t a w e
a l a r n x z n s o c b e u t a k
r h e s o u l c a l i b u r a a o
d b i g b r a i n a c a d e m y p
d e b n u p e g d e b d u k a d e
n a d h e s l h w e l b b a r c s
a p p l e s t o a p p l e s i d t
s o a r n a b u g l i k r e d r e
n g u i t a r h e r o e a a a o k
o s l w d l a h r m l d w k m c o
e t i - e n e c s b b r o r a k a
g o x i a s t r o p s i i w c b r
n a d n e i o s a s r a r a y a a
u b u r r p n n b a b c a n r n k
d o i m x o l b m o o b w t s d r
```

APPLES TO APPLES	BIG BRAIN ACADEMY
BOOM BLOX	BUZZ
DDR	DUNGEONS AND DRAGONS
FLUXX	GUITAR HERO
HALO	KARAOKE
KATAMARI DAMACY	MARIO KART
PAC MAN	PICTUREKA
POKEMON	ROCK BAND
RUNESCAPE	SCENE-IT
SCRABBLE	SOUL CALIBUR
SSBB	WARIO WARE
WII SPORTS	WITS AND WAGERS

Level 4 Strategy Guide: Forms and Flyers for Video Gaming Programs

Figure 4SG.1. Program Survey

Program title: _____ Program date: _____
Library: _____
City, State: _____
Coordinator's name: _____
Coordinator's e-mail: _____
Web site address: _____

Who attended?

What equipment was required?

What games did you play?

What happened at the event?

Who did you partner with?

How much did the program cost (budget breakdown)?

Please share any quotes from participants:

What advice would you give to other librarians who might want to replicate this program?

Do you have any photos or documents to share (i.e., program flyer, scoring sheet, press release)? If so, please attach.

Source: Beth Gallaway.

Figure 4SG.2. Collection Survey

Collection contents (age range, consoles supported, genres purchased):

Collection development policy (selection, purchase, cataloging, weeding procedures):

Circulation policy (limits, fee, replacement costs):

Most popular titles:

Least popular titles:

Issues, concerns, successes:

How much did the collection cost (budget breakdown)? How does it compare to your total materials budget?

Circulation statistics:

Please share any quotes from users:

What advice would you give to other librarians who might want to collect games?

Source: Beth Gallaway.

Figure 4SG.3. Video Game Evaluation Checklist

Title: _____

Designer:_____

Publisher: _____

Date: _____

Platform(s): _____

Genre: _____

ESRB Rating:_____

Plot:

Engaging premise:

Conflict: What compels you to continue playing?

(Cont'd.)

Figure 4SG.3. Video Game Evaluation Checklist *(Continued)*

Characters:
  Nonstereotypical characters?
  Diverse characters?
  Customizable characters?
  Unique non-player characters (NPCs)?
  How do NPCs interact with your character?

Multiplayer modes:

Setting: Complete and believable world building?

Realistic physics:
  Game space exists on physically plottable map?
  Terrain is fun and interesting to explore?
  Real environmental and geographic details are accurately rendered?
  What environmental details flesh out the setting?

Graphics:
  Fast loading with smooth motions and actions?
  Clipping or ghosting of images?

Relevant cut scenes:

Sound:
  Ambient sound adds to the setting?
  Musical score sets mood and tone?
  Speech is clear, with facial expressions synchronized to audio?
  Voiceover acting is well executed?
  Music is licensed and credited?

Game design:
  Multiple storylines or modes of play?
  The design includes a logical rewards system?
  Leveling up is reasonably challenging?
  What is the experience curve? How long will it take to get the game? To master it? Is the game replayable?

Modifications:
  Game code is open to manipulation?
  Options are customizable?

Support:
  Online and/or phone support is available from the publisher?
  Online and/or phone support is available through fan forums?

Source: Beth Gallaway.

Figure 4SG.4. Survey: Game and Console Preferences for Gaming Night

Directions: Please select one top game choice for each console. You may write in a suggestion for library play. Game suggestions must be rated E, E10+, or T for teen and consist of short rounds that are good for groups to play! For example, all of the games listed below are 2–4 player with songs, trials, or sessions lasting from between 3 and 10 minutes. Consoles are limited to GameCube, PlayStation 2, Wii, or Xbox 360.

1. **Console # 1: Sony PlayStation 2**
   - *American Idol Karaoke* (2 player)
   - *Dance Dance Revolution: Supernova 2* (2 player)
   - *EyeToy Play* (4 player)
   - *Guitar Hero I* (2 player)
   - *Guitar Hero II* (2 player)
   - *Guitar Hero III* (2 player)
   - *Katamari Damacy* (2 player)
   - *Namco Museum* (*Pac Man, Pole Position*, etc.; 2 player)
   - *Ratchet & Clank: Up Your Arsenal* (4 player)
   - *Rock Band* (4 player)
   - Other (please specify): _____

2. **Console # 2: Sony PlayStation 2**
   - *American Idol Karaoke* (2 player)
   - *Dance Dance Revolution: Supernova 2* (2 player)
   - *EyeToy Play* (4 player)
   - *Guitar Hero I* (2 player)
   - *Guitar Hero II* (2 player)
   - *Guitar Hero III* (2 player)
   - *Katamari Damacy* (2 player)
   - *Namco Museum* (*Pac Man, Pole Position*, etc.; 2 player)
   - *Ratchet & Clank: Up Your Arsenal* (4 player)
   - *Rock Band* (4 player)
   - Other (please specify): _____

3. **Console #3: Nintendo Wii**
   - *Big Brain Academy*
   - *DDR: Hottest Dance Party* (2 player)
   - *Mario Kart N64* (4 player)
   - *Mario Kart Wii* (4 player)
   - *Rayman Raging Rabbids* (2 player)
   - *Wii Play Wii Sports* (2 player)
   - Other (please specify): _____

4. **Console #4: Nintendo GameCube**
   - *Donkey Konga* (3 player)
   - Other (please specify): _____

5. **Console #5: Xbox 360**
   - *Beautiful Katamari* (2 player)
   - *LEGO Star Wars: The Complete Saga*
   - *Scene It?* (4 player)
   - Other (please specify): _____

6. **Nintendo DS**
   - *Brain Age 2*
   - *Drawn to Life*
   - *Guitar Hero: On Tour*
   - *LEGO Star Wars*
   - *Mario Kart*
   - *Nintendogs*
   - *Pokémon Diamond*
   - Other (please specify): _____

7. **OPTIONAL: Write-in.**
Is there a 2–4 player game with short rounds (3–10-minute turns) that is rated T for Teen or lower (sorry, no *Halo*!) for the Wii, PlayStation 2, or Xbox 360 console that you would rather play?

Please list title and console preference:

Title: _____

Console:
   - GameCube
   - PlayStation 2
   - Xbox 360
   - Wii

Source: Beth Gallaway.

Figure 4SG.5. Survey: Console Preference

Directions: The library is going to offer gaming programs! Please give us your input for consoles, video games, and tabletop games to purchase!

1. **Console Options:** Please rate your console preferences by numbering your first, second, and third choices:
   - GameCube
   - 2–4 Player Nintendo DS
   - PlayStation 2
   - PlayStation 3
   - 2–4 Player PlayStation Portable
   - Xbox
   - Xbox 360
   - Other (please specify): _____

2. **Video Game Types:** Please rate the style of game you prefer by numbering your first, second, and third choices:
   - Action/Adventure Games (*LEGO Star Wars, Pokémon, Super Monkey Ball*)
   - Band Games (*Rock Band, Guitar Hero: World Tour, Rock Revolution*)
   - Dancing Games (*Dance Dance Revolution*)
   - *Guitar Hero* (I–III)
   - Karaoke Games (*American Idol, SingShot, High School Musical*)
   - Party Games (*Rayman Raging Rabbids, WarioWare, Scene It?, Wii Play*)
   - Puzzle Games (*Big Brain Academy*)
   - Racing Games (*Mario Kart, Gran Turismo*)
   - Retro Games (*Pac Man, Pole Position, Centipede*)
   - Shooter Games (*Ratchet & Clank, Halo*)
   - Other (please specify): _____

3. **Tabletop Game Types:** Please rate the style of game you prefer by numbering your first, second, and third choices:
   - Playing Card Games (war, bridge, poker)
   - Battle Games (*Magic, Pokémon*)
   - Card Games (*Apples to Apples, Settles of Catan, Fluxx, Uno, Nanofictionary*)
   - Classic Board Games (*Monopoly, Scrabble, Risk*)
   - Dice Games (*Dungeons & Dragons*)
   - Modern Board Games (*Pictureka!*)
   - Train Games (*Ticket to Ride*)
   - Jigsaw Puzzles
   - Other (please specify): _____

4. **OPTIONAL: Write-in.**

Title (and console if applicable): _____

_____

Source: Beth Gallaway.

Figure 4SG.6. Gaming Program Evaluation with Pre/Post Survey

Program title: _____ Program date: _____

What did you think of the program?

Excellent   Very Good   Fair   Bad   Awful

How often do you use the library?

Never   Rarely   Monthly   Weekly   Twice a week or more

PRE SURVEY:

Please rate the following on a scale of 1–5, 1 = disagree strongly and 5 = agree strongly:

The library is a place for books:	1	2	3	4	5
The library is a place for homework:	1	2	3	4	5
The library is a place for games:	1	2	3	4	5
The library is a place to hang out and relax:	1	2	3	4	5
The library is a place to meet friends:	1	2	3	4	5
The library is a place to play on the computer:	1	2	3	4	5
The library is a place for research on the computer:	1	2	3	4	5
The library is a boring place:	1	2	3	4	5
The library is an exciting place:	1	2	3	4	5

How would you rate your knowledge of playing games BEFORE the program?

Total n00b   I knew a little   I knew some   I was an expert

POST SURVEY:

Please rate the following on a scale of 1–5, 1 = disagree strongly and 5 = agree strongly:

The library is a place for books:	1	2	3	4	5
The library is a place for homework:	1	2	3	4	5
The library is a place for games:	1	2	3	4	5
The library is a place to hang out and relax:	1	2	3	4	5
The library is a place to meet friends:	1	2	3	4	5
The library is a place to play on the computer:	1	2	3	4	5
The library is a place for research on the computer:	1	2	3	4	5
The library is a boring place:	1	2	3	4	5
The library is an exciting place:	1	2	3	4	5

How would you rate your knowledge of playing games BEFORE the program?

Total n00b   I knew a little   I knew some   I was an expert

Please complete this sentence:

Gaming at the library was . . .

Source: Beth Gallaway.

Figure 4SG.7. Sample Permission Slip/Photo Release

Game Boy SP Night

Event Permission Slip

Date: _____

Time: _____

Background Information

At this event, participants will have the opportunity to link up their games and battle each other in a relaxed and fun environment. Participants should bring their Game Boy Advance or Game Boy Advance SP, favorite multiplayer games, and cords or wireless adaptors to link. Gaming books, magazines, and other resources for tips and cheats are also welcome.

There will be a tournament using Pokémon games (Emerald, Sapphire, Leaf Green, Ruby, and Fire Red), for those who bring them. Participants will be under the supervision of a Sellers Library staff member at all times.

Sign-ups are available on a first-come, first-served basis. This permission slip must be returned to participate.

Personal Information

Participant's Name: _____

Age: _____ Grade: _____

Phone Number: _____

E-mail Address: _____

Rules

1. Participants must behave in a manner respectful of the other participants, their personal property, and library property. Participants who do not follow directions or who behave inappropriately will be asked to leave.

2. All participants must provide their own game equipment, including Game Boy, cords, and games.

3. The library is not responsible for participants' personal belongings.

4. **ALL** participants must have a signed permission slip on file with the library. No visitors are allowed, even if they are not playing.

5. **ALL** participants must be entering grades 6 through 12.

Parent Signature

My child may participate in Game Boy SP Night. I understand and agree with the rules of this event.

Signature of Parent/Guardian: _____ Date: _____

☐ Please check here if you do not want photos of your child from this event used in library publicity.

Source: Gretchen S. Ipock, Sellers Memorial Library, Upper Darby Township, PA.

Figure 4SG.8. Game Boy Night Poster

GAMEBOY NIGHT!

Friday, September 29★★★6:30 to 8:30 pm

★★★For Students in Grades 6 to 12!★★★

If you plan to attend, bring your:
- GameBoy Advance or GameBoy Advance SP
- Cords or wireless adaptors to link up
- Games
- Game Books or Magazines

During the event, there will be a Pokemon tournament using the games Sapphire, Ruby, Fire Red, Leaf Green, and Emerald. If you have those games, bring them along and prepare to duel!

Register Now!

BATTLE OTHERS! SHARE YOUR KNOWLEDGE!
SELLERS LIBRARY ★★★ 76 S. STATE RD. ★★★ UPPER DARBY ★★★ 610-789-4440

Source: Gretchen S. Ipock, Sellers Memorial Library, Upper Darby Township, PA.

Figure 4SG.9. Video Game User Guidelines

Important Rules

- **No eating or drinking is allowed during play or near the games. Hands must be clean before playing.**

- **The volume of the game will be determined by staff. The user is not allowed to adjust the volume without consent.**

- **No overly aggressive trash-talking is allowed. Players are required to keep their boasting to a minimum and to think about the other players in the room.**

- **General After-School Zone rules are in effect. These include (but are not limited to) the following: no screaming, shouting, throwing, or hitting.**

- **Players may not touch the game console itself, the software (including cases), or anything else related to their operation for any reason, unless given explicit permission to do so.**

Responsibilities

- **The Benicia Public Library is not responsible for any theft of or damage to the user's games and/or devices. Please watch your belongings with care.**

- **It is strongly recommended that the user seek parental consent prior to participating. Parents are advised to be aware of their children's activities and are encouraged to visit.**

- **If you are sensitive to different light patterns, use your own discretion. The Library will not be responsible for any of the consequences that might result from play.**

- **Games are provided as a free service. As such, the Library makes no guarantee of functionality, quality, or the availability of these games.**

- **Disagreement with, unwillingness, or failure to follow the rules as outlined will result in elimination from play and possibly also expulsion from the Library. No exceptions will be made.**

Benicia Public Library

Videogame User Guidelines

Benicia Public Library
150 East L Street
Benicia, CA 94510
707-746-4343
http://www.ci.benicia.ca.us/library.html

Players

-Children 8 and older are allowed to play games rated E. Those younger than 8 years of age are not allowed to participate unless accompanied by an adult at all times.

-Teens are allowed to play E and T-rated games.

-Adults are welcome; however, keep in mind priority use of this service will be given to those aforementioned groups.

Games

- Participants are allowed to bring in their own games, TVs, and systems, within reason, but they must be screened for general use. Be prepared to share equally whatever game equipment is brought in.

- All games rated M or above are banned, unless otherwise noted. The Library reserves the right to restrict or allow play of any game, regardless of rating.

Turns

-Order will be determined on first-come, first-serve basis. Players are expected to line up and wait for their turn in a civilized manner.

- Loser leaves and the winner stays. The winner may continue for up to 10 minutes (or at the discretion of Library staff). Losers go to the end of the line and wait for their turn again.

- In the event of a tie, all players involved will be required to leave the game.

- Players must finish their turn in the time given to them. No pausing, stalling, or breaks are allowed. Once the game has started, there will be no do-overs or restarts.

- If the above rules are broken, the player will lose his or her turn.

Source: Allison Angell, Benecia Public Library, Benecia, CA.

Figure 4SG.10. Tournament Chart

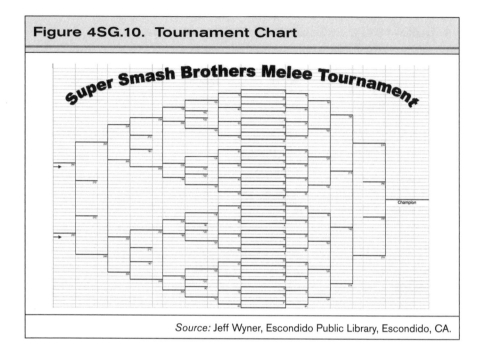

Source: Jeff Wyner, Escondido Public Library, Escondido, CA.

Figure 4SG.11. Game Day Floor Plan

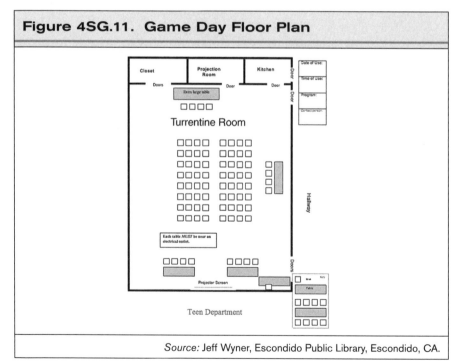

Source: Jeff Wyner, Escondido Public Library, Escondido, CA.

Figure 4SG.12. Tournament Intake Form: Long Version

Super Smash Brothers Melee Tournament
Intake Form

Please *PRINT* neatly

Name _____ Age _____

Phone Number _____

Mailing Address _____ Apt # _____

   Escondido, CA 920_____ (or): _____

School _____ Grade _____

Source: Jeff Wyner, Escondido Public Library, Escondido, CA.

Figure 4SG.13. Tournament Intake Form: Short Version

Super Smash Brothers Melee Tournament
Intake Form

Please *PRINT* neatly

Name _____

Age ____

School _____

Grade _____

Source: Jeff Wyner, Escondido Public Library, Escondido, CA.

Figure 4SG.14. Official Tournament Rules

Official Tournament Rules

Double Elimination
4 stock, 8-minute limit
Ties broken by lives/percentage, NO sudden death
Items OFF

Stages:
Stages limited to the 7 neutral stages for random others open for counter picks.

Neutral stages: Final Destination, Battlefield, Yoshi's Story, Fountain of Dreams, Rainbow Cruise, Kirby 64, and Pokémon Stadium

Stages banned: Hyrule Temple, Fourside, Flatzone, Brinstar Depths, Icicle Mountain, Yoshi's Island 64, Big Blue, Yoshi's Island (Pipes), and Termina

Knockout: Each person knocks out one stage for entire set. This stage must be selected at the beginning of the match, after initial characters have been chosen.

Advanced Slob Picks: Loser may choose the next stage or elect to go random, then winner may choose to change characters, then loser may change characters.

Special Team Rules:
Team Attack ON
Life stealing allowed
During teams, Mute City is banned, due to lag/slowdown

Other Rules & Special Issues:
−Controller mods of ANY kind (short-hop mod, L-trigger mod, etc.), except for cosmetic changes (paint job, different-colored plastic), are banned. If you are caught using a banned controller you will be disqualified from the tournament.

−Turbo or programmed buttons of any kind are banned. You may use third-party controllers or pads that have these features, but if you are suspected of using the banned features you will not be allowed to use that controller any longer.

−Glitches used to stop your opponent from controlling their character or indefinitely freezing them (Mewtwo's Soul Stunner, the Ice Climber freeze glitch), or any glitch or trick that freezes the match or makes it in any way unable to be finished are banned. Using them will result in the immediate forfeit of the match.

−Tactics such as Peach's Wallbombing and Jiggly's Rising Pound are allowed as methods of recovery or to maneuver around the stage. Using them (or any similar tactics) to excessively stall a match, such as dropping below levels intentionally and stalling underneath, is banned. Judges, who will be on the tournament floor, can be called in at any time to enforce this rule during a match.

−You are responsible to BRING YOUR OWN CONTROLLER.

No games between authorized matches. **DO NOT TOUCH** the game settings or system hardware or you may be disqualified from the tournament.

Source: Jeff Wyner, Escondido Public Library, Escondido, CA.

Figure 4SG.15. Tournament Chart with Game Numbers

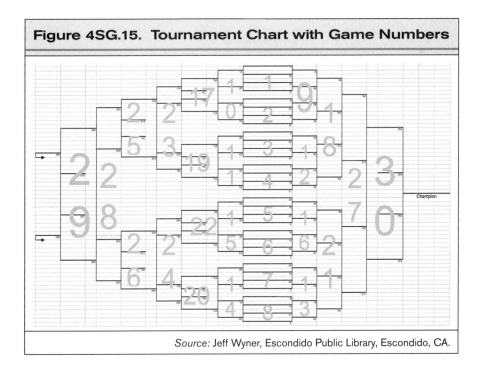

Source: Jeff Wyner, Escondido Public Library, Escondido, CA.

Figure 4SG.16. Sign-up Seeding Form

Name	Grade	School (optional)

Source: Jeff Wyner, Escondido Public Library, Escondido, CA.

Figure 4SG.17. Automatic Tournament Play Chart

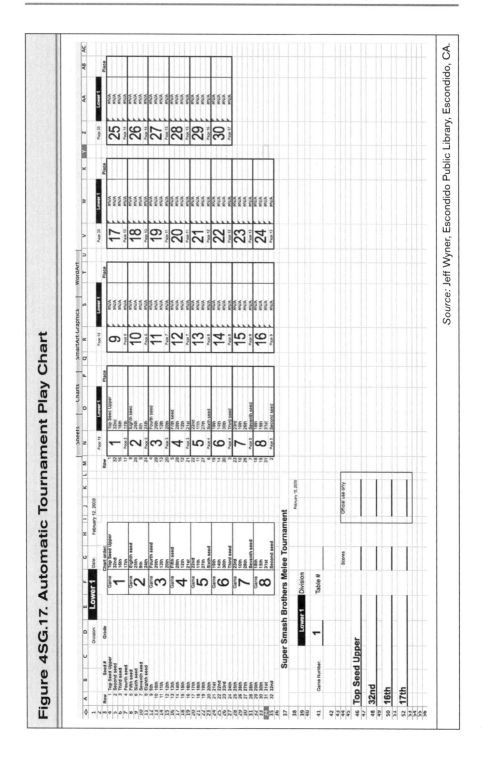

Source: Jeff Wyner, Escondido Public Library, Escondido, CA.

Figure 4SG.18. Team Tournament Chart

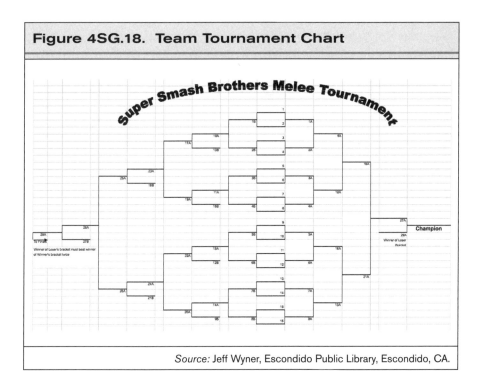

Source: Jeff Wyner, Escondido Public Library, Escondido, CA.

Figure 4SG.19. Team Tournament Intake Form

Please *PRINT* neatly

Name _____ Grade _____

Name _____ Grade _____

Team Name (optional) _____

Source: Jeff Wyner, Escondido Public Library, Escondido, CA.

Figure 4SG.20. Team Tournament Chart with Game Numbers

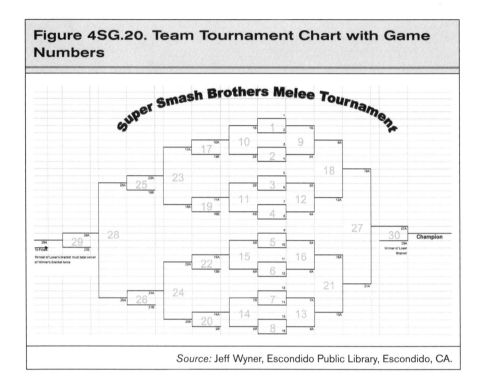

Source: Jeff Wyner, Escondido Public Library, Escondido, CA.

Figure 4SG.21. Sign-up Team Seeding Form

Team Name (or last/names)	Grades added together	Schools (optional)

Source: Jeff Wyner, Escondido Public Library, Escondido, CA.

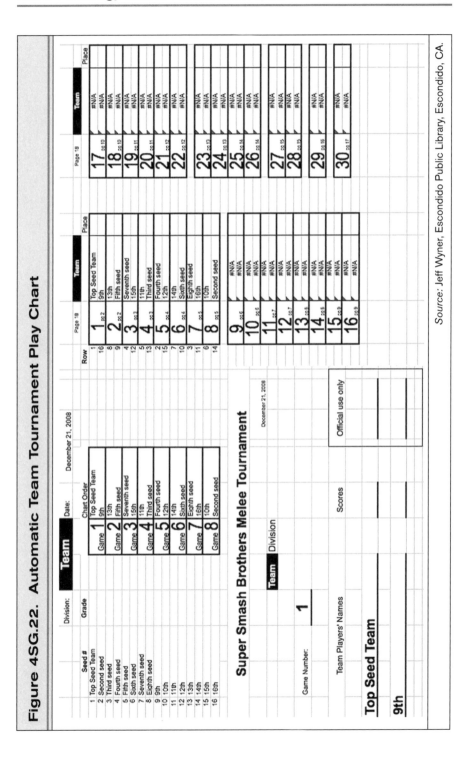

Figure 4SG.22. Automatic Team Tournament Play Chart

Source: Jeff Wyner, Escondido Public Library, Escondido, CA.

Figure 4SG.23. Tournament To-Do List

Super Smash Brothers Melee Tournament Agenda*

*Note: This program is designed for any game (not just SSBMT) that allows four people to compete in a head-to-head-to-head-to-head competition. The TEAM program can be used for any game that has two teams or two individual players competing head-to-head.

1. Announcing SSBMT
   a. Produce a flyer
      i. Distribute to schools
      ii. Place in libraries
      iii. Post other places?
   b. Send announcement to media
   c. Contact your sponsor (EB Games?) to confirm their assistance
   d. Ask Friends group for prize money—suggestions:
      i. $20 gift card to EB Games for 1st place for each division
      ii. $10 gift card to EB Games for 2nd place for each division

2. Send the **Tournament Chart** to the Graphics Dept.
   a. Ask them to make at least 4 copies, each 36" high by 48" (approx.) wide
   b. This and all other steps will be similar for **Team Tournament** play

3. Print the **Game Day Floor Plan** and place into set-up book

4. Print one copy of the **Intake Form: Long Version** (or two copies of the **Intake Form: Short Version**)
   a. This will produce two intake forms per piece of paper
   b. Print enough for as many participants that you expect
   c. Cut the double forms in halves

5. Sign-in table(s)
   a. Have half-sized intake forms on table
   b. Have golf pencils
   c. Volunteers to assist sign-in
      i. At least one will be a runner to periodically bring forms to main tournament table

6. Volunteers/Workers needed
   a. One to announce which game is to be played at which station
   b. One (or two) to write results on the wall charts
   c. One for each game table
   d. Optional: one to assist at tournament table

7. Equipment needed at tournament site/table
   a. Laptop computer
   b. Jump drive/flash drive loaded with game-day programs
   c. Printer w/cable
   d. Paper for printer
   e. Scissors
   f. Pens
   g. Microphone

(Cont'd.)

Figure 4SG.23. Tournament To-Do List *(Continued)*

8. Print the **Official Tournament Rules**
   a. Keep one at tournament table
   b. Place one at each competition station
   c. Post one near tournament wall charts
   d. Important: this is a double-elimination tournament; everyone will play a minimum of two games!
      i. Explain how a double-elimination tournament works, as most do not understand this concept; also explain what a BYE means (see 10.iii.1.a below)

9. Print the **Tournament Chart with Game Numbers**
   a. Keep one at tournament table
   b. Post one or more near tournament wall charts

10. Seeding and division distribution
    a. Using the intake forms:
       i. Enter name and grade into the **Sign-up Seeding Form**
          1. School name is optional for statistical reasons only
          2. Note: Column B MUST remain hidden
       ii. Highlight all entrants and then sort by grade level (descending); this will allow 12th graders to be seeded ahead of 11th graders, and so on
       iii. Divisions:
          1. Only 32* (or fewer) names can be entered into any given division (*16 for team play)
             a. If fewer than 32 names are placed into a division, the remaining spaces should have the word BYE placed into the "empty" slots; a BYE automatically loses
             b. If you want to "seed" someone, place his/her name(s) at the top of the division list [ex: someone who won a previous tournament can be seeded in the #1 spot]
          2. In the past I have had the following divisions:
             Upper: grades 10–12
             Middle: grades 8–9
             Lower: grade 7 [I had two lower divisions]
    b. The names and grades should be copied from the **Sign-up Seeding Form** and placed into the proper location in the **Automatic Tournament Play Chart**
       i. To copy: highlight columns A–C and no more than 32 names
       ii. Make certain that one **Automatic Tournament Play Chart** is kept untouched!
       iii. Use one **Automatic Tournament Play Chart** for each division (give each a different name; see 11.a.ii. below)

11. Using the **Automatic Tournament Play Chart**
    a. First division/start of tournament
       i. The names from the Sign-up Seeding Form will be placed into the proper grids (B4–D35) [copy and paste]
       ii. Replace the title in E1 with the Division Title [your choice]

(Cont'd.)

Figure 4SG.23. Tournament To-Do List *(Continued)*

---

   b. Round 1
      i. Go to FILE
      ii. Go to PRINT
      iii. Print pages 1–5
      iv. Cut pages 2–5 in half
         1. Page 1: use list in column G to enter names on wall chart
         2. Pages 2–5: games 1–8 (the page number is listed with the game number on page 18 & page 35)
   c. Repeat 11.a. and 11.b. for each additional division
      i. Can play in following pattern
         Games 1–8 of first division (suggest starting with the oldest-aged division), followed by
         Games 1–8 of second division, followed by
         Games 1–8 of third division, etc.
         Games should ALWAYS be played in numerical order (Game 1 followed by Game 2 followed by Game 3, etc.)
      ii. Can have a different competition table for each division
      iii. Personally, I prefer 11.c.i (with age [12th graders] comes privilege)
      iv. Scoring
         1. Enter the game finishing positions on the **Automatic Tournament Play Chart** (page 18): **1**, **2**, **3**, or **4**
         2. Go to FILE
         3. Go to PRINT
         4. PRINT page 18
         5. Post names on tournament wall charts
   d. Round 2
      i. After games 1–8 are played for each division, print games 9–16
         1. Go to FILE
         2. Go to PRINT
         3. PRINT pages 6–9
         4. Cut pages in half
      ii. Repeat 11.d.i. for each additional division
      iii. Scoring
         1. Enter the game finishing positions on the **Automatic Tournament Play Chart** (age 18): **1**, **2**, **3**, or **4**
         2. Go to FILE
         3. Go to PRINT
         4. PRINT page 35
         5. Post names on tournament wall charts
   e. LUNCH BREAK
      i. Depending on the tournament start time, and the number of participants, this may be the best time to take a lunch break:
         AFTER Round 2 is completed and
         BEFORE Round 3 begins

(Cont'd.)

Figure 4SG.23. Tournament To-Do List *(Continued)*

---

f. Round 3
   i. After games 9–16 are played for each division, print games 17–22
     1. Go to FILE
     2. Go to PRINT
     3. PRINT pages 10–12
     4. Cut pages in half
   ii. Repeat 11.f.i. for each additional division
     1. Enter the game finishing positions on the **Automatic Tournament Play Chart** (page 35): **1, 2, 3,** or **4**
     2. Go to FILE
     3. Go to PRINT
     4. PRINT page 35
     5. Post names on tournament wall charts
g. Round 4
   i. After games 17–22 are played for each division, print games 23–24
     1. Go to FILE
     2. Go to PRINT
     3. PRINT page 13
     4. Cut page in half
   ii. Repeat 11.g.i. for each additional division
     1. Enter the game finishing positions on the **Automatic Tournament Play Chart** (page 35): **1, 2, 3,** or **4**
     2. Go to FILE
     3. Go to PRINT
     4. PRINT page 35
     5 Post names on tournament wall charts
h. Round 5
   i. After games 23–24 are played for each division, print games 25–26
     1. Go to FILE
     2. Go to PRINT
     3. PRINT page 14
     4. Cut page in half
   ii. Repeat 11.h.i. for each additional division
     1. Enter the game finishing positions on the **Automatic Tournament Play Chart** (page 35): **1, 2, 3,** or **4**
     2. Go to FILE
     3. Go to PRINT
     4. PRINT page 35
     5. Post names on tournament wall charts
i. Round 6
   i. After games 25–26 are played for each division, print games 27–28
     1. Go to FILE
     2. Go to PRINT
     3. PRINT page 15

(Cont'd.)

Figure 4SG.23. Tournament To-Do List *(Continued)*

    4. Cut page in half
  ii. Repeat 11.i.i. for each additional division
    1. Enter the game finishing positions on the **Automatic Tournament Play Chart** (page 35): **1**, **2**, **3**, or **4**
    2. Go to FILE
    3. Go to PRINT
    4. PRINT page 35
    5. Post names on tournament wall charts
 j. Round 7
  i. After games 27–28 are played for each division, print game 29
    1. Go to FILE
    2. Go to PRINT
    3. PRINT page 16
  ii. Repeat 11.j.i. for each additional division
    1. Enter the game finishing positions on the **Automatic Tournament Play Chart** (page 35): **1**, **2**, **3**, or **4**
    2. Go to FILE
    3. Go to PRINT
    4. PRINT page 35
    5. Post names on tournament wall charts
 k. Round 8/final game(s):
  i. Wait a few minutes to let suspense build
  ii. Print game 30 (final game)
    1. Go to FILE
    2. Go to PRINT
    3. PRINT page 17
  iii. Repeat 11.k.ii. for each additional division. Each division will play at its own table if there are a sufficient number of tables for all championship rounds to play simultaneously; if not (or optionally), I would suggest playing this round in reverse order, i.e., the upper (oldest) division will play last
  iv. If possible, project this last round on a large screen for the audience
  v. Explain to everyone how the last game(s) is to be played
    1. The championship round (game 30) could have as many as 4 games played to determine the champion
    2. Those coming in from game 29 already have one loss each
    3. Any player placing first or second is still considered as having won until there are only 2 players remaining; then, and only then, is second place considered to be a loss
    4. With only 2 players left, the first to acquire two losses will be the division's second place winner, the other player will be the division CHAMPION
      a. Post names on tournament wall charts
      b. Present any prizes at this time
      c. Take pictures (in front of wall posters?)
      d. Give the wall posters to the champion

Source: Jeff Wyner, Escondido Public Library, Escondido, CA.

CHAPTER 5

Level 5:
Selecting, Collecting, and Circulating Video Games

Selecting, collecting, and circulating video games isn't much different from the processes used with other collections. In many cases, librarians can draw on previous knowledge to make good decisions. For example, video games can be evaluated by the same categories (genres) and elements used to evaluate books (plot, character, setting) and media (sound, graphics).

Games are the same size as music CDs, multimedia CDs, and movie DVDs, so, from a processing standpoint, the technical services department can use similar storage units and/or security cases. Circulation policies may have some special considerations, or libraries can choose to circulate games with the same loan period and fines as other media.

New Media/New Technology

Librarians are about providing access to information and story, not concerned with the packaging that the stories come in. The first public libraries contained hardbound collections of information resources, and there was likely an uproar over the inclusion of pulp fiction paperbacks and again over the introduction of children's books. Librarians have fought format wars over integration of media, too: music (records, cassettes, CDs), film (videos, DVDs), comic books, graphic novels, and even the Internet. Games are no more than stories and information presented in a three-dimensional (3D) digital, interactive, multimedia format, playable on a variety of platforms.

We can take all the same arguments for why videos, music, comics, and the Internet belong in today's libraries and apply them to video games by examining library mission statements. Many libraries have mission statements that proscribe them to provide a breadth and depth of materials in a variety of formats, levels, and points of view or that put the patron first, promising that the library be a community place that delivers what the local community wants and needs. Some missions mandate that the library provide items with instructional, educational, entertainment, and/or recreational purposes.

Just like novels, games have viewpoints! As you read game reviews, here are some terms you might come across:

First person perspective is usually connected with shooter games. The game is perceived through the point of view of the character, with the feeling that one is looking out of the character's eyes.

Isometric is a two-dimensional (2D) perspective that appears 3D due to the angles used in the game; the movements in the game are on a diagonal axis, such as in *The Sims* (EA, 2002).

Aerial View games are nearly synonymous with "god" games. This viewpoint is used most often in strategy and simulation games in which the player controls the actions of the characters or systems within the game. As an omniscient player, having a top-down view of the action is common, as in *Spore* (EA, 2008). *Spore* allows the player to manipulate the universe at the single-celled organism level (see Figure 5.1).

Figure 5.1. *Spore* Screenshot

Source: Spore creature created by Beth Gallaway, using Spore: Creature Creator (EA, 2008); available online for free download at www.spore.com.

Game Genres

Action Games

The most popular style of game is action. Action games dominated sales in 2006, with 30.1 percent of the market. Action games emphasize movement and quick thinking. Fighting games and shooting games are action games.

Fighting action games are combat oriented. Gameplay may involve formal matches, as in *Fight Night Round 3* (EA, 2006), a boxing game featuring historic matches. Others involve street fighting, like *Mortal Kombat vs. DC Universe* (Midway Games, 2008). Shooting games can be historically based, such as *Medal of Honor: Allied Assault* (EA, 2002); survival oriented, such as the zombie shooter *Left 4 Dead* (Valve, 2008); or based in postapocalyptic science fiction, like *Fallout 3* (Bethesda Softworks, 2008).

Superhero games that emulate superhero comics are also action games. Larger than life characters solve local and global problems in classic good versus evil scenarios. Of late, games are modeled after their popular movie blockbuster counterparts, so players can become the hero by navigating through the plot of the film in digital pixels. *Spider-Man 3* (Activision, 2007) and *Superman Returns* (EA 2006) are two popular examples. The massively multiplayer online game (MMOG) *City of Heroes/City of Villains* (NCsoft, 2005) takes the concept a step further; instead of playing existing characters from the DC or Marvel universe, players can invent their own heroes and villains, customizing abilities and costumes to save the world. In *Mortal Kombat vs. DC Universe* (Midway, 2008), worlds collide as heroes from two fighting franchises go head-to-head (see Figure 5.2).

Figure 5.2. *Mortal Kombat vs. DC Universe Screenshot*

Source: www.worldscollide.com/us/main.html (accessed: April 16, 2009).

Adventure Games

Adventure games are characterized by an exploration model. A player must discover the world around him, continuing through a story as the main character. Some examples are the *Super Mario Brothers* games (Nintendo) and *Kirby's Dreamland* (Nintendo, 1992).

Construction and Management Games

In construction and management games, players control certain variables, with limited resources; the computer takes over to apply the variables. Sometimes called "god" games, construction and management games frequently have an ethics or morality subtext to them. Some have an economic focus, such as *RollerCoaster Tycoon* (Hasbro, 1999) and *Sim City 4* (EA, 2003). Others, such as *Cake Mania* and *Diner Dash*, are based on a profession.

Black and White (Lionhead, 2001) is a "god" game with an ethical slant; players choose to rule as a benevolent or a malevolent entity. *Spore* (Maxis, 2008) is another "god" game that allows players to manipulate the universe at the single-celled organism level.

Life Simulation Games

In life simulation games, the player micromanages virtual creatures as opposed to manipulating systems. Gameplay is via control of specific variables, with limited resources; the computer takes over to apply the variables. Pet management games like *Nintendogs* (Nintendo, 2006), biology and ecology games like the classic *Sim Earth* (Mindscape, 2002), and social simulations like *The Urbz: Sims in the City* (EA, 2004) are all characterized by controlling living things.

Role-playing Games

In role-playing games (RPG), character development is the primary focus of the gameplay. Players create, and sometimes assume, a persona based on the stock character types they customize. As they play the game, they earn points from their experiences: discovering new areas, killing monsters, and completing quests. Some RPGs have anime/manga themes (like *Final Fantasy X*; Square Enix, 2001), and others have fighting themes (like *Age of Conan: Hyborian Adventures*; Eidos, 2008). Medieval and fantasy themes are the most popular; *World of Warcraft* (Blizzard, 2004) is an excellent example. Other themes include shooting, as in *BioShock* (2K Games, 2007), and science fiction. *EVE Online* (CPC Games, 2003) is a science fiction MMOG (see Figure 5.3) in which players take the role of spaceship pilots seeking fame, fortune, and adventure in a complex, exciting, and sometimes hostile galaxy.

Figure 5.3. *Eve Online* Screenshot

Source: www.eve-online.com/screenshots/05122007/04m.jpg (accessed: April 16, 2009).

Game Styles

The style most talked about in the media is **first person shooter** (FPS), named for its unique "looking down the barrel of a gun" perspective. The player has a first person point of view, making the action more immediate, dramatic, and realistic than from any other vantage. The *Halo* series is the most popular FPS of all time.

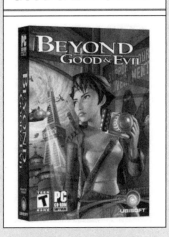

Figure 5.4. *Beyond Good & Evil* **Game**

In most FPS storylines, players are spies or soldiers in the midst of a conflict, but not all storylines involve guns. Many have classified *Beyond Good & Evil* (Ubisoft, 2003) as an FPS, but the main character, Jade, takes pictures instead of firing bullets (see Figure 5.4).

Massively multiplayer online games (MMOGs) are games that require an Internet connection. Defined as virtual persistent-state environments created and maintained by a number of computer game companies, MMOGs are characterized by their communities made up of thousands of players, online simultaneously in persistent worlds that exist on computer servers; when the player is offline, the world still exists and changes. In some MMOGs, the players take on new personas based on stock character types as they play their game, thereby adding a role-playing element to the game. Many MMOGs are based on the *Dungeons & Dragons* style of play. A leveling system means that advancement in the game is based on points earned from experience—discovering new areas, killing monsters, and completing quests. Team play is rewarded, and gamers often play in groups called "clans" or "guilds." Examples of MMOGs include *World of Warcraft* (Blizzard, 2004), *City of Heroes* (NCsoft 2004), and *EVE Online* (CPC Games, 2003).

A **platformer** is an action game in which the character moves from location to location. Jumping and climbing are often part of the action. Platformers can be 2D, like *Mario Brothers* (Nintendo, 1983), or 3D, like *Super Paper Mario* (Nintendo, 2007). Platformer themes include action, adventure, and horror.

A **sandbox**-style game is one in which the player builds the story based on the choices made in the game. These are sometimes called "open-ended games," because the plot is nonlinear; chunks of the story can be ordered in several ways. The *Grand Theft Auto* titles are all sandbox-style games.

Music Games

Sometimes called "rhythm games," music games are defined by their music and movement components. Often, the games are bundled with special controllers, such as dance pads, drum sticks, or instrument shapes that encourage physical activity. Most can be played without these accessories, but they are not as engaging. These games lend themselves well to programs for all ages. Watching the action is often as much fun as competing, and spectators can dance or sing along without actually playing. Some versions offer multiplayer modes for up to 8 to 16 players, but it's important to note that they are not simultaneous-use games; unless you network consoles together, play is limited to two to four people at a time. Music games include *In the Groove* (Roxor Games, 2004), *Donkey Konga* (Namco 2004), and *Karaoke Revolution Party* (Konami, 2005). MTV's acquisition of Harmonix in 2006 resulted in a marriage of *Guitar Hero* and *Karaoke Revolution*. Incorporating drums, vocals, bass, and guitar, *Rock Band* (Harmonix 2007) has been a hit in homes and libraries. *Guitar Hero* was the most popular video game played in libraries in 2007.[1] *Wii Music* is a new addition to the rhythm game scene; players emulate playing up to 50 different instruments, and the game responds with music (see Figure 5.5).

Figure 5.5. *Wii Music* Screenshot

Source: http://media.nintendo.com/nintendo/bin/KqJT3elJxkyZMh DJdli2AYGh4Ydl7GXO/15gMEGRXgy8B7gqiNvp9O1tECkFZ0p 4u.jpg (accessed: April 16, 2009).

Puzzle Games

Puzzle games emphasize creative and/or logical problem solving. Puzzle games tend to be short or to have many short rounds. Often, they are simply designed and port well to mobile devices. *Boom Blox* (EA, 2008) and *Tetris DS* (Nintendo, 2007) are examples of puzzle games.

Sports Games

Sports have had a long and rich history in video games. The competitive nature of sports lends itself well to video games, because winners and losers clearly emerge and the outcome of the game is point based. Sports games sales account for 17.3 percent of the console game sales market, and the top-selling game of 2005 was *Madden NFL Football 2005* (EA, 2004) for the PlayStation 2. *Madden* has been around since the late 1980s, and there is a version for every platform.

Sports games are easily recognizable as games that simulate competitive sports, such as golf, baseball, football, wrestling, and the Olympics. Sports games have several subgenres. Fantasy games might focus on compilation of "dream teams" composed of players who may not be real-life teammates, based on real-life statistics like batting average. The teams play against other dream teams put together by other players. Management games place the player in an administrative role, with the player planning gameplay strategy and team building as well as finances.

Fantasy games may take real-life games and extend them in hyperbolic ways, such as *Dead or Alive Xtreme Beach Volleyball* (Tecmo/Team Ninja, 2003) in which the focus is split equally on a gambling premise and a volleyball game with eye candy in the form of scantily clad beach babes. Or as fantasy sports, such as *Harry Potter: Quidditch World Cup* (EA Games, 2003). In *Harry Potter: Quidditch World Cup*, gameplay centers on the inventive mix of polo on broomsticks created by Harry Potter author J.K. Rowling (see Figure 5.6).

Figure 5.6. *Harry Potter: Quidditch World Cup* **Game**

Strategy Games

Strategy games focus on decision making. They are designed to make the player analyze a situation and determine a solution. One of the better features of having such situations in an electronic format is the ability to hit a reset button and attempt to solve a problem again. Popular strategy games include profession simulations like *Cake Mania* (Majesco, 2007) and *Diner Dash* (PopCap, 2006). The most beloved example of a strategy game is *Myst* (Broderbund, 1993).

Strategy games are usually either real time or turn based. In real-time strategy games, actions are simultaneous; while your army is advancing, so is your opponent's, as in *Empire Earth III* (Sierra Studios, 2007). *Empire Earth III* is a real-time strategy war game focused on conquering to build an empire (see Figure 5.7). In turn-based strategy games, players alternate actions incrementally in turns, as in *Sid Meier's Civilization IV: Complete* (2K Games, 2007).

Figure 5.7. *Empire Earth III* Screenshot

Source: http://empireearth.com/us/index.html (accessed: April 16, 2009).

Best Methods for Selection

What Makes a Good Game?

Librarians unfamiliar with video games may come to understand them better by relating them to an older immersive technology we know and love: books. Like books, video games can be grouped by audience (children, teen, adult), genre (sports, action/adventure, puzzle, role-playing, first person shooter), and format (CD or cartridge). Just as book authors (Clancy), book series (*Harry Potter*), and book genres (mystery) attract a loyal reader base, game fandoms materialize around designers, such as Sid Meier, Will Wright, and American McGee; around series, such as *Final Fantasy* or *Warcraft*; around franchises, such as Tony Hawk or John Madden; and around platforms, such as Nintendo and PlayStation. We can apply the same evaluation criteria to games that we use for books and multimedia by examining details such as plot, setting, tone, character, line, color, transitions, and design.

Games evolved from the simple graphics of *Asteroids* (Atari, 1981) to the text-based play of interactive fiction games presented in the second person point of view, such as *Adventure* (CRL, 1976), *Zork* (Infocom, 1982), and *Hitchhiker's Guide to the Galaxy* (Infocom, 1984). The focus on narrative forced designers to focus on story, not just button mashing, and challenged them to become vivid writers as well as good programmers.

The backstory or premise of the game must make sense and have strong roots, such as in the history of a realm, a mythology, and so forth. Like any solid work of fiction, the plot must be fleshed out with character, dialogue, and actions that further the adventure and immerse the player as an active participant who contributes to the story. The best games offer multiple storylines in which each choice leads in a new direction. Story is key. While the plot doesn't have to be linear, each choice should lead in a new direction to increase replayability. The plot should incorporate a rewards system in addition to "leveling up" (the process of advancing your character in the game). Leveling up activities should be fun, interactive, and creative and go beyond the traditional "get items, earn experience" round. Interesting quests that focus on the journey, not on the destination, are preferred. A graded experience curve makes leveling up fair; pacing is important.

Complete world building, a characteristic of fantasy, science fiction, and historical fiction novels, makes the settings come alive. Whether the story is set in the past, present, or future, in space, on the isle of *Myst* (Broderbund, 1993) or in the kingdom of Britannia (in the *Ultima* series), the physics and other rules governing the world of the game must be believable and consistent. A physically plottable map like the map of Britannia in *Ultima V* (Team Lazarus, 2006; see Figure 5.8) lends realism and eases

Figure 5.8. *Ultima V* Map

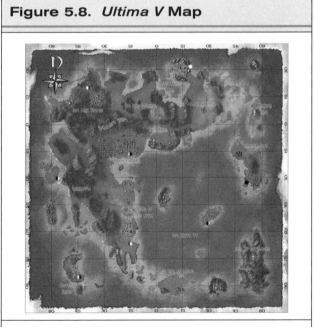

Source: http://lazarus.thehawkonline.com/downloads/clothmap
.pdf (accessed: April 16, 2009).

play. The terrain must be fun to explore and interesting. Attention to detail in realistic settings enhances game play. Any settings based on real locations should have strict attention to detail and stay as true to real life as possible.

Some MMOGs are made up of enough players to populate a small country and have customs, governments, and an economy all their own. In 2008, the MMOG *World of Warcraft* (Blizzard, 2004) users passed the 11 million mark.[2]

Most games, from *Mario Kart: Double Dash* (Nintendo, 2003) to *Project Gotham Racing 3* (Microsoft Game Studios, 2005), require the player to choose or create a representative avatar that on the player's behalf performs the action of the game and interacts with creatures, objects, and the setting in the game. Often, familiar stock characters from literature, mythology, and psychology appear as the hero, the princess, the wizard, the fool. A nonplayer character (NPC) that is computer generated might have a set of 5 stock phrases or 50 and might move in ways that grow repetitive and predictable. Another NPC might react to the player's moves. The smarter and less predictable the artificial intelligence (AI) is, the more challenging and fun the game play becomes.

Games have perspective—the immediacy of first person makes a player feel part of the game. The ability to go "meta" (switch between first and third person, zoom in and out, and view a map) is often vital to the gamer's success. Players demand customizable characters in the form of avatars with a variety of nonstereotypical choices in look, personality, trade, skills, dress, and ethics. Traditional characters (archetypes such as the hero, the guide, the trickster, etc.) are expected, and creative options beyond this are a nice touch.

Multiplayer capacity is an important element to creating character. Gaming with and against other people adds several dimensions to character, including chat, development of community through support or assistance, or by banding together to solve problems. Playing against other people adds a certain degree of unpredictability that is thrilling.

Economics are a key feature in some world-building games. In his book *Synthetic Worlds* (University of Chicago Press, 2005), economist Edward Castronova addresses digital economics and microtransactions (see

Figure 5.9. *Synthetic Worlds* Book

Figure 5.9). Based on the theory that as soon as there is an exchange rate, there is an economy, he provides examples of online games that gross more than third world nations.

Smart AI is more challenging and more fun. Unpredictability means that the enemy reacts in surprising ways and can out-think a player; for example, a wizard might attack with his staff instead of a spell. Balance of power between character and the enemies must be fair. Bosses to beat should be diverse from level to level and increase in difficulty as the player levels up.

Graphics can make or break a game. The game engine (the set of program code and software that gives a game its look and style of play) should have the capability to turn elements off and on, so players can compete more fairly. A game shouldn't require the best or newest hardware to run properly.

Game physics are related to graphics in that striking range should be realistic, and motion, such as walking, should be smooth. Graphics must be fast loading, meaning there should be zero lag time to cause stuttering or skipping. High-quality graphics means no clipping or ghosting (seeing characters or objects through walls). Beautiful, seamless, and cinematic images are nice, as in *Riven* (Brøderbund Software, Inc., 1997; see Figure 5.10), but content—story, character, etc.—must back up the pretty pictures. Generally gamers want to participate, not watch long cut scenes, as in *Final Fantasy X* (Square EA, 2001). Content and presentation are of equal value.

Figure 5.10. *Riven* Screenshot

Source: www.mysterium.ch/riven/pictures/riven_03.jpg (accessed: April 16, 2009).

A player's ability to interact with the environment, such as trampling grass or causing lasting damage, can be as impressive as explosions or other special effects. Cool digital effects and name-brand designers can be a draw, but convincing execution is more important. Environmental details like shadows and weather add to the setting, tone, and mood; environmental impact such as sustained damage is impressive.

More than just random background noise, ambient sound adds to the setting and gives clues about what might happen next. A musical score sets the mood and tone. Speech imparts information about character by what is being said and the tone used. As graphics continue to improve, facial expressions synchronize with the audio. Emerging musicians and up-and-coming bands are finding that getting a song onto a video game soundtrack can be a stepping stone to success; *Guitar Hero* (RedOctane, 2005) features both classic and new contemporary rock songs for players to master. Voiceover acting by celebrities made for an award-winning soundtrack for *Grand Theft Auto: Vice City* (Rockstar, 1995; see Figure 5.11). Listen in at www.vicecityradio.com.

Figure 5.11. *Grand Theft Auto: Vice City* Game

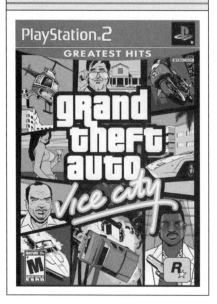

Games are also rated on the amount of online support and number of communication options to play against computer or against other people. Flexibility—the openness of the code and to what extent a hacker player can customize his or her game—is desirable. The ability to modify the game, or "mod," is more widespread thanks to the open-source movement and share-alike licensing. The game engine (the set of program code and software that gives a game its look and style of play) should include custom options. Many games are now packaged with tools that allow players to film their in-game play, modify in-game objects, or take apart the game's code and use the engine to create their own games. End User License Agreements (EULAs) and Terms of Service (ToS) vary in their permissions for gamers to make changes to copyrighted content (and profit from it); they must always read the fine print.

All of this adds up to the most important feature: replayability. At $50 or more per game, players don't want to beat a game in a few hours or to play it only once. Many features mentioned earlier, such as flexibility in plot or custom characters, allow the game to be played over and over with different choices yielding different results. These seemingly infinite permutations means endless replay possibilities and more play for the money.

Overview of Online and Print Resources

Online Resources

1Up.com (www.1Up.com) publishes the online *Electronic Gaming Monthly* and other console and computing magazines. 1Up has extensive features that include blogs and podcasts in addition to reviews, forums, and news.

Calendar of Video Game Awards

January

Game of the Year (IGN): Awards broken down by console, then genre. Winners determined by IGN Staff. Announced at http://Bestof.ign.com

February

ELAN: Canadian awards for electronic and animated art, given in 15 categories, including Video Game Hall of Fame. Includes a student award category. Winners determined by member vote. Winners selected by industry jurors. Announced at www.theelans.com

Game of the Year (Academy of Interactive Arts and Sciences): Awards for outstanding achievement in various fields of excellence for the games of the past year, including artistic design, music, and more. Announced at www.interactive.org

March

Game Developer's Choice Awards (Game Developer's Association): Awards in ten categories, as well as awards to people who further the game industry; and three choice awards, both nominated and voted on by the development community. Nominees also listed on the Web site. Nominations accepted from members, finalists selected by advisory committee, winners voted by membership. Announced at www.gamechoiceawards.com

May

Game Critics Awards (Game Critics): Awards in 15 categories. Winners determined by poll of members from over 30 media outlets that cover gaming. Announced at www.gamecriticsawards.com

October

Excellence in Video Games (British Association of Film and Television Arts): All nominations judged in each of 13 categories by a jury of industry practitioners, including a range of developers and publishers. Announced at www.bafta.org

November

Video Game Report Card (National Institute on Media and the Family): Guide meant to be used to select appropriate titles for holiday gifts. Announced at www.mediafamily.org

December

Game of the Year (GameSpot): Game of the Year award selected by editor; Reader's Choice awarded from poll. Announced at www.gamespot.com

Game of the Year (GameSpy): Awards broken down by console; all games receiving five-star reviews during the year are eligible. Winners selected by editorial staff. Announced at http://goty.gamespy.com

Gay Gamer Video Game Awards: Multiple categories, winners determined by polls in 2006, by staff in 2007. Announced at http://gaygamer.net/2008/01/gaygamer_video_game_awards_200.html

Video Game Awards (Spike TV Network): Announced at www.spike.com\About-show/23733

The Entertainment Software Ratings Board (ESRB; www.esrb.org) is a self-regulating body established by the Entertainment Software Association (ESA). ESRB applies and enforces game ratings, advertising, and online privacy principles. They are primarily known for evaluating games for violence, sex, language, and substance abuse.

The American Library Association's (ALA) gaming Web site (http://gaming .ala.org) is the portal for the ALA Games and Gaming Member Initiative Group and community. It features a blog, wiki, and gaming toolkit.

GameSpot (www.gamespot.com), not to be confused with GameStop, offers news, reviews, cheat codes, and more for every platform. Games in Libraries (www.games inlibraries.org) has a monthly podcast that features news, reviews, interviews, and how-tos for tabletop games and video games in all types of libraries. GameSpy (www .gamespy.com) is an ad-heavy site that offers news, reviews, cheat codes, and more for every platform. It has an affiliation with FilePlanet for downloads and free trials.

Library Successes: A Best Practices Wiki is a Web site created by Meredith Farkas "to be a collaborative space for librarians to share success stories and inspire each other to do great things in our own libraries" (http://www.libsuccess.org/index.php? title=Library_Success:_A_Best_Practices_Wiki: About). The site contains a Gaming page (www.libsuccess.org/index.php?title=Gaming) containing resources from within the library community that includes entries on core collections, journal articles, and lists of libraries hosting gaming events and circulating games.

Finally, Video Game Magazines Breakdown (www.animeted.org/4librarians/video-games/game-mags.htm) highlights the pros, cons, and audiences of numerous video game magazines. It was compiled by two gaming reviewers who are also librarians.

Video Game Magazines

One frequent question is, "There are so many video game magazines on the market; how do I choose just one to subscribe to?" The answer is that there is not a one size fits all gaming magazine. Taking needs of the local community into consideration is key. Sometimes the ads in the magazines are age inappropriate for youth collections. Many of the gaming magazines appear to target the 18–35-year-old male demographic.

One strategy is to purchase one copy of each of the magazines and conduct a poll during a community-style meeting. For example, ask your teen advisory board or gaming club to browse through and pick their top three choices. Another strategy is to create a simple online poll to determine what console is favored in the community and then purchase a magazine that supports that specific platform (see Figure 5.12). Purchasing at least one magazine that covers all consoles is also a good place to start (see Figure 5.13).

A third strategy would be to save your money and create a list of links to gaming magazine Web sites (a number of which are listed in the Level 3 Strategy Guide). Many feature reviews and cheat codes, if not feature-length articles, free online. Some have added online-only content, such as blogs or podcasts.

Don't forget that there are other kinds of gamers who would appreciate gaming support. *Dungeons & Dragons* campaigners, MMOG gamers, and board and card game players also have magazines dedicated to their pursuits (see Figure 5.14).

Figure 5.12. Platform- and Style-Specific Magazines

PC Gamer, Beckett Massive Online Gamer, PlayStation and Nintendo Power all have niche audiences.

Source: Photo by Beth Gallaway.

Figure 5.13. Comprehensive Gaming Magazines

Game Informer and *Game Pro* cover all platforms.

Source: Photo by Beth Gallaway.

Figure 5.14. Gaming Culture Magazines

Play and *Edge* cover gaming industry and culture.

Source: Photo by Beth Gallaway.

Vendors

Like books, most games are not purchased directly from publishers or manufacturers, but there are many options for acquisition. Wal-Mart, Best Buy, and the like sell games in addition to other goods. CompUSA (www.compusa.com) accepts purchase orders through their business services unit and carries most major games and accessories.

If you are looking for truly knowledgeable staff, a local specialty game store is your best bet. Game Crazy stores (www.gamecrazy.com), part of the Hollywood video franchise, are prevalent in Texas and California, but GameStop (www.gamestop.com) is the largest retailer of video games in the United States and the only retailer with a specific video game focus. GameStop sells new and used games, consoles, and console accessories in addition to action figures, trading cards, and strategy guides. Their e-commerce site offers online ordering, reviews at your fingertips, and a locater for their 4,400 stores. They don't accept purchase orders, so be prepared to pay cash or use your personal credit card and get reimbursed. One advantage of using a game store is that you can purchase used games (in working condition) at a discount. Another benefit of using a local store is that they may offer a small discount for games, consoles, or equipment. Purchasing direct from manufacturers may be another option for some games. For example, RedOctane (www.redoctane.com) offers discounted bundles for their popular *Guitar Hero* game. They also sell dance pads and other items that accompany their popular video games (see Figure 5.15).

Beth Gallaway is a RedOctane Affiliate, which means she gets a kickback in the form of a 5 percent commission on the purchase of gaming accessories such as *Dance Dance Revolution* pads and *Guitar Hero* games and controllers for each transaction completed through the following address: www.jdoqocy.com/click-3357180-10493465.

One disadvantage of buying from a local or independent retailers is that they may not be able to do a purchase order. Best Buy for Business: Government and Education (www.bestbuybusiness.com) is one store that does accept library purchase orders. Librarians that use Best Buy to purchase games have said that equipment arrives quickly, but that software does not. More vendors of games, equipment, storage and security, computers, and projectors are listed in the Level 2 Strategy Guide.

Online bookstores, including Amazon (www.amazon.com) and Barnes and Noble (www.bn.com), also sell games at a small discount. "I purchase our games through Amazon.com. Not only do they carry almost any title you can think of, they have decent prices and you can set up a corporate account so that your library is billed for the titles you order. It's worked very well for us. They also will take back defective items, even if you have already cataloged them. We're now using Amazon.com for almost all our DVD, music CD, and game purchases. And their Customer Service is amazing. One of the best vendors my library uses."

–Sarah Sogigian, Young Adult Librarian/Volunteer Coordinator, Shrewsbury (MA) Public Library

Figure 5.15. RedOctane.com—The Official Guitar Hero Store Homepage

Source: Red Octane Referral. Available: http://www.jdoqocy.com/click-3357180-10493465 (accessed: April 16, 2009).

Library jobbers are slowly getting into the act and distributing games—Baker & Taylor (www.btol.com) offers standing order plans and sells titles for PC, Nintendo Wii and DS, PlayStation 2, PlayStation 3, PlayStation Portable, and Xbox 360. They also sell some accessories. Julie Dyson, Manager of Music & Video Services at Baker & Taylor, sends out periodic e-mails about new releases and price drops; e-mail Julie at dysonj@btol.com to receive weekly Excel spreadsheets of titles available through Baker & Taylor (see Figure 5.16). Ingram began distributing video games in March 2009.

Thomas Klise/Crimson Multimedia (www.crimsoninc.com) provides CD-ROM products and console games. One additional service they provide is labeling and cataloging. Another alternative is S&S Worldwide (www.ssww.com), a craft and activity supply distributor; they sell *Dance Dance Revolution* as a fitness activity.

Digital Downloads

For libraries thinking about creating an in-house, noncirculating collection, digital downloads may be the answer. Playfirst (www.playfirst.com) and IGN's Direct2Drive (www.direct2drive.com) will save you a trip to the store and prevent loss and damage.

Figure 5.16. Baker & Taylor New Releases

DATE AVAILABLE AT B&T	TITLE	SYS	TY	MANUFACTURER	UPC CODE	MSR	ESRB	COMMENTS
4/15/09	Dark Spire	DS	SW	Atlus	730865400287	$29.99	E10+	
4/15/09	Dokapon Journey	DS	SW	Atlus	730865400317	$29.99	RP	
4/16/09	Guitar Hero Metallica (SAS)	PS2	SW	Activision	047875957077	$39.99	T	
4/16/09	Gravity	DS	SW	Destineer	895678002056	$29.99	RP	
4/16/09	Gravity	Wii	SW	Destineer	895678002063	$29.99	RP	
4/21/09	Major League Baseball 2K9	PSP	SW	Take-Two	710426335365	$29.99	E	
4/22/09	Dynasty Warriors: Gundam 2	PS2	SW	Koei	722674100748	$29.99	T	
4/22/09	Dynasty Warriors: Gundam 2	PS3	SW	Koei	722674110259	$59.99	T	
4/22/09	Excitebots: Trick Racing	Wii	SW	Nintendo	045496901523	$39.99	E	
4/23/09	101 in 1 Explosive Megamix	DS	SW	Atlus	730865400300	$19.99	RP	
4/23/09	Dynasty Warriors: Gundam 2	X360	SW	Koei	722674210270	$59.99	T	
4/24/09	Damnation	XBOX 360	SW	Codemasters	767649402274	$59.99	M	
4/24/09	Damnation	PS3	SW	Codemasters	767649402298	$59.99	M	
4/28/09	Elite Forces:Unit 77	DS	SW	Destineer	895678002047	$29.99	RP	
4/29/09	Velvet Assassin	X360	SW	Southpeak	612561700263	$59.99	M	
4/29/09	Garfield Gets Real	DS	SW	Zoo Games/Destination	802066101404	$19.99	E	
4/30/09	Backyard Baseball 2010	PS2	SW	Atari	742725277427	$19.99	RP	
4/30/09	Super Root taisen OG Saga: Endless Frontier	DS	SW	Atlus	730865400324	$34.99	RP	
4/30/09	Dynasty Warriors: Strikeforce	PSP	SW	Koei	040198002611	$39.99	RP	
5/3/09	X-Men Origins: Wolverine	PS2	SW	Activision	047875836013	$29.99	T	
5/3/09	X-Men Origins: Wolverine	PS3	SW	Activision	047875835993	$59.99	RP	
5/3/09	X-Men Origins: Wolverine	X360	SW	Activision	047875836051	$59.99	RP	
5/3/09	X-Men Origins: Wolverine	Wii	SW	Activision	047875836099	$49.99	T	
5/3/09	X-Men Origins: Wolverine	PSP	SW	Activision	047875836037	$39.99	T	
5/3/09	X-Men Origins: Wolverine	DS	SW	Activision	047875836075	$29.99	E10+	
5/5/09	Klonoa	Wii	SW	Namco-Bandai	722674000161	$29.99	RP	
5/7/09	Jagged Alliance	DS	SW	Southpeak	744788029265	$29.99	T	
5/7/09	Night at the Museum Battle of the Smithsonian	DS	SW	Majesco	096427010501	$29.99	E	
5/7/09	Night at the Museum Battle of the Smithsonian	Wii	SW	Majesco	096427010918	$39.99	E10+	
5/7/09	Night at the Museum Battle of the Smithsonian	X360	SW	Majesco	096427010925	$39.99	E10+	
5/7/09	Patapon 2	PSP	SW	Sony	711719873226	$19.99	E	
5/12/09	Puzzle Kingdom	DS	SW	Zoo Games/Destination	802066102074	$19.99	E10+	
5/12/09	Pirates vs Ninjas Dodgeball	Wii	SW	Southpeak	612561002268	$29.99	E	
5/12/09	Desktop Tower Defense	DS	SW	THQ	785136362762	$19.99	E	
5/12/09	Girl Time	DS	SW	THQ	785136362663	$19.99	E	
5/12/09	Mission Runway	DS	SW	THQ	785136362374	$19.99	E	
5/12/09	My Farm Around the World	DS	SW	THQ	785136362960	$19.99	E	
5/12/09	Short Track Racing Trading Paint	PS2	SW	THQ	752919461440	$19.99	E	
5/13/09	Sacred 2:Fallen Angel	PS3	SW	Atari	894388002010	$59.99	M	
5/13/09	Sacred 2:Fallen Angel	X360	SW	Atari	894388002097	$59.99	M	
5/13/09	Fuel	X360	SW	Codemasters	767649402595	$59.99	E	
5/13/09	Fuel	PS3	SW	Codemasters	767649402567	$59.99	E	
5/13/09	Dreamer: Shop Owner	DS	SW	Dreamcatcher	625504721914	$29.99	E	
5/13/09	Dreamer:Babysitter	DS	SW	Dreamcatcher	625500719911	$29.99	E	
5/13/09	Battlestations Pacific	X360	SW	Eidos	788687200615	$59.99	T	
5/13/09	Help Wanted	Wii	SW	Konami	083717400813	$29.99	E10+	
5/13/09	Magicians Quest: Mysterious Times	DS	SW	Konami	083717241522	$29.99	E10+	
5/14/09	Shin Megami Tensei I: Devil Summoner	PS2	SW	Atlus	730865630373	$39.99	M	
5/14/09	Drama Queens	DS	SW	Ubisoft	096427015833	$19.99	T	
5/14/09	Imagine Music Fest	DS	SW	Ubisoft	008888165132	$29.99	E	
5/14/09	Puzzle Kingdom	Wii	SW	Zoo Games/Destination	802066102067	$19.99	E	
5/15/09	Little King's Story	Wii	SW	XSeed	853466001510	$49.99	T	
5/20/09	Steel Princess	DS	SW	Atlus	730865400270	$34.99	E	
5/20/09	EA Sports Active (Bundle)	Wii	SW	EA Games	014633190458	$59.95	RP	with resistance band and leg strap
5/20/09	Left 4 Dead Game of the Year Edition	X360	SW	EA Games	014633098761	$49.99	M	
5/20/09	Rock Band Track Pack: Classic Rock	Wii	SW	EA Games	014633191752	$29.99	T	

Source: Extended forecast of New Release video games via e-mail from Julie Dyson at Baker & Taylor, April 14, 2009.

Another alternative is GameTap, owned by mega media mogul Turner Broadcasting Corporation. GameTap (www.gametap.com) delivers arcade classics, console favorites, PC bestsellers, and machinima. For $9.95 a month, GameTap provides a legal gaming-on-demand service. Instead of scouring the Internet for old favorites illegally hosted online, users log in to a remote server to access a library of over 500 titles (as of this writing) and game-related content including news and reviews. Games are hosted on a single computer, not circulated; the Terms of Service permit creation of one backup copy.

OverDrive (www.overdrive.com) provides online versions of games direct to library patrons at home. Modeled on their successful e-book, e-audio, and e-movie format, the concept as applied for games is that patrons download a viewer/player and log in with their library card number. They download an always-available game or productivity software title to their PC, and it expires automatically at the end of the preset lending period. The system eliminates issues of theft and damage.

OverDrive promises over 70 program titles in every educational curriculum category for every age group from preschool to adult. A few titles are recognizable by name: *Hallmark Create-a-Card* (Sierra, 2007), *Mavis Beacon Teaches Typing* (Broderbund, 2008), and *Sudoku Puzzle Addict* (Global Software Publishing, 2006). One won't find Xbox 360 releases or arcade classics here. Watch for demos at library conferences, and check OverDrive's Web site for more information.

Establish a Collection Policy

Your general video game collection development policy will cover a number of the issues addressed in your general collection development policy. Because every community is unique, no two policies should be the same, and simply copying another library's policy may not be effective. Instead, it's better to come up with a list of key questions your policy has to address and tailor the policy to your specific library and community.

Key Questions: Prompts for Writing Your Collection Development Policy

- Who is the collection for (children, teens, adults)?
- What platforms will you collect (consoles: Wii, PlayStation 3, Xbox 360; handhelds: DS, PlayStation Portable, and/or PC)?
- What genres will you collect (action/adventure, sports, puzzle, first person shooter, role playing)?
- What are your selection criteria (Rating, Content descriptors, Awards, Reviews, and/or Recommendations/Patron requests)?
- What resources will you use to select titles (gaming magazines, gaming Web sites, library journals, patron recommendations)?
- Is there a donation policy?
- How will the collection be classified and cataloged?
- Where will the collection be stored?
- How will it be displayed?
- What security measures need to be taken?
- What is the procedure for materials challenge?

Sample Video Game Selection Policy

The library will purchase Wii, PlayStation 3, and Xbox 360 games for teens. All games must be rated T for Teen or lower (E, E+10). Sources for review include trade publications such as *Voice of Youth Advocates* (*VOYA*) and *School Library Journal*, computer magazines such as *PC Gamer*, general gaming magazines such as *Game Informer*, and console-specific publications such as *Nintendo Power*. Reviews may also be weighed from GameFAQs.com, G4 TV, and others. Patron recommendations should be given highest priority.

Expenditures will be between $20 and $60 per game. Purchases will be from jobbers such as Baker & Taylor, Ingram, and Crimson Multimedia. To reduce theft, we do not purchase popular games immediately, waiting six months to a year.

Games will be classified as Rental Software, scat 415, and labeled Game Rental/ Title of Game. The MARC record should include the game synopsis, genre, and platform. Codebooks will be classified 793.1/Title of Game and may be checked out separately. Games will be stored like DVDs in security cases. The packaging may be used to create cases for marketing purposes. Games will be stored on wire rack carts on wheels, face out for display purposes. They will be shelved in the DVD/Video area, close to the computer lab. (Adapted from Video Game Collection Development Policy, Haverhill, MA)

Keep Games Circulating

Cataloging

Steven Bellotti, an MLS candidate at the Queens College, examined the cataloging of video games at the University of Illinois at Urbana-Champaign in 2007 and came up with more questions than answers. Issues include vocabulary (Does "electronic resource" for a GMD and "Game" in the Nature and Scope note suffice to identify a game in the catalog, or is a more concise expression, such as a GMD for "electronic game" required? Is there a difference between the title screen and main menu?); system requirements (Do we go with what the publisher states, or do we have to amend them if there's also something required that the publisher didn't mention? Is it necessary to account for backwards-compatibility in the SysReqs note?); and the start of the content (What constitutes AACR2's "formally presented information"? Anything before the game starts from the main menu? Anything before game play proper begins? For that matter, just what is "game play proper"? Does pushing a button to advance lines of dialog count as being "in the game"? Does a character-creation screen?).

For gathering information not evident at the start of the game or within accompanying manuals, Steve recommends visiting what he calls database-oriented Web sites such as MobyGames (www.mobygames.com/home), a game documentation project that attempts to "catalog" all video games; GameFAQs (www.gamefaqs.com); or even ReplacementDocs (www.replacementdocs.com), an archive of game manuals, for content. It should be noted that these sites are compiled of user-generated content, but, as Bellotti points out, "Fan-maintained Web sites like this are the only thing we have that approaches a viable reference source for video games." And, since it is highly unrealistic to expect a cataloger to play a game to the end to get the information presented in the final credits, database Web sites may be a good source for that information.

Looking to the future, and the increasing prevalence of video games in libraries, Bellotti notes, "We're going to need new subject headings eventually, especially for access by genre—and on the subject, does the genre of the game play or the genre of the setting and storyline have precedence?"

Storage and Display

Storage depends on budget, space, and staff. The most secure method, storing the actual video game behind the desk and requiring patrons to turn in the case or box to get the item, is most likely the cheapest but also the most staff and space intensive. Staff need to take valuable time to retrieve the game and to match up the case with the video game disk or cartridge. Storage is required behind the scenes for the CDs, and marketing-style storage is needed in public spaces to display titles. Archival three-ring binders with pages for 100 CD-sized disks cost around $50.

A more efficient method is to store your video games in secure, see-through, durable, locked packaging. The patron takes the locked item to the circulation desk, and the librarian unlocks upon checkout. Because today's games come on CDs, frugal libraries can store video games in the same secure devices being used for DVD collections. Three options are described.

Gressco Kwik Cases are unlocked with a strong magnet that can be bolted to your circulation desk. The cases cost a few dollars each; the unlocking device is quite expensive. Gressco recommends placing an order based on your circulation statistics. Get a quote direct from Gressco online (www.gresscoltd.com/kwikcase/demo).

Nexpak DVD security strips fit over standard-size cases, preventing the case from being opened. The straps are about $3 each, and the unlocking device is around $70 from Demco (www.demco.com).

D-Fence Security Caps fit over the CD to prevent its removal. The CD needs to be stored in a larger than usual DVD case. The caps cost about $.50 each; the decoupler to remove the cap from the disc is around $70 from Video Store Shopper (www.shopperinc.com). A similar item from library jobbers costs about $1.50 apiece, and the device remover is around $85.

Marketing

Very little needs to be done in terms of marketing—store games on face-out display shelves, the type your library may be using for graphic novels, videos, and magazines. Post a list of all available titles online, with links to the catalog so patrons can place holds, and post a list in the library near the storage shelves. Hosting a gaming night to introduce your new collection to the public is a great way to publicize the video games—load circulating titles into borrowed consoles or library PCs, and scatter gaming magazines and "suggestion for purchase" forms around the room.

Preservation

Game collections are often self-weeding. That is to say, by the time a game is damaged, it has worn out its welcome or the library has gotten its money's worth. To ensure preservation of games, check for damage and scratches upon return. Cleaning CD, CD-ROM, and DVD games in a CD-Doctor device (handheld ones sell for around $70, while desktop models retail for around $250) may be an option; be aware that you can't buff out scratches on Blu Rays using the usual machines. Cleaning dust and debris by hand with a cotton cloth and rubbing alcohol may help to keep game disks clean.

When patrons complain about a nonworking game, the biggest cause seems to be that they tried to play a game that is not backward compatible. Some patrons also try to use an inappropriate console, like putting a PlayStation 2 game into a regular PlayStation. Clearly labeling game formats is one simple solution.

Thanks to recycling efforts, games are coming in smaller, more standardized packaging. Console games come in DVD-sized cases, and the boxes for PC games can be cut down to a similar size and inserted into DVD cases. The library may need to make a choice about game manuals for PCs—shelve and circulate separately, or place all items in a bag and circulate as a kit.

Best Practices

Helen McGraw Branch of the Irondequoit Public Library
The all-ages collection at the Helen McGraw Branch of the Irondequoit Public Library (Rochester, NY) contains video games rated E, E10+, and T. At present, no Mature

(M)–rated games are allowed, although the library does purchase R-rated movies. Currently, Wii and PlayStation 2 are the only supported consoles; an older collection of PC games that spans from E- to T-rated games rounds out the collection. Video games circulate for two weeks, with an overdue fine of $0.25 per day (not counting Sundays). Patrons are allowed to check out two games per visit per day.

If a game is damaged, the patron is fined the replacement cost of the game plus a $5 processing fee. To help determine whether game damage was caused by the patron, make sure someone on staff has the same console at home that you purchase games for so that you can easily test problem disks. Most problems are just a patron's poorly maintained machine spitting out error messages. On the other hand, the games will get beaten up a lot, so keep disk cleaner and scratch wipes in supply.

Theft is an issue. About 6 to 12 games have been stolen and only a few recovered.

Some older patrons have expressed "Pfft, games in a library!" sentiments but mainly only to themselves. No formal complaints were ever made, but a patron did include "Games" on a list of bad things happening at the library that the patron mailed to the director. Patrons of all ages seem to love the collection. Games are constantly on hold, and the circulation numbers are great.

The library has no official collection development policy; selection is fueled by what is available at the time of purchase. Games are purchased from AEC One Stop (www.aent.com), and donations in good working order are accepted. Priority is given to unique and quirky titles (such as *Katamari Damacy* [Namco, 2004], *Culdcept* [NEC Interchannel, Ltd., 2003], and *Destroy All Humans!* [THQ, 2005]) that people might not otherwise play. Helen McGraw Branch librarian John Scalzo (aka "The Video Game Librarian" at www.videogamelibrarian.com) recommends that gamer librarians buy games that they themselves would want to play. "A friendly voice that can describe in detail what a game is like or can recognize a title from a child's less-than-perfect description will go a long way in making games feel like a part of the library." One major goal is to keep every game purchase under $30 to stretch the tiny game budget that much further. Games average about $25 each, and the Helen McGraw Branch's total game budget of $1,500 is less than 1 percent of the total materials budget.

> "I try to get a healthy mix of genres, but I focus mostly on compilations (for the sheer number of games they contain), sports titles (for their mass appeal), racing games (for their "pick up and play" style), and platformers (because really, who doesn't love a platformer?)."
>
> –John Scalzo, Helen McGraw Branch librarian, aka the Video Game Librarian

With the small size of the game collection (roughly 130 titles), most popular and least popular blur together. The most popular games seem to be the *Harry Potter* and other licensed titles, EA Sports fare (*Madden, NBA Live, FIFA Soccer* [EA, 1993–2007]), and compilations of older games.

Scalzo advises other librarians who might want to collect games, "Start small, but make sure the patrons know exactly which games you have in your collection. A list goes an extremely long way to smooth over the cries of 'Everything's always checked out when I come in!' And it'll probably increase your hold count as well."

Rockridge Branch of the Oakland Public Library

By contrast, the Rockridge Branch of the Oakland (CA) Public Library established a collection of PlayStation 2 games (this seemed to be the most widely owned console) for 13–18-year-olds in response to patron surveys. With $700 dollars—10 percent of her total budget—librarian Susy Moorhead purchased over 30 games (see Figure 5.17). She focused on sports, adventure, racing, fighting, and shooter games, with no games rated M or higher. In the collection's infancy, patrons expressed a desire for M-rated games and more formats. Title purchases were based on patron requests and suggestions and on gaming magazine reviews.

Figure 5.17. Rockridge Branch Opening Collection

Titles		
NBA Live 06	Kingdom Hearts	The Lord of the Rings–
Final Fantasy X-2	Midwar Arcade	The Fellowship of the
Fullmetal Alchemist 2	Treasures	Ring
Jak 3	Finny the Fish & the	NBA Live 2001
Shadow the Hedgehog	Seven Waters	NHL 2001
Tony Hawk's American	Madagascar	Madden NFL 2002
Wasteland	Gians Citizen Kabuto	Fight Night Round 2
Smack Down vs. Raw	Dragon Rage	The Sims 2
Rachet & Clank	Tomb Raider–The Angel	Samurai Champloo
Madden NFL 06	of Darkness	Tekken 5
Star War Battlefront	Oni	SSX on Tour
Dark Cloud	Summoner	Tomb Raider–Legend
Inuyasha–The Secret of	Escape from Monkey	Harvest Moon–A
the Cursed Mask	Island	Wonderful Life

The circulation policy limits patrons to two games at a time; there are no holds and no renewals. Items circulate for seven days, and the overdue fine is $1 per day. The game replacement fee is now set at $50; this may change in the future. They are still experimenting with the details. The most popular titles as of this writing are *Soul Calibur* (Namco, 1999), *Tekken 5* (Namco, 2005), *Madden Football* (EA, 1989–present), *NBA Live* (EA, 1995–2007), and *Sims 2* (EA, 2005). Some of the older sports titles and E-rated adventure games aren't too popular. Moorhead advises librarians interested in starting collections to ask their patrons what they want.

> "I can't believe you have games. I love this library."
> –Rockridge Branch patron

Notes

1. Nicholson, Scott. 2008. "Library Gaming Census Report." *American Libraries* 40, no. 1/2: 44. Available: site.ebrary.com/lib/ala/docDetail.action?docID=10268897&page=46 (accessed April 16, 2009).
2. MMOG Chart. Available: www.mmogchart.com/charts (accessed: April 16, 2009).

Bonus Round 5:
Word Scramble

Figure 5.18. Word Scramble

1. SOOHBKCI	11. SRETSORAGWAL
2. AIBEGNAR	12. EFDMNLNAD
3. NTAVIELCAAS	13. OIAKM
4. CINVLAOTIIIZ	14. LORATP
5. ANDOWRLEFTI	15. OCNRFRIEPEASIP
6. RLTPKEONLCEAOTN	16. SSAHOUYCPTN
7. SFFTYLNAAIN	17. UTREPIORYRASPMA
8. AAMAATMYRDACIK	18. DYUOTDHEUNNRNAOGRWK
9. OIAHMENKSTDRG	19. NAEETCTUARMR
10. AZFNELDELOEGD	20. ANATIVPIAV

Figure 5.19. Word Scramble Solution

1. SOOHBKCI = BIOSHOCK
2. AIBEGNAR = BRAIN AGE
3. NTAVIELCAAS = CASTLEVANIA
4. CINVLAOTIIIZ = CIVILIZATION
5. ANDOWRLEFTI = DRAWN TO LIFE
6. RLTPKEONLCEAOTN = ELECTROPLANKTON
7. SFFTYLNAAIN = FINAL FANTASY
8. AAMAATMYRDACIK = KATAMARI DAMACY
9. OIAHMENKSTDRG = KINGDOM HEARTS
10. AZFNELDELOEGD = LEGEND OF ZELDA
11. SRETSORAGWAL = LEGO STAR WARS
12. EFDMNLNAD = MADDEN NFL
13. OIAKM = OKAMI
14. LORATP = PORTAL
15. OCNRFRIEPEASIP = PRINCE OF PERSIA
16. SSAHOUYCPTN = PSYCHONAUTS
17. UTREPIORYRASPMA = SUPER MARIO PARTY
18. DYUOTDHEUNNRNAOGRWK = TONY HAWK UNDERGROUND
19. NAEETCTUARMR = TRAUMA CENTER
20. ANATIVPIAV = VIVA PINATA

Level 5 Strategy Guide: Recommended Gaming Collections

A Core Collection of Essential Games

A solid game collection is well-rounded, deep in breadth and scope, and contains a mixture of genres and styles: action, fantasy, puzzle, rhythm, shooter, simulations, sports, strategy, two dimensional (2D), three dimensional (3D), side-scrollers, and sandbox (genres, styles, and themes are discussed in detail in Level 5). The discerning librarian will select titles based on both merit (award winners, games with high ratings and positive reviews, and games that will enrich the lives of people in the community) and popularity (requests from members of the community, bestsellers and classics, and titles that may increase circulation statistics).

This Strategy Guide offers core collection recommendations. They are divided by major platform (PC, Microsoft, Sony, Nintendo, Internet) and then by targeted audience age groups, with suggestions for expansion where appropriate. Because prices vary (new vs. used, library discount, price drop for sales for bestsellers) no prices are given. New games for PlayStation (PS) 3, Wii, and Xbox 360 range from $50 to $60; games that come with special controllers, like *Mario Kart* with Wii, *High School Karaoke Revolution* with PS2, and *Guitar Hero: Rock the 80s* with Xbox 360, may cost an additional $20 to $30. Games for handhelds range from $20 to $40. Digital downloads range from $10 to $50. Used games range from $10 to $50.

Each citation has publisher, date, and genre information, verified at MobyGames (www.mobygames.com); the Entertainment Software Rating Board (ESRB) rating, verified at the ESRB's Web site (www.esrb.org); and a short description, verified with Game Rankings (www.gamerankings.com), sponsored by CNET. Titles followed by an asterisk are games published in 2008 and are first choices for a collection focused on brand new games. Award winners are noted.

No titles are duplicated, although in some cases a sequel or the next game in a series or franchise may be recommended for a later version of a console. In most cases, if a game is recommended for one system, it is a good choice for another system as well, if available. Additional versions are noted; some games are exclusive to one console. The URLs that follow the annotations of console, handheld, and PC games are provided for more information about the game; in most cases, these games are not available for online play. PC games require users to enter a key code to install and register the software, and digital rights management may prevent multiple installations on numerous computers. More details are found in the End User License Agreement (EULA) or Terms of Service; each publisher's policy is unique.

A complete list of online games is posted on the author's Delicious Web site at www.delicious.com/informationgoddess29/games. The list is annotated and continually updated. All links are bundled at www.delicious.com/information goddess29/bundle:gameonbook. Also, check out these core collection lists compiled by other librarians:

Johnson, Megan. Available: www.animeted.org/4librarians/video-games/circ-count.xls (accessed: April 16, 2009).

Scalzo, John. "The Video Game Librarian." Available: www.gamingtarget.com/article.php?artid=3982 (accessed: April 16, 2009).

Schwarzwalder, Jami. "Video Game Collections." Available: www.mbmpl.org/vg/hcollect.pdf (accessed: April 16, 2009).

Young Adult Library Services Association. "Top 50 Core Recommended Collection." Available: http://wikis.ala.org/yalsa/index.php/Gaming_Lists_%26_Activities# Top_50_Core_Recommended_Collection_Titles (accessed: April 16, 2009).

Digital collections are listed separately. You can link to these games from your library's Web site or download and install them on a library machine. Note that online games are not rated by the Entertainment Software Association, and some Web pages feature advertisements or additional content inappropriate for general audiences.

PC

Read the fine print! Many games for personal computers work only on the Windows platform. A gaming computer requires a fast processor, graphics accelerator, available memory, and the most up-to-date graphics and sound cards. Gaming computers cost $1,000 to $3,500 and are available from vendors listed in Level 2 Strategy Guide.

Games for Tweens

CivCity: Rome (Take Two Interactive, 2006). Strategy. Rated E10+ for Alcohol Reference and Mild Violence.

This is a fairly complicated game for upper elementary and middle school students. Players experience Roman life by creating and building a Roman city. They can play the main mission, side quests, or building mode. Special features allow players to see the insides of buildings and to get an up-close look at day-to-day city life in ancient Rome through simulation (see Figure 5SG.1). Available: www.2kgames.com/civcityrome/civcity.html

Figure 5SG.1. *CivCity* **Screenshot**

Source: "Screenshots." Civ City Rome. Firaxis. www.2kgames.com/
civcityrome/civcity.html (accessed: February 8, 2009).

LEGO Batman* (Warner Brothers, 2008). Also available for Nintendo DS, PS2, PS3,
PSP, Wii, and Xbox 360. Action. Rated E10+ for Cartoon Violence.

> This game contains familiar LEGO building and brick-busting action, this time focused on
> Gotham City and the caped crusader. The story is original, allowing players to play as a
> hero or villain, and pulls from the comics and television series rather than from a specific
> film. Available: http://legobatmangame.com

Lemony Snicket's A Series of Unfortunate Events: Mini Games (Activision, 2004). Also
available for GameCube, Game Boy Advance, PS2, and Xbox. Action. Rated E for
Mild Violence.

> This puzzle-solving action game for upper elementary students successfully carries through
> the tongue in cheek dreariness of the book series and films. The goal is to foil Count Olaf
> in 16 missions, playing each of the characters. Available: www.activision.com/index.html#
> gamepage|en_US|gameId:LemonySnick&brandId:LemonySnick

Nancy Drew: Legend of the Crystal Skull (Her Interactive, 2007). Adventure. Rated E
for Mild Violence.

> Characters based on the children's mystery series embark on an updated set of adventures
> in this puzzle-solving action game for upper elementary students. When the owner of a
> crystal skull is found dead, Nancy is on the case, exploring New Orleans to find the skull
> and the murdered. Expand your collection with others in the series from Her Interactive.
> Available: www.herinteractive.com/game.php?game_id=17&platform=pc

RollerCoaster Tycoon 3: Gold (MicroProse Software, 2005). Strategy. Rated E for
Comic Mischief, and Mild Violence.

Run your own theme park and design your own rollercoasters—then ride them!—in this business simulation. The *Gold* edition comes with two expansion packs for building more complex coasters and new themes, with rides and landscaping details; circulate as a set. Expand your collection with expansion packs like *RollerCoaster Tycoon 3: Soaked!* (Microsoft Game Studios, 2005; see Figure 5SG.2), which adds a water park simulation, or *Zoo Tycoon 2* (Microsoft Game Studios, 2001), which continues to release expansion packs featuring increasingly exotic, endangered, and extinct animals. Available: www.atari .com/rollercoastertycoon.

Figure 5SG.2. *RollerCoaster Tycoon 3: Soaked!*

Source: "Screenshots." Roller Coaster Tycoon. Atari. www.atari.com/ rollercoastertycoon/us/downloads (accessed: April 16, 2009).

SEGA Rally (Sega of America, 2008). Also available for PS3, PlayStation Portable (PSP), and Xbox 360. Racing simulation. Rated E.

This off-road racing game features amazingly realistic responses to varying terrains. Available: www.sega.com/games/?g=2

The SimCity Box* (Maxis/EA, 2008). Strategy. Rated E.

This deluxe civics simulation includes all the tools to manage growth and development of your megalopolis. Zoom out to sculpt land, zoom in on the lives of individual Sims, or focus on attractions or transportation systems. This edition contains *SimCity Societies* (EA, 2007) and *SimCity 4: Rush Hour* (EA, 2003). Available: http://simcitysocieties.ea.com

Spider-Man: Web of Shadows (Activision, 2008). Also available for PS2, PS3, PSP, Wii, and Xbox 360. Action. Rated T for Animated Blood, Drug Reference, Mild Language, Mild Suggestive Themes, and Violence.

Battle Spidey's inner demons and a deadly alien menace that is threatening to take over Manhattan. The players' choices and play style preferences develop the character as a hero...or a villain. Available: http://seizecontrol.marvel.com

Spore: Creature Creator* (Maxis, 2008). Life simulation. Rated E.

This evolutionary simulation is simply a tool to make creatures to import to *Spore* (see Figure 5SG.3). Because creating creatures is the most fun part of the *Spore* game, it works well as a standalone title. Consider expanding your collection with *Spore** (EA, 2008) to lead your creations from primordial swamp to space travel; be aware that the End User License Agreement (EULA) limits installations of *Spore*, and you'll need to contact EA for permission to reinstall. Available: www.spore.com

Figure 5SG.3. Spore Creature Creator Game

Games for Teens

Age of Empires III: Gold Edition (Microsoft Game Studios, 2007). Strategy. Rated T for Animated Blood and Violence.

This game of empire building focuses on myth and legend rather than on historical fact. This edition includes *The War Chiefs*; circulate as a set. Expand your collection with the expansion packs and *The Asian Dynasties* (Microsoft Game Studios, 2007). Available: www.ageofempires3.com

Guild Wars: Platinum Edition (NCsoft, 2007). Role playing, action. Rated T for Use of Alcohol, Violence, and Suggestive Themes.

The unique mission-based design of *Guild Wars* makes for instant access to quests and easy formation of affinity groups for quests. The game has player versus player action and guild warfare servers. The *Platinum Edition* includes *Eye of the North*; circulate as a set. Expand your collection with *Guild Wars: Factions* (NCsoft, 2006) and the *Bonus Mission Pack* (NCsoft, 2007). Available: www.guildwars.com

The Lord of the Rings: The Battle for Middle Earth II (EA, 2006). Also available for Xbox 360. Role playing. Rated T for Violence.

This game was inspired by J.R.R. Tolkien's bestselling fantasy novels set in Middle Earth. Players assume command of an army on the side of good or evil, build castles and hold lands, and participate in battles. Expand your collection with *Rise of the Witch-King* (EA, 2006). Available: www.ea.com/games/lotr-the-battle-for-middle-earth-2

Medal of Honor: Allied Assault (EA Games, 2002). Action. Rated T for Violence.

In this World War II–themed first person shooter game, players fight 20 historical battles, with authentic landscaping, uniforms, and weaponry. Other titles in the series are available for other platforms. Now available in tenth anniversary edition that contains two expansion packs. Available: www.ea.com/games/medal-of-honor-anniversary

The Movies: Complete Pack (Lionhead, 2007). Also available for Xbox 360. Strategy. Rated T for Blood and Gore, Crude Humor, Mild Language, Sexual Themes, Use of Alcohol and Tobacco, and Violence.

> Players become movie moguls in this movie-making business game. They manage talent, cast players, and create a film to upload and share online. This is easy machinima creation. The *Complete Pack* includes *The Movies: Stunts and Effects* (Lionhead, 2006). It won the British Association of Film and Television Arts' (BAFTA) Best Simulation award. Available: www.lionhead.com/themovies

Neverwinter Nights 2 (Atari/Obsidian Entertainment 2006). Role playing. Rated T for Blood, Violence, Mild Language, and Sexual Themes.

> This game is fantasy themed, based on the rules of *Dungeons & Dragons* 3.5, and set in the *Forgotten Realms* universe. Players can control the level of blood and violence. Expand your collection with *Neverwinter Nights 2: Mask of the Betrayer* (Atari, 2007). Available: www.atari.com/nwn2/

NHL 09* (EA, 2008). Also available for PS2, PS3, and Xbox 360. Sports. Rated E10+ for Mild Violence.

> This ice hockey simulation game features NHL and international teams, a draft mode to create a dream team, and up-to-date team uniforms. Available: www.easports.com/nhl09/

Psychonauts (Majesco, 2005). Also available for PS2, Xbox, and Xbox 360. Puzzle. Rated T for Cartoon Violence, Crude Humor, and Language.

> In this platform game, a boy with psychic powers escapes the circus to join up with others of his kind, undergoing psychonaut training. It has witty dialogue and a strong story. It won BAFTA's Best Game Screenplay award. Available: www.psychonauts.com.

Sid Meier's Civilization IV: Complete Edition (Firaxis/Infogames, 2007). Strategy. Rated E10+ for Violence.

> In this turn-based historical simulation and strategy game, the goal is to build an empire from scratch starting in ancient times and progressing through modern day. The Complete Edition includes *Warlords* and *Beyond the Sword*; circulate as a set. Available: www.civilization.com

Sid Meier's Pirates! (Atari, 2004). Also available for PSP, Xbox, and Xbox 360. Action. Rated E for Alcohol Reference, Blood, Suggestive Themes, and Violence. (Note: other versions of the game, for other platforms, have a higher rating than the PC version).

> Swashbuckling adventure and treasure await as players earn their own fleet through gaining skill and reputation through battles on the high seas and complete missions to deliver people and goods from one port to another. The game incorporates history and geography, with role-playing and strategy elements. Available: www.2kgames.com/pirates/pirates/home.php.

Adult Games for Young Adults

This category includes complex video games intended for an adult audience, featuring mature content that has a high appeal for teens.

Battlefield 1942: Deluxe Edition (EA, 2003). Action. Rated T for Blood and Violence.

> This World War II–themed shooter features historical battle settings. The Deluxe Edition includes the expansion pack *The Road to Rome* (EA, 2003). *Battlefield 1942* won the

Academy of Interactive Arts & Sciences' (AIAS) Game of the Year award. Available: www.battlefield.ea.com/official/battlefield/bf

Crackdown (Microsoft, 2007). Also available for Xbox 360. Action. Rated M for Blood and Gore, Intense Violence, Sexual Themes, Strong Language, and Use of Drugs.

In this sandbox-style game, the object is to defeat drug kingpins and break up three different crime rings. It won BAFTA's Best Action and Adventure. Available: http://crackdownoncrime.com

Crysis: Warhead (EA, 2008). Action. Rated M for Blood, Strong Language, and Violence.

In this combat-driven first person shooter game, players fight against Korean forces and extraterrestrials. Available: www.ea.com/games/crysis-warhead

Darwinia (Cinemaware, 2006). Strategy. Rated E for Fantasy Violence.

A tribe of video game sprites are trapped in a 3D game world that is like a fantasy theme park. A deadly virus breaks out, and players must battle it to save the simulated lives of the Darwinians. The gameplay is inspired by retro-arcade games—hence the adult appeal. Available: www.ambrosiasw.com/games/darwinia

*Dead Space** (EA, 2008). Also available for PS3 and Xbox 360. Action. Rated M for Blood and Gore, Intense Violence, and Strong Language.

Responding to a distress call from a space station, Isaac Clark finds himself fighting various enemy necromorphs and searching for clues in multimedia left behind in the space station in this cyberpunk survival horror game. Available: http://deadspace.ea.com

*Left 4 Dead** (Valve, 2008). Action. Rated M for Blood and Gore, Intense Violence, and Language.

This multiplayer zombie shooter game won Video Game Librarian's Bookmark award. Available: www.l4d.com

Microsoft Flight Simulator X (Microsoft, 2006). Flight simulation. Rated E.

Players fly a variety of aircraft on dozens of missions, land at real-world airports, and engage with other players online. Available: www.microsoft.com/games/flightsimulatorx

SWAT 4: Gold Edition (Sierra, 2006). Action. Rated M for Blood, Intense Violence, and Strong Language.

The point of *SWAT 4*, a first person shooter game, is to *not* shoot. It is to diffuse hostage situations through securing citizens and controlling potential terrorists and to learn to delegate and work as a team. The Gold Edition includes the expansion pack *SWAT 4: The Stetchkov Syndicate*. Available: www.activision.com/index.html#gamepage|en_US|gameId:swatGold&brandId:swat

---

Subscription Massively Multiplayer Online Games

Although many of the massively multiplayer online games (MMOGs) are now available free online, using the original discs makes the installation go more quickly. An Internet connection is required to download updates. Include a note with these games instructing patrons to go to the game publisher's Web site to set up a free trial account.

(Cont'd.)

Subscription Massively Multiplayer Online Games *(Continued)*

City of Heroes/City of Villains: Good Versus Evil Edition (NCsoft/Cryptix, 2006). Role playing. Rated T for Violence and Suggestive Themes.

> Players create their own superhero, with costume, powers, and backstory and then save the world! Or, they can choose to fight on the side of evil and destroy the world. The sidekick play mode is a great option for casual gamer friends to join in regardless of level. Available: www.cityofheroes.com

Dungeons & Dragons Online: Stormreach (Turbine/Hasbro, 2006). Role playing. Rated T for Alcohol Reference, Blood, and Violence.

> This version of *Dungeons & Dragons* is based on the popular pencil, paper, and dice game, with familiar races and classes. It won BAFTA's Best Multiplayer Game award. Available: www.ddo.com

Figure 5SG.4. *Warhammer Online* **Homepage**

Source: www.warhammeronline.com (accessed: March 9, 2009).

Warhammer Online: Age of Reckoning* (Mythic Entertainment, 2008). Role playing. Rated T for Mild Blood, Suggestive Themes, Use of Alcohol and Tobacco, and Violence.

> *Warhammer Online: Age of Reckoning* is a fantasy MMOG with a variety of character classes (see Figure 5SG.4). Players can play individually or in large group quests versus other players (PvP) or versus the environment (PvE). It won both XPlay's and GameSpy's Best MMO of the Year awards. Available: www.warhammeronline.com

World of Warcraft (Blizzard, 2004). Role-playing. Rated T.

> This fantasy game allows player to choose good or evil (Alliance or Horde) and play a range of traditional classes and races. Gameplay may change online. Expand your collection with *World of Warcraft: Burning Crusade** (Blizzard, 2007) and *World of Warcraft: Wrath of the Lich King** (Blizzard, 2008). *World of Warcraft* won the Video Game Librarian's Bookmark award. Circulate as a set. Available: www.worldofwarcraft.com

Microsoft Xbox

Games for Tweens

Fusion Frenzy (Microsoft Game Studios, 2001). Action. Rated E.

This party game features 45 futuristic style minigames, including fight matches in round cages and collecting items. Available: www.xbox.com/en-US/games/f/fuzionfrenzy

Geometry Wars: Retro Evolved (Bizarre Studios, 2005). Also available for Nintendo DS, PC, and Wii. Action. Rated E.

Similar to the arcade classic *Asteroids*, players kill or are killed in this fast-paced shooter game as they fly triangular ships around the galaxy, fighting hordes of other shapes. Expand your collection with *Geometry Wars: Retro Evolved 2** (Bizarre Studios, 2008). Available: www.bizarrecreations.com/games/geometry_wars_retro_evolved/

Harry Potter: Quidditch World Cup (EA, 2003). Also available for GameCube, PC, and PS2. Sports. Rated E.

J.K. Rowling's inventive ballgame played on flying broomsticks comes to life. Players join one of the four house teams in international locations and compete for the Quidditch World Cup. Expand your collection with other titles in the *Harry Potter* series for Xbox, such as *The Sorcerer's Stone* (EA, 2002) and *Chamber of Secrets* (EA, 2003). Available: www.mobygames.com/game/harry-potter-quidditch-world-cup

Karaoke Revolution Party (Konami, 2005). Also available for GameCube and PS2. Music. Rated E10+ for Mild Lyrics and Suggestive Themes.

Players dance and sing to 50 musical numbers, solo or with a competitor. Expand your collection with other singing games, such as *Karaoke Revolution* (Konami/Harmonix, 2004), or dancing games such as *Dance Dance Revolution Ultramix 1–4* (Konami, 2003–2006). Available: www.harmonixmusic.com/kr1.html

NCAA Football 2003 (EA, 2002). Also available for GameCube and PS2. Sports. Rated E.

Unique in its college football scope, the game features 100 teams with unique uniforms and fight songs. Available: www.mobygames.com/game/ncaa-football-2003

Project Gotham Racing (Microsoft Game Studios, 2001). Racing simulation. Rated E.

This Xbox launch title features over 20 customizable cars and tracks in cities all over the world. It won BAFTA's Best Racing Game award. Expand your collection with the sequel, *Project Gotham Racing 2* (Microsoft Game Studios, 2003), or *Need for Speed: Underground* (EA, 2003). Available: www.xbox.com/en-US/games/p/projectgotham racing

SpongeBob SquarePants: Lights, Camera, Pants! (THQ, 2005). Also available for GameCube and PS2. Adventure. Rated E for Mild Cartoon Violence.

In this intellectual property game, SpongeBob wants a part in a movie; minigames make up his audition process. Although SpongeBob is marketed to young children, it has a cult following with teens and adults. Available: www.spongebobthevideogame.com

Games for Teens

Dance Dance Revolution Ultramix 4 (Konami, 2004). Music. Rated E10+ for Mild Lyrics and Suggestive Themes.

Players follow the arrows up, down, left, and right in time to the beat to earn points and unlock new songs. Expand your collection with earlier versions featuring different songs: *Dance Dance Revolution Ultramix 3* (Konami, 2005), *Dance Dance Revolution Ultramix 2* (Konami, 2004) and *Dance Dance Revolution Ultramix* (Konami, 2003). Available: http:// www.konami.com/games/ddr

Gauntlet: Seven Sorrows (Midway, 2005). Also available for PS2. Action. Rated T for Violence.

This is classic *Gauntlet*, with hack and slash play in a fantasy setting. Available: www .xbox.com/en-US/games/g/gauntletlivearcadexbox360/

Justice League Heroes (Warner, 2006). Also available for PS2 and PSP. Action. Rated T for Fantasy Violence and Mild Language.

Comic book heroes from the Justice League fight Brainiac in this dungeon crawler–styled action adventure. Available: http://justiceleagueheroes.warnerbros.com

Prince of Persia: The Sands of Time (Ubisoft, 2003) Also available for GameCube, PC, PS2 Action. Rated T for Blood and Violence.

The classic platformer game is now in 3D. In this action/adventure game, players complete minipuzzles as they work their way through the Sultan's palace. Available: http://prince-of-persia.us.ubi.com

Prisoner of War (Codemasters, 2002). Also available for PC and PS2. Action. Rated T for Mild Violence.

Authenticity in setting and rewarding of stealth over violence make this a winner. The gamer plays a captured pilot who must escape from Hitler's war camps; each successful attempt leads to recapture and internment in another camp. Available: www.codemasters .com/games/?gameid=754

The Simpsons: Hit & Run (Vivendi, 2004). Also available for GameCube, PC, and PS2. Action. Rated T for Comic Mischief, Mild Animated Violence, and Mild Language.

This mission-based driving game features running around outside of the car to complete tasks. The sandbox-style play encourages the players to explore Springfield, creating many opportunities to reference the 15-plus-year history of the hit animated television series. Voiceovers are provided by the actors from the cast. Available: www.xbox.com/en-us/games/s/simpsonshitandrun/

Star Wars: Knights of the Old Republic (LucasArts, 2003). Also available for PC. Role-playing. Rated T for Blood and Violence.

This turn-based action game is set in the familiar Star Wars universe (see Figure 5SG.5). Through open-ended choices, players create their own adventure-style gameplay. Players must decide which side to choose: the dark, or the light. It is highly replayable, though, because you decide anew for each game. It won BAFTA's Best Xbox Game award in 2003. Expand your collection with Star Wars: Knights of the Old Republic II: The Sith Lords (LucasArts, 2005). Available: www.bioware.com/games/knights_old_ epublic

Figure 5SG.5. *Star Wars: Knights of the Old Republic* **Screenshot**

Source: Star Wars: Knights of the Old Republic Screenshots. Team X Box May 3, 2003. http://screenshots.teamxbox.com/ screen/12386/Star-Wars-Knights-of-the-Old-Republic (accessed: April 16, 2009).

Tony Hawk's Underground 2 (Activision/Neversoft, 2004). Also available for GameCube, Game Boy Advance, PC, and PS2. Sports. Rated T for Blood, Crude Humor, Language, Suggestive Themes, Use of Alcohol, and Violence.

In this sandbox-style skating game, players become part of Tony Hawk's "World Destruction" tour. They learn tricks, tour the world, and compete in a scavenger hunt to unlock new goals. Available: www.activision.com/index.html#gamepage|en_US|gameId: THUnderGrnd2&brandId:TonyHawk

Adult Games for Young Adults

This category includes complex video games intended for an adult audience, featuring mature content that has a high appeal for teens.

Fable (Microsoft Game Studios, 2004). Role-playing. Rated M for Blood, Strong Language, Violence, and Sexual Themes.

This action-oriented game plays out a dark fairytale that features moral choices and archetypal heroes. It is highly replayable, because players can alternate, in separate games, between being a villain or a hero. Expand your collection with *Fable: The Lost Chapters* (Lionhead, 2006). Available: www.lionhead.com/FableGame/

Halo 2 (Microsoft Game Studios, 2004). Also available for PC. Rated M for Blood and Gore, Language, and Violence.

This exceptional first person shooter game with several gameplay modes has a science fiction theme. The premise is that the mission from the first game is incomplete, and the main character, the Master Chief, returns to space to investigate the Covenant elite. Available: www.microsoft.com/games/halo2

Jade Empire (BioWare, 2003). Also available for PC and Xbox 360. Action. Rated M for Blood and Gore and Violence.

In this role-playing game set in an alternative China, players seek to rescue their martial arts trainer. The choices they make evolve their combat style to be heroic or villainous. Available: http://jade.bioware.com

MVP Baseball 06 (EA, 2005). Also available for PS2. Sports. Rated E.

Players create their own university and develop their own team in this college baseball game. Then they get on the road to the championships, playing in realistic stadiums against real teams along the way. Games are called by ESPN broadcasters, and players choose one of two official rule sets to play by. Available: http://games/easports.com/mvp06/

Tom Clancy's Rainbow Six 3 (Ubisoft, 2003). Also available for PS2, GameCube, and PC. Shooter. Rated M for Violence.

In this realistic first person shooter game with a terrorist theme, the mission is to rescue kidnapped scientists, stop development of weapons of mass destruction, and prevent a global war. Expand your collection with *Tom Clancy's Splinter Cell* (Ubisoft, 2003). Available: http://rainbowsixgame.us.ubi.com

Trivial Pursuit: Unhinged (Atari, 2004). Also available for PC and PS2. Puzzle. Rated T for Comic Mischief and Suggestive Themes.

This electronic version of the popular family board game has multiple modes of play. It goes beyond the traditional version by offering opportunities to bet and steal. Available: www.xbox.com/en-US/games/t/trivialpursuitunhinged/

Microsoft Xbox 360

Figure 5SG.6. Xbox 360 and Games

Source: Photo by Beth Gallaway.

Microsoft's Xbox 360 (see Figure 5SG.6) debuted in November 2005 and features online multiplayer gaming and exclusive downloadable content and gamer profiles via Xbox Live, a subscription service. The console serves as a DVD and CD player as well. The Xbox 360 retails for between $400 and $500, depending on extras like hard drive and external HD-DVD player.

Games for Tweens

Banjo-Kazooie: Nuts & Bolts* (Microsoft Game Studios, 2008). Action. Rated E10+ for Cartoon Violence and Comic Mischief.

The infamous bear and bird team return to defeat the evil witch, Gruntilda, to gain control of Mountain. Players earn new vehicles through achievements, or they can build their own from parts at Mumbo's garage. Available: http://banjo-kazooie.com

Beautiful Katamari (Namco, 2007). Strategy. Rated E for Mild Fantasy Violence.

The father, the King of all Cosmos, has accidentally broken the galaxy. Players restore the cosmos by rolling over objects that stick to their Katamari. When they meet their goal (for size or type of object), the Katamari turns into a heavenly body. Available: http://katamari.namco.com

Beijing 2008: The Official Video Game of the Olympic Games* (Sega, 2008). Also available for PC, PS3, and Wii. Sports. Rated E.

This officially licensed game features competition in over 30 Olympic events in ten stadiums. Players can try their hand at gymnastics, track and field, cycling, swimming, and more as representatives of their favorite countries. Available: www.sega.com/beijing olympics/us/index.html

Harry Potter and the Half-Blood Prince* (EA, 2009). Also available for DS, PC, PS2, PS3, PSP, Wii, and Xbox 360. Rating pending at time of publication.

Harry returns to Hogwarts in this movie-based game. Authenticity stems from voiceover acting by cast members. Available: http://harrypotter.ea.com/us/

Harry Potter and the Order of the Phoenix (EA, 2007). Also available for Game Boy Advance, Nintendo DS, PC, PS2, PS3, PSP, and Wii. Adventure. Rated E10+ for Fantasy Violence.

Figure 5SG.7. *Harry Potter and the Order of the Phoenix* Game

The game follows the plot of the popular movie (see Figure 5SG.7). Authenticity stems from voiceover acting by cast members and attention to detail in settings. Players can choose to attend classes, recruit for Dumbledore's Army, and play minigames out of sequence. Available: www.ea.com/harry potter and theorderofthephoenix/features.jsp?platform= xbox360

LEGO Star Wars: The Complete Saga (LucasArts, 2007). Also available for Nintendo DS, PS3, and Wii. Action/adventure. Rated E for Animated Violence.

This is a charming and humorous retelling of *Star Wars* episodes I–VI, with Lego characters. Features include short cut scenes from the films and the ability to swap characters as their unique powers are needed. Expand your collection with *LEGO Indiana Jones: The Original Adventures** (LucasArts, 2008). Available: www.lucasarts.com/games/legostarwarssaga

RoboBlitz (Naked Sky Entertainment, 2006). Also available for PC. Action. Rated E10+ for Fantasy Violence.

In this game with elements of shooting, puzzle solving, and science fiction, a robot named Blitz saves the galaxy from space pirates with inventive gizmos. Available: www.roboblitz.com

SEGA Superstars Tennis* (Sega 2008). Also available for Nintendo DS, PS2, PS3, and Wii. Sports. Rated E10+ for Mild Blood, Mild Fantasy Violence, and Mild Suggestive Themes.

This game features four tournaments across ten courts with 16 different characters that span Sega's history. Minigames are intended to improve player skills. Available: www.sega .com/gamesite/segasuperstarstennis

Viva Piñata (Microsoft, 2006). Also available for PC. Strategy. Rated E.

Players develop a plot of land to attract piñatas to collect, manage, and interact with. Expand your collection with *Viva Piñata: Party Animals* (Microsoft Game Studios, 2007). Available: www.vivapinata.com

Games for Teens

Bully: Scholarship Edition* (Rockstar, 2008). Also available for PC and Wii. Action. Rated T for Use of Tobacco and Alcohol, Sexual Themes, Language, Crude Humor, Animated Blood, and Violence.

A mischievous boy, expelled from a number of boarding schools, gets transferred to another and has to claw his way up the social ladder, playing both bully and victim in a variety of situations (see Figure 5SG.8). *Bully* was a controversial game before its release, with publisher Rockstar still under scrutiny for its *Grand Theft Auto* media snafu. People were convinced *Bully* was going to focus on the player solely taking on the role of the bully, encouraging and rewarding bullying behavior. Available: www.rockstargames.com/bully/home

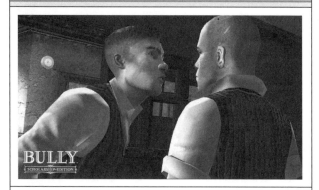

Figure 5SG.8. *Bully: Scholarship Edition* **Screenshot**

Source: "Campus Scenery." Bully: Scholarship Edition. http://www. rockstargames.com/bully/home/scenery/360/scenery6.html (accessed: April 16, 2009).

Call of Duty 4: Modern Warfare* (Activision/Infinity Ward 2008). Also available for Nintendo DS, PC, and PS3. Action. Rated T for Blood, Mild Language, and Violence.

This World War II army shooter game includes a chronology of varied tasks. It won the AIAS's Game of the Year award. Available: www.callofduty.com

Iron Man* (Sega, 2008). Also available for Nintendo DS, PS2, PS3, PSP, and Wii. Action. Rated T for Alcohol Reference, Mild Language, and Violence.

> This game follows the story of Iron Man, a superhero in the Marvel universe. It is based on the recent film with the same name. Available: http://ironmanthegame.marvel.com

Kameo: Elements of Power (Microsoft, 2005). Role-playing. Rated T for Animated Blood and Violence.

> Kameo, an elf, must rescue captured family members and warriors from the evil Thorn. Available: http://kameo.com/default.htm

Lost Odyssey* (Mistwalker/Microsoft Studios, 2008). Role-playing. Rated T for Language, Suggestive Themes, Use of Alcohol, and Violence.

> In this Japanese turn-based game, a 1,000-year-old man can't recall his past and doesn't know his destiny. It has an epic good versus evil theme, masterful storytelling, and beautiful graphics. Available: www.xbox.com/en-US/games/l/lostodyssey

PES2009: Pro Evolution Soccer* (Konami, 2008). Also available for PC, PS2, PS3, and Wii. Sports. Rated E for mild lyrics.

> This engaging soccer game includes league and club play. Available: www.pesunites .com/us/index.htm

Star Wars: Force Unleashed (LucasArts, 2008). Also available for PS3. Action. Rated T for Violence.

> Set in the *Star Wars* universe between *Revenge of the Sith* and *A New Hope*, the story sets the player as Darth Vader's apprentice. It won the Video Game Librarian's Bookmark award. Available: www.lucasarts.com/games/theforceunleashed/

Tomb Raider: Legend* (Core Design/Eidos, 2006). Also available for Game Boy Advance, GameCube, Nintendo DS, PS2, and PSP. Action. Rated T for Animated Blood and Animated Violence.

> This adventurous third person shooter game has an archaeology theme. The game features the bodacious Lara Croft. It won BAFTA's Best Original Score award. Expand your collection with *Tomb Raider: Underworld* (Core Design/Eidos, 2008). Available: www.tombraider.com/legend

Adult Games for Young Adults

This category includes complex video games intended for an adult audience, featuring mature content that has a high appeal for teens.

BioShock (2K Games, 2007). Also available for PC and PS3. Action. Rated M for Blood and Gore, Drug Reference, Intense Violence, Sexual Themes, and Strong Language.

> *BioShock* is a sophisticated first person shooter game with an art-deco tone and eerie soundtrack. Set in the future, the gamer plays a castaway in an underwater world called "Rapture," caught in a civil war. Gameplay is a mix of adventure/exploration, shooting, and puzzles. Its lush graphics, haunting soundtrack, and gore are a surprisingly engaging combination. It won BAFTA's Best Game of the Year award (see Figure 5SG.9). Available: www.bioshockgame.com

Figure 5SG.9. *BioShock* Screenshot

Source: "Screenshots." Bioshock. 2K Games, 2009. http://
downloads.2kgames.com/bioshock/site/us/_media/_img/screenshots/
screenshot_15_xl.jpg (accessed: April 16, 2009).

Culdcept SAGA* (Namco, 2008). Also available for Game Boy Advance, GameCube, Nintendo DS, PC, PS2, PS3, PSP, and Wii. Strategy. Rated T for Mild Fantasy Violence, Mild Language, Partial Nudity, and Suggestive Themes.

This game blends the real estate concepts of *Monopoly* with the depth of cards in *Magic*. Players accumulate property to boost their mana. Landing on another player's occupied space results in battle. Available: www.namcobandaigames.com/games/culdceptsaga

Dead Rising (Capcom, 2006). Action. Rated M for Blood and Gore, Intense Violence, Language, Partial Nudity, and Use of Alcohol.

The gamer takes on the role of a photojournalist, trapped in a mall full of zombies. Its sandbox-style play means everything can—and does—become a defensive weapon. Missions are also accomplished via photography assignments, giving new meaning to the term "first person shooter." Available: www.dead-rising.com

Gears of War (Microsoft/Epic Games, 2007). Action. Rated M for Blood and Gore, Intense Violence, and Strong Language.

This third person perspective tactical shooter game has a horror slant. It won the AIAS's Game of the Year Award. Available: http://gearsofwar.com

Halo 3 (Microsoft/Bungie Software, 2007). Shooter. Rated M for Blood and Gore, Language, and Violence.

This exceptional first person shooter game has several gameplay modes. Available: http://halo.xbox.com/halo 3

Madden NFL 2009* (Electronic Arts, 2008). Also available for PS2, PS3, PSP, Nintendo DS, and Wii. Sports. Rated E.

Madden NFL 2009 is the twentieth anniversary edition in the best-selling *Madden* franchise, featuring realistic gameplay, commentary, and multiple ways to play. Available: www.ea .com/games/madden-nfl-09

Mass Effect* (BioWare, 2008). Also available for PC. Role-playing. Rated M for Blood, Language, Partial Nudity, Sexual Themes, and Violence.

Mass Effect is an interactive game interspersed with fight scenes. Available: http://mass effect.bioware.com

The Orange Box (Half-Life 2: The Orange Box) (Valve, 2007). Also available for PC and PS3. Action. Rated M for Blood and Gore, Intense Violence, and Language.

The Orange Box includes three games in the *Half-Life* series—*Half-Life 2, Half-Life 2: Episode One*, and *Half-Life 2: Episode 2*—as well as *Portal* and *Team Fortress 2*. *Team Fortress 2* is a multiplayer team shooter game. *Portal* is both a shooter and a puzzle game; players solve physical puzzles and challenges by opening portals to maneuver objects (and themselves) through space (see Figure 5SG.10). Despite its short length, *Portal* won accolades for its dark humor and inventive gameplay; it won both GDC's and GameSpy's Game of the Year awards. The *Half-Life* franchise has a free download, *Counter-Strike*, for multiplayer LAN parties. Available: http://orange.half-life2.com

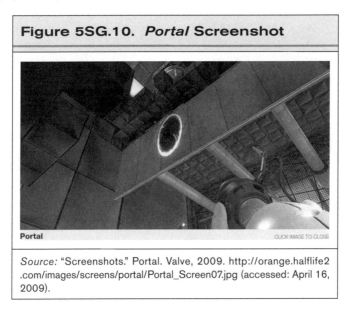

Figure 5SG.10. *Portal* **Screenshot**

Portal

Source: "Screenshots." Portal. Valve, 2009. http://orange.halflife2
.com/images/screens/portal/Portal_Screen07.jpg (accessed: April 16,
2009).

Overlord (Codemasters, 2007). Also available for PC. Action. Rated T for Blood and Gore, Crude Humor, Suggestive Themes, Use of Alcohol, and Violence.

Players command an army of minions to help them in their goals of rebuilding a tower and subduing the peasant vassals. Available: www.codemasters.com/overlord

Viking: Battle for Asgard* (Sega, 2008). Also available for PS3. Action. Rated M for Blood and Gore and Intense Violence.

Historical battle and sandbox exploration combine in this game as the player goes on a quest to conquer the queen of the underworld for the goddess, Freya. Available: www.sega .com/gamesite/viking

WWE SmackDown! vs. RAW 2007 (THQ, Inc./Yukes, 2006). Also available for PS2 and PSP. Sports. Rated T for Blood, Language, Sexual Themes, Simulated Gambling, and Violence.

> This fighting game, based on the popular wrestling franchises, features professional wrestlers. It has loads of pair-ups, match types, and slick moves. Available: www.smackdownvsraw.com

Nintendo DS

Figure 5SG.11. Nintendo DS and Games

Source: Photo by Beth Gallaway.

Figure 5SG.12. *Electroplankton* Screenshot

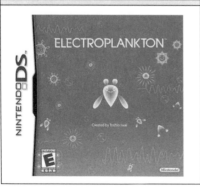

The DS ("Developer's System" [for ease of programming] or "Dual Screen" [for its two screens]) is Nintendo's handheld, mobile gaming device (see Figure 5SG.11). It features standard WiFi and exclusive WiFi that allows machines in proximity to talk to one another; it retails for about $129.99. The DSig, which debuted in April 2009, features a built-in camera and touch-screen technlogy; it retails for $169.99.

Games for Tweens

Animal Crossing: City Folk* (Nintendo, 2008). Life simulation. Rated E.

> Players create and populate a town, socialize, and perform a variety of tasks and activities, such as sports, shopping, and adventuring. Expand your collection with *Animal Crossing: Wild World* (Nintendo, 2005). Available: www.animal-crossing.com/wildworld

Bella Sara (Codemasters, 2008). Life simulation. Rated E.

> Every little girl's fantasy is to own a pony. In this DS game based on the *Bella Sara* self-esteem–building trading card game for girls, players train up to five horses and explore the magical world they live in. Available: www.codemasters.com/bellasara

Electroplankton (Nintendo, 2006). Music. Rated E.

> Players interact with and control musical plankton in Performance or Audience mode, creating their own musical patterns or playing back their own composition or a randomly generated one (see Figure 5SG.12). It won BAFTA's Best Soundtrack award. Available: www.nintendo.com/games/detail/db2f8da6-2e1b-48cb-b142-a90899e8a1a8

*Final Fantasy IV** (Square Enix/Matrix, 2008). Role-playing. Rated E10+ for Language, Mild Fantasy Violence, and Mild Suggestive Themes.

The game features 3D effects and animated cut scenes. Expand your collection with *Final Fantasy: Crystal Chronicles: Ring of Fates** (Square Soft/Equinox, 2008). Available: http://na .square-enix.com/ff4

*N+** (Atari, 2008). Also available for PSP. Action. Rated E for Mild Fantasy Violence.

Players must avoid traps and make their way through increasingly difficult maze-like puzzles in this platformer with stylized stick figure graphics. Available: www.atari.com/ us/games/n_plus/ds

New Super Mario Brothers (Nintendo, 2006). Platform. Rated E for Comic Mischief.

The classic 2D side-scrolling adventure is restyled for the DS and features familiar characters combating new worlds with new enemies. Expand your collection with other revamped *Mario* classics like *Mario Kart DS* (Nintendo, 2005) and *Super Princess Peach* (Nintendo, 2006). Available: http://mario.nintendo.com

*Ninja Town** (Southpeak Games, 2008). Strategy. Rated E for Crude Humor and Mild Cartoon Violence.

Players build dojos to protect themselves from invaders while working through more than 30 level of cute ninjas and fighting action. Available: www.ninjatown.com

Nintendogs (Nintendo, 2006). Life simulation. Rated E.

Players train their virtual puppy and then socialize him or her (and collect up to 20 breeds!) by connecting wirelessly to other DS machines. Available: http://nintendogs.com

Pokémon Diamond (Nintendo, 2007). Role-playing. Rated E.

In this third person turn-based game, the player, as a trainer, accepts quests to capture and train Pokémon for battle. Expand your collection with the companion title *Pokémon Pearl* (Nintendo, 2007), the puzzle game *Pokémon Trozei!* (Nintendo, 2006), or the nature adventure *Pokémon Ranger* (Nintendo, 2006). Available: http://origin.pokemon.com/ videogames_27

WarioWare: Touched! (Nintendo, 2004). Puzzle. Rated E for Cartoon Violence and Crude Humor.

The game includes over 150 microgames. Ten different characters, each with their own set of games that range from dentistry to pizza delivery to karaoke, encounter many homages to classic Nintendo games along the way. Expand your collection with *MarioWare: Twisted!* (Nintendo, 2005). Available: www.nintendo.com/games/detail/2cbad24c-51fe-4d3f-bf7b-b9ca5a6751c5

Games for Teens

*Castlevania: Order of Ecclesia** (Konami, 2008). Also available for Wii. Action/Adventure. Rated T for Blood, Fantasy Violence.

In this puzzle-solving, side-scrolling sequel to *Castlevania: Dawn of Sorrow* (Konami, 2005) and *Castlevania: Portrait of Ruin* (Konami, 2006), fight Dracula and his minions. Expand your collection with *Castlevania: Aria of Sorrow* (Konami, 2003). Available: www.konami .com/games/cvooe/

Death Jr. and the Science Fair of Doom (Konami, 2007). Action. Rated E10+ for Animated Blood, Cartoon Violence, Crude Humor, and Mild Language.

> Players are challenged with minigames set in a science fair gone wrong. Available: www .nintendo.com/games/detail/XQm_QvocURFuqOwMWebyFr8gKRywIPrR

Drawn to Life (THQ, 2007). Action. Rated E for Mild Cartoon Violence.

> Content creation is the play style of this game. Players must save their village by drawing everything they need and then play as their creations (see Figure 5SG.13). Available: www.thq.com/games/gameinfo.php?id=1283

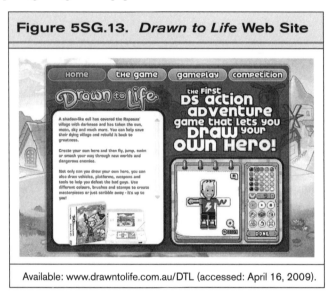

Figure 5SG.13. *Drawn to Life* **Web Site**

Available: www.drawntolife.com.au/DTL (accessed: April 16, 2009).

Figure 5SG.14. *Lost in Blue 3* **Game**

Fullmetal Alchemist: Dual Sympathy (Bandai, 2006). Rated T for Blood, Fantasy Violence, and Mild Language.

> Players brawl their way through this side-scrolling adventure as they search for the Philosopher's Stone. Available: www.nintendo.com/games/detail/ 7nbhdsyc_CifJT6IeM2XzEnWoOKmSMLL

Lost in Blue 3 (Konami, 2005). Role-playing. Rated E10+ for Mild Violence.

> Players must survive after a shipwreck (see Figure 5SG.14). Gameplay is a mix of acquiring survival skills, hunting and swimming with dolphins, exploring the island, and playing minigames. Expand your collection with the sequels *Lost in Blue 2* (Konami, 2007) and the original *Lost in Blue* (Konami, 2005). Available: www.nintendo.com/games/detail/-5sbl GSTWQEDMzquxQTsoctI42KXYE7H

Orcs & Elves (EA, 2007). Role-playing. Rated T for Blood and Gore, Fantasy Violence, and Use of Alcohol.

Players are challenged with 12 levels of "good versus evil" dungeon crawling. Available: www.orcsandelves.com

Puzzle Quest: Challenge of the Warlords (Infinite Interactive, 2007). Also available for PC, PS2, PS3, PSP, Wii, and Xbox 360. Role-playing. Rated E10+ for Suggestive Themes.

Players must rid the kingdom of evil by playing some of PopCap's famous games, like *Bejeweled*. Available: www.puzzle-quest.com/warlords

*Teenage Zombies: Invasion of the Teenage Brain Thingys** (Ignition Entertainment, 2008). Action. Rated E10+ for Animated Blood, Crude Humor, and Mild Cartoon Violence.

Zombies are the heroes in this comical horror game, rescuing Earth from an invasion of Thingys controlled by an Alien Brain. Available: www.teenagezombiesgame.com

*The World Ends With You** (Square Enix, 2008). Action. Rated T for Fantasy Violence, Mild Language, and Mild Suggestive Themes.

Text message riddles are the only clues in this adventure role-playing game that takes the hero racing through the streets, trying to save his own life before it is extinguished. Available: www.theworldendswithyou.com

Adult Games for Young Adults

This category includes complex video games intended for an adult audience, featuring mature content that has a high appeal for teens.

*Assassin's Creed: Altair's Chronicles** (Ubisoft, 2008). Action. Rated T for Violence.

A thirteenth-century crusader searches for the chalice through four Middle Eastern cities. Acrobatic movies delight in this counterpart to the console version. Pickpocket training is provided via minigames. Available: www.ubi.com/US/ Games/Info .aspx? pId=6306

Brain Age (Nintendo, 2006). Puzzle. Rated E.

Players exercise their brains with math puzzles and logic games (see Figure 5SG.15). *Brain Age* records players' progress over time. Those who stick with it will unlock more games. Expand your collection with *Brain Age 2* (Nintendo, 2007) or similar training titles like *Brain Assist** (Sega, 2008), *Brain Voyage* (Eidos, 2008), and *Flash Focus* (Nintendo, 2006). Available: www.brainage .com

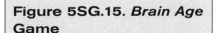

Figure 5SG.15. *Brain Age Game*

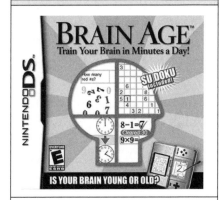

Source: Brain Age at Nintendo Games: http://media.nintendo.com/nintendo/bin/ BCMF8dCyXSZAaO-X5x7hQ9GuLX8 nbup/yo4HpZEQ009EMzRpOicY7cYX0i7l inm3.jpg (accessed: February 8, 2009).

Contra 4 (Konami, 2007). Action. Rated T for Blood and Gore, Fantasy Violence, and Language.

The sequence "up, up, down, down, left, right, left, right, A, B, A, B (select) start" is the code that unlocks unlimited lives in the platformer/shooter game *Contra* (NES, 1988).

Four soldiers must be found and transported to fight Black Viper. Marking the twentieth anniversary of the classic combat game, *Contra 4* is sure to raise nostalgia for those who can remember what "up, up, down, down, left, right, left, right, A, B, A, B (select) start" does. Available: www.konami-data .com/ officialsites/ contra4

Crosswords DS* (Nuevo Retro Games, 2008). Puzzle. Rated E.

Over 1,000 crosswords, plus anagrams and word searches, with multiple skill levels, can be played on the go. Available: www.nintendo.com/games/detail/EMhTj-8YQ4ebfxAJCm6 UrYn567YLGU24

Sudoku Gridmaster (Nintendot, 2006). Puzzle. Rated E.

This game contains over 400 combinatorial number-based puzzles with four difficulty settings. The objective is to fill the blanks in a partially completed 9 × 9 grid so that each column, each row, and each of the nine 3 × 3 boxes contains the digits from 1 to 9 only one time each. Available: www.nintendo.com/games/detail/P-2REUUT2n056n21Vx3p4n3z8L mq_nd_

Tetris DS (Tetris/Elorg, 2006). Puzzle. Rated E.

Features include Nintendo characters and music, multiplayer gaming, and new modes of play, such as pushing and catching pieces. Available: www.tetrisds.com

Trauma Center: Under the Knife (Atlas, 2005). Action. Rated T for Blood, Mild Language, and Mild Violence.

The stylus becomes an intern's syringe and knife in this medical drama. Players learn how to diagnose diseases and perform in the operating room, advancing their skills to fight a new deadly disease. Expand your collection with *Trauma Center: Second Opinion* (2006). Available: www.atlus.com/tcso

Nintendo Wii

The Nintendo Wii debuted in 2007, with a wireless, kinetic set of controllers (see Figure 5SG.16, next page). Marketed as a multigenerational gaming system, the Wii is backward compatible with Nintendo GameCube, and Nintendo and Sega classics can be downloaded directly to the console. The Wii retails for about $250.

Games for Tweens

BlastWorks: Build, Trade, Destroy* (Majesco, 2008). Shooter. Rated E for Mild Fantasy Violence.

Geometry is this game's premise. Battling their way across land, sea, and air, players shoot opponents to add pieces or ships to their own ships. Available: www.blastworks game.com

Figure 5SG.16. Nintendo Wii and Games

Source: Photo by Beth Gallaway.

Figure 5SG.17. *Boom Blox* Game

Source: Boom Blox at Nintendo Games: http://media.nintendo.com/nintendo/bin/ 0ozNAR5rivKbyTLsoQl218bcPOgPxkTD/ DoWE3AGUzVW_NVBwixG-tLMln Q4Y jzkh.jpg (accessed: April 16, 2009).

Boom Blox* (EA, 2008). Puzzle. Rated E.

Players destroy their way through a number of brainteasers or create their own (see Figure 5SG.17). Steven Spielberg helped develop this brick builder/blaster. Available: http:// games.ea.com/ boomblox

Deca Sports* (Hudson Entertainment Inc, 2008). Sports. Rated E.

Players compete in ten sports games, including badminton, beach volleyball, supercross, snowboard cross, archery, and figure skating. Recommended for *Wii Sports* fans, it is also great as a party game. Available: www.decasports.com

Disney Sing It* (Disney, 2008). Music. Rated E.

Vocalists from Disney Channel's hit shows, such as *Hannah Montana*, and original movies, such as *Camp Rock* and *High School Musical*, sing squeaky-clean lyrics in this karaoke game. Players can sing solo or compete with up to seven friends. It has both competitive and collaborative modes of play. Available: http://disney.go.com/disneyinteractivestudios/singit

Elebits (Konami, 2006). Action. Rated E for Cartoon Violence.

In this hide-and-seek game, players search for Elebits across 30 levels of minigames. Available: www.konami-data.com/officialsites/elebits

Endless Ocean (Nintendo, 2007). Adventure. Rated E.

A scuba diver explores life under the sea, searching for treasure and ocean wildlife. Available: www.endlessocean.com

Figure 5SG.18. *Mario Party 8* Game

Mario Party 8 (Nintendo, 2007). Action. Rated E for Mild Cartoon Violence.

Games include cake decorating, a game show, an obstacle course, bowling, and more, with all the beloved Mario characters. The Star Carnival setting adds to the party atmosphere (see Figure 5SG.18). Available: www.nintendo.com/sites/mp8

Pokémon Battle Revolution (Nintendo/Creature Inc., 2007). Role-playing, fighter. Rated E for Mild Fantasy Violence.

Pokémon battles in Pokétopia in a dozen different stadiums. The game features online gameplay and 16 player tournaments over a WiFi connection. Available: http://origin.pokemon.com/ #videogames_28

Super Mario Galaxy (Nintendo, 2007). Adventure. Rated E for Mild Cartoon Violence.

With traditional characters and plot—rescuing Princess Peach, this time—the gameplay is 3D and the action takes place across several planets. Available: www.supermariogalaxy.com

Games for Teens

Legend of Zelda: Twilight Princess (Nintendo, 2006). Role-playing. Rated T for Animated Blood and Fantasy Violence.

Link travels to the land of Twilight to attend the Hyrule summit, encountering enemies along the way. The Wii remote is inventively used for archery and fishing. Available: www.zelda.com/ universe/game/twilightprincess

*Mario Kart Wii** (Nintendo, 2008). Racing simulation. Rated E.

Thirty-two tracks! Ten battlegrounds! New and classic bloopers! Baby and villainous characters! Four at a time can play; when set up as a Wii LAN 12 people can play. The game comes with a wheel-shaped controller that houses the Wii remote; additional wheels can be purchased separately (see Figure 5SG.19). It won the Video Game Librarian's Bookmark award. Available: www.mariokart.com

NBA Live 08 (EA, 2007). Sports. Rated E.

This basketball game features multiple play modes (such as quick play or a whole season) smooth moves, and realistic plays by NBA stars. Available: http://games.easports.com/nba live08

Figure 5SG.19. *Mario Kart Wii*

Rayman Raving Rabbids (Ubisoft, 2006). Also available for Game Boy Advance, Nintendo DS, PS2, and Xbox 360. Action. Rated E for Cartoon Violence and Comic Mischief.

Rayman and his friends have been kidnapped by bunnies and must compete in a variety of minigames to win freedom. Play can be stand-alone or in story mode. Gems include a cow toss game, a rhythm game, and a plunger shooting game. Expand your collection with the sequel, *Rayman Raging Rabbids 2** (Ubisoft, 2008), and *Rayman Raving Rabbids TV Party** (Ubisoft, 2008). Available: http://raymanzone.us.ubi.com

Shaun White: Snowboarding Road Trip (Ubisoft, 2008). Sports. Rated E10+ for Comic Mischief, Lyrics.

Players use the innovative Wii Fit Balance Board to control their rider, integrating jumps and tricks with advice from Olympic Gold Medalist Shaun White as they travel the world to participate in snowboarding competitions. Available: http://shaunwhitegame.us.ubi.com/

Super Paper Mario (Nintendo, 2007). Adventure. Rated E.

The classic side-scroller action breaks out from 2D to 3D action as gameplay demands, combining traditional action with puzzle and role-playing elements. New characters have to be earned. Available: www.nintendo.com/sites/spm

Super Smash Bros. Brawl* (Nintendo, 2008). Action. Rated T for Cartoon Violence and Crude Humor.

This side-scrolling fighting game involves beating up a cast of characters and knocking them out of the screen, using signature moves and objects. It features a cast of characters from other Nintendo franchises. It won the Video Game Librarian's Bookmark award. Available: www.smashbros.com

Tony Hawk's Downhill Jam (Activision, 2006). Also available for Game Boy Advance, Nintendo DS, and PS2. Sports. Rated E10+ for Mild Violence, Comic Mischief, and Mild Language.

Players race downhill, from the streets of San Francisco to courses laid out in cities all over the world. Available: www.thdownhilljam.com

WarioWare: Smooth Moves (Nintendo, 2007). Puzzle. Rated E10+ for Crude Humor and Mild Cartoon Violence.

Minigames include nose picking, sawing wood, jumping for coins, and fishing. All require handling the Wiimote, providing great practice for application in other games. Available: www.nintendo.com/sites/software_warioware.jsp

Wii Music* (Nintendo, 2008). Music. Rated E.

No musical skill needed—players just mimic playing and the game responds! There are over 50 instruments to choose from. Additional modes include conductor and a variety of musical minigames. Available: www.wiimusic.com

Adult Games for Young Adults

This category includes complex video games intended for an adult audience, featuring mature content that has a high appeal for teens.

Big Brain Academy: Wii Degree (Nintendo, 2006). Also available for Nintendo DS. Puzzle. Rated E.

Players can play alone or compete with a friend in a variety of pattern recognition and matching games. Available: www.bigbrainacademy.com

CSI: Crime Scene Investigation: Hard Evidence* (Ubisoft, 2008). Also available for PC and Xbox 360. Action. Rated M for Blood and Gore, Sexual Themes, and Violence.

Figure 5SG.20. CSI: Hard Evidence Game

In this crime-solving game based on the popular *CSI* TV show, players solve five puzzles with a variety of forensic and investigative tools. *Hard Evidence* (see Figure 5SG.20) is the fifth game in the series—expand your collection with the other titles. Available: http://csi.us.ubi.com/hardevidence

House of Dead: Overkill* (Sega 2009). Rated M for Blood and Gore, Intense Violence, Partial Nudity, Sexual Themes, Strong Language.

Kill hordes of zombies in various modes in this B-movie styled game. It received an Editor's Choice Award from IGN.com. Available: www.sega.com/hodoverkill

Metroid Prime 3: Corruption (Nintendo, 2007). Shooter. Rated T for Animated Blood and Violence.

This is the final installment in a trilogy featuring galactic bounty hunter Samus Aran. Available: www.nintendo.com/sites/metroidprime3/index.jsp

Red Steel (Ubisoft, 2006). Action. Rated T for Language, Mild Suggestive Themes, and Violence.

Players must rescue a man from the Japanese mafia in this globe-trotting fighting game. Available: http://redsteelgame.us.ubi.com

Resident Evil 4 (Capcom, 2007). Also available for GameCube, PC, and PS2. Action. Rated M for Blood and Gore, Intense Violence, and Language.

A Secret Service agent is on a mission to rescue the President's kidnapped daughter by slaughtering crowds of enemies in this third person shooter. Available: www.capcom.com/re4

Trauma Center: Second Opinion (Atlas, 2006). Action. Rated T for Blood, Mild Language, and Mild Violence.

A medical intern leans how to operate and perform triage, advancing his skills to become a doctor and battling against a deadly biological weapon. Expand your collection with *Trauma Center: New Blood** (Atlas, 2008), set in Fairbanks, Alaska. Available: www.atlas.com/tcso

Wii Fit (Nintendo, 2007). Sports. Rated E.

A series of kinetic games—including yoga, step aerobics, balance games, and strength training—requires a special balance board. Increase your collection of games for the balance board with *Shaun White Snowboarding** (Ubisoft, 2008), *Wii Music* (Nintendo, 2008), and *Rayman Raving Rabbids TV Party** (Ubisoft, 2008). Available: www.nintendo.com/wiifit

World Series of Poker: Tournament of Champions (Activision, 2006). Also available for PS2, PSP, and Xbox 360. Sports. Rated T for Alcohol Reference, Language, and Simulated Gambling.

> Story-based gameplay takes players through a series of poker competitions against professional gamers at the Rio in Las Vegas. Available: www.activisionvalue.com/titles/WSOPTOC

Party Games

Buzz: The Mega Quiz (Relentless/Sony 2006). PS2. Puzzle. Rated E10+ for Alcohol and Tobacco Reference, Comic Mischief, Mild Language, Mild Suggestive Themes, and Mild Violence.

> Up to eight players can participate in this animated game show hosted by a Guy Smiley type. It includes over 5,000 general interest questions. It won BAFTA's Best Casual/Social Game award. Available: www.us.playstation.com/Buzz

EyeToy Play (Sony, 2003). PS2. Action. Rated E for Violence.

> This innovative collection of minigames features a range of activities, from window washing to boxing to plate spinning to dancing. The quirk? The controller is a camera that sits on the television, reading the movements of the player's body. Expand your collection with *EyeToy Play 2* (Sony, 2004) and *EyeToy Play 3* (Sony, 2005), both also featuring minigames; and *EyeToy: Antigrav* (Sony, 2004), featuring sports. Available: www.eyetoy.com

Scene It? Lights, Camera, Action (Microsoft, 2007). Xbox 360. Puzzle. Rated T for Blood, Language, Suggestive Themes, Use of Alcohol and Tobacco, and Violence.

> Movie trivia is presented in over 20 minigame formats—sequence films by date, attribute quotes, answer questions based on film clips, match actors to their yearbook pictures, recognize films by their posters, and more. Circulate *Scene It?* with the four buzzer controllers (see Figure 5SG.21), or keep it in your teen area for in-house use. Available: www.xbox.com/en-US/games/s/sceneitlightscameraaction

---

Figure 5SG.21. *Scene It?* Game and Controller

Sony PlayStation 2

In early 2008, Sony was still releasing an average of two new titles a month for the PS2, which debuted in 2000 (see Figure 5SG.22). Many games are backward compatible and will also run on a PS3. For a complete list of PS2 games, visit www.us .playstation .com/PS2. The Web site features an e-mail list, PlayStation Underground.

Figure 5SG.22. PS2 and Games

Source: Photo by Beth Gallaway.

Games for Tweens

Crash Bandicoot: The Wrath of Cortex (Sierra, 2001). Also available for Xbox. Action. Rated E for Mild Violence.

In this cartoony platformer, Crash must fight against Crunch, a supervillian created by his nemesis, Dr. Cortex. Available: www.wrathof cortex.com

Dragon Ball Z: Budokai Tenkaichi 3 (Atari, 2004). Action. Rated T for Cartoon Violence and Mild Language.

This 3D fighting game is modeled after a popular Japanese series. Available: www.atari .com/us/games/dbz_budokai_tenkaichi3/ playstation2

Gran Turismo 4 (Polyphony, 2005). Racing simulation. Rated E for Mild Lyrics.

Gran Turismo 4 is a driving game with real-life physics and a unique licensing system for upgrading vehicles. Available: www.us .playstation.com/GranTurismo4

Grim Grimoire (Vanillaware, 2007). Rated E10+ for Fantasy Violence, Mild Language, and Mild Suggestive Themes.

In this time-traveling mystery for upper elementary school students, a girl magician must go back to the past when all of the students at her academy are killed. Available: www.nisamerica.com/games/grimgrimoire

Harry Potter and the Goblet of Fire (EA/Griptonite Games, 2005). Action. Also available for GameCube, Nintendo DS, Game Boy Advance, PC, PSP, and Xbox. Action. Rated E10+ for Fantasy Violence.

This spell-casting action/adventure game is based on J.K. Rowling's fourth fantasy novel. Available: www.mobygames.com/game/ps2/harry-potter-and-the-goblet-of-fire

Katamari Damacy (Namco, 2004). Strategy. Rated E for Mild Fantasy Violence.

The father, the King of all Cosmos, has accidentally deleted all the stars from the sky. Players re-create the constellations by rolling over objects that stick to their Katamari; when the goal is met (for size or type of object), the Katamari is turned into a star. A whimsical soundtrack and comedic dialogue add charm and humor to this offbeat game (see Figure 5SG.23). Expand your collection with We Katamari (Namco, 2006). Available: http://katamari.namco.com

Kingdom Hearts (Square Enix, 2002). Action. Rated E for Violence.

Disney characters meet *Final Fantasy* characters in this action-oriented role-playing game. Expand your collection with the sequel, *Kingdom Hearts II* (Square Enix, 2005). Available: http://na.square-enix.com/games/kingdomhearts

SpongeBob SquarePants: Creature From the Krusty Krab (Viacom, 2006). GameCube, Game Boy Advance, Nintendo DS, Wii, and PC. Adventure. Rated E for Mild Cartoon Violence.

Figure 5SG.23. *Katamari* **Web Site**

Source: "Screenshots." *Katamari Damacy.* Namco, 2007. http://katamari.namco.com/content/gallery/index.php?id=6&gid=1 (accessed: February 8, 2009).

This silly horror spoof adventures through nine levels, with all of the favorite characters from under the sea. Available: www.spongebobthevideogame.com

Games for Teens

Burnout 3: Takedown (EA, 2004). Also available for Xbox. Racing simulation. Rated T for Mild Language and Mild Violence.

In this aggressive racing game, players are rewarded for knocking out opponents and creating massive vehicle pileups. It won BAFTA's Best Racing Game award. Available: http://info.ea .com/products/ title.php?id=396

Dance Dance Revolution: SuperNOVA 2 (Konami, 2007). Music. Rated E 10+ for Mild Lyrics and Suggestive Themes.

Kids dance along to a mix of over 40 pop and rock songs from the United States and Japan. Available: www.konami.jp/bemani/ddr/na/am/sn

Final Fantasy XII (Square Enix, 2006). Role-playing. Rated T for Alcohol Reference, Fantasy Violence, Mild Language, Partial Nudity, and Suggestive Themes.

Figure 5SG.24. *Final Fantasy XII* **Game**

This turn-based, role-playing, "explore and battle" game has Japanese manga/anime characteristics (see Figure 5SG.24). Expand your collection with others in the Final Fantasy series. The Final Fantasy series is notable for its gorgeous graphics and lengthy cut scenes.

Final Fantasy XII has more balanced cut scenes and real-time battle, as opposed to turn-based gameplay. Available: www.finalfantasyxii.com

The Incredibles (THQ, 2004). Also available for GameCube, Game Boy Advance, PC, and Xbox. Action. Rated T for Cartoon Violence.

The premise follows the plot of the award-winning Pixar film of the same name. Expand your collection with *The Incredibles: Rise of the Underminer.* (THQ, 2005). Available: www.mobygames.com/game/ps2/incredibles

Okami (Capcom, 2006). Also available for Wii. Adventure. Rated T for Blood and Gore, Crude Humor, Fantasy Violence, Suggestive Themes, and Use of Alcohol and Tobacco.

A legendary monster spreads a curse over the land; the sun god, in wolf form, comes to the rescue by recovering 13 Celestial Brush powers through solving a series of puzzles. *Okami* features a unique art style—the game looks like it has been rendered in watercolors and calligraphy brushstrokes (see Figure 5SG.25). It won BAFTA's Artistic Achievement award. Available: http://ww2.capcom.com/okami

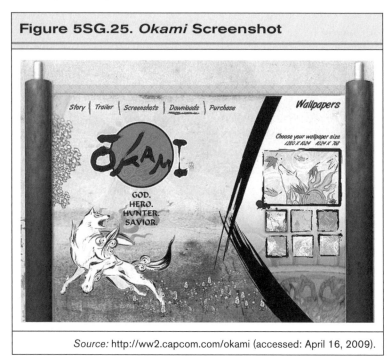

Figure 5SG.25. *Okami* **Screenshot**

Source: http://ww2.capcom.com/okami (accessed: April 16, 2009).

Shadow of the Colossus (Sony, 2006). Adventure. Rated T for Blood and Fantasy Violence.

Wander, the hero, must defeat 16 giants to rescue a girl. It won BAFTA's Best Action and Adventure award. Available: www.us.playstation.com/PS2/Games/Shadow_of_the_Colossus/OGS

The Sims 2 (Maxis/EA 2005). Also available for PC. Life Simulation. Rated T for Crude Humor, Sexual Themes, Comic Mischief, and Violence.

This sequel to the best-selling game of all time allows several different methods of play, including building and interior design and guiding a character from babyhood through old age. Available: http://thesims2.ea.com

Tony Hawk's Pro Skater 4 (Neversoft, 2002). Also available for GameCube, PC, PS1, and Xbox. Sports. Rated T for Blood, Comic Mischief, Mild Lyrics, and Suggestive Themes.

Players advance level by level to professional skater status first by practicing and then by seeking a pro, who provides a goal to meet. Expand your collection with other *Tony Hawk* titles, such as the sandbox-style *Tony Hawk's Underground* (Activision, 2003). Available: www.neversoft.com/site/?#/THPS4

Adult Games for Young Adults

This category includes complex video games intended for an adult audience, featuring mature content that has a high appeal for teens.

24: The Game (2K Games, 2007). Action. Rated M for Blood and Violence.

This adventuresome game resembles the storytelling style of the TV show *24* through 100 missions that are a mix of interrogation, shooting, driving, and puzzles during a day in the life of Jack Bauer. *24: The Game* is notable because it extends the story arcs of *24* by tying up loose ends and bridging seasons two and three (see Figure 5SG.26). Available: www.2kgames .com/index.php?p=games&platform=&title=24

Figure 5SG.26. 24: The Game

God of War (Sony Computer Entertainment America, 2006). Action. Rated M for Blood and Gore, Intense Violence, Nudity, Sexual Themes, and Strong Language.

In this Greek mythology–themed game, Kratos seeks redemption for his sins by serving the gods. It won AIAS's Game of the Year award. Expand your collection with *God of War II* (Sony Computer Entertainment America, 2007). Available: www.godofwar.com

Metal Gear Solid II: Sons of Liberty (Konami, 2001). Action. Rated M for Animated Blood and Animated Violence.

A variety of weapons and moves and a carefully applied musical score are highlights of this stealth-based first person shooter game. Available: www/konami.jp/gs/game/mgs2english/index.html

Namco Museum 50th Anniversary Arcade Collection (Namco, 2006). Also available for Nintendo DS and PS2. Arcade. Rated E10+ for Cartoon Violence and Mild Lyrics.

Namco's collection of classic games includes *Pac-Man, Ms. Pac-Man, Pole Position,* and *Dig Dug,* among other titles. Available: www.mobygames.com/game/ps2/namco-museum-50th-anniversary

Silent Hill: Origins (Konami, 2007). Also available for PSP. Action. Rated M for Blood and Gore, Language, Suggestive Themes, and Violence.

> This survival horror game prequel adds to the popular *Silent Hill* series. Fight your way out of a city of horrific inhabitants, in the dark, surrounded by scary noises. Guaranteed to make players jump! Expand your collection with *Silent Hill 2* (Konami, 2001), *Silent Hill 3* (Konami, 2003), and *Silent Hill 4: The Room* (Konami, 2004). Available: www.konami-silenthillorigins.com

Sony PlayStation 3

Figure 5SG.27. PS3 and Games

Source: Photo by Beth Gallaway.

The PlayStation 3 debuted in 2006 and retails for $400 to $500, depending on options such as hard drive (see Figure 5SG.27). Like the Xbox 360, it has HD, DVD, and CD capabilities; and it has an Internet connection to an online community.

Games for Tweens

FIFA Soccer 09 (EA, 2008). Also available for DS, PC, PS2, PS3, Wii, Xbox 360. Sports. Rated E for Everyone.

The premiere professional soccer game offers increasingly realistic physics and an overwhelming variety of players, teams, leagues, and locations. Available: www.ea.com/games/fifa-soccer-09

Karoaki Revolution: American Idol Encore 2* (Konami Digital Entertainment, 2008). Also available for Wii and Xbox 360. Rhythm. Rated E10+ for Lyrics.

> Over 140 solo and duet songs span forty years of pop. Compete with whole songs or medleys in a variety of venues as you struggle to get to Hollywood. Paula, Randy and Simon lend their voices, compliments and criticism. Expand your collection with other karaoke titles like *Singshot* (SCEA, 2007). Available: www.konami.com/games/kraie2/

Kung Fu Panda* (Activision, 2008). Also available for Nintendo DS, PC, PS2, Wii, and Xbox 360. Action. Rated E10+ for Fantasy Violence and Mild Language.

> Players embark on an epic journey as they master Kung Fu in this martial arts comedy. Available: www.kungfupandagame.com

The Legend of Spyro: Dawn of the Dragon* (Sierra, 2008). Action. Rated E for Comic Mischief.

> Spyro the dragon continues to have adventures. He is a bit less rounded and babyish for his next-gen console debut. Available: http://lair.spyrothedragon.com/us

Mega Man 9 (Capcom, 2008). Also available for Wii and Xbox 360. Action. Rated E for Mild Cartoon Violence.

In this 3D side-scrolling platformer, players fight past robots to reach the boss of each stage, earning new weapons in each stage. Additional modes include short "challenge" missions and timed levels. It won the Video Game Librarian's Bookmark award. Available: http://megaman.capcom.com

MX vs. ATV: Untamed (THQ, 2007). Also available for Nintendo DS, PS2, PSP, Wii, and Xbox 360. Racing simulation. Rated E for Mild Violence.

Professional riders compete in off-road competitions on a variety of three- and four-wheeled vehicles. Unique for the way it brings together multiple types of off-road racing into one tournament. Available: http://mxvsatv.com

Ratchet & Clank Future: Tools of Destruction (Sony/Insomniac, 2007). Action. Rated E10+.

Two friends—an alien and a robot—save the galaxy from the forces of evil with the help of numerous gadgets in this platformer shooter. Available: www.us.playstation.com/ratchet andclank/tools_of_destruction.html

Ridge Racer 7 (Namco, 2006). Racing simulation. Rated E for Mild Language and Mild Suggestive Themes.

The game involves drift racing, with 40 customizable cars and 22 tracks that can be played in reverse. Available: www.namcobandaigames.com/games/ridgeracer7

Sonic Unleashed (SEGA, 2008). Action/Adventure game. Rated E10+ for Animated Blood, Fantasy Violence. Also available for PS2, Wii, and Xbox 360.

This text-heavy platformer combines combat and puzzle solving as Sonic turns from a hedgehog in daytime to a "Werehog" at night. Available: www.sonic-unleashed.com

Tiger Woods PGA Tour 10 (EA, 2009). Also available for PS2, PSP, Wii, and Xbox 360. Sports. Rated E Everyone.

Realistic features of over a dozen real courses and many top players, plus inclusion of the US Open Tournament for the first time! Expand your collection with *Tiger Woods PGA Tour 09** (EA, 2008) or the *Hot Shots* golf series (SCEA, 2007). Available: http://tigerwoods pgatour.easports.com/home.action

Games for Teens

Civilization Revolution, aka *Sid Meier's Civilization Revolution* (Take 2 Interactive, 2008). Strategy. Rated E10+ for Alcohol and Tobacco Reference, Mild Suggestive Themes, Violence. Also available for Xbox360 and Nintendo DS.

In this turn-based strategy game the player builds, trains, researches, attacks, or consults an expert for advice; then, the simulation kicks in to execute the choices. There are sixteen civilizations to choose from, and multiple end game scenarios to appeal to different types of players. Available: www.civilizationrevolution.com

Lair (SCEA, 2007). Action. Rated T for Blood and Gore and Violence.

As a dragon-riding warrior, the player fights an age-old battle of good versus evil by land, sea, and air. Available: www.us.playstation.com/lair

LittleBigPlanet* (SCEA, 2008). Action. Rated E for Comic Mischief and Mild Cartoon Violence.

Players solve puzzles and pick up stickers in this 50-level platformer. Players can even create and upload their own levels. It won the Video Game Librarian's Bookmark award. Available: www.littlebigplanet.com

Naruto: Ultimate Ninja Heroes (Namco, 2006). Action. Rated T for Cartoon Violence and Comic Mischief.

In this game, based on a popular anime series, players create a powerful Ninja fighting team. Expand your collection with *Naruto: Ultimate Ninja Heroes 2: The Phantom Fortress** (Namco, 2008). Available: http://narutoheroes.namcobandaigames.com

Rock Band 2* (MTV Games, 2008). Also available for PS2, Wii, and Xbox 360. Music. Rated T for Lyrics and Mild Suggestive Themes.

Players become rock stars in this sequel that marries *Guitar Hero* to *Karaoke Revolution* and throws in a drum kit (see Figure 5SG.28). Up to four players compete or collaborate to play through a variety of current and classic punk, rock, and pop songs from—AC/DC to the Who. Expand your collection with the original *Rock Band* (MTV Games, 2007) or *Guitar Hero: World Tour** (RedOctane, 2008). (Assume patrons have the first game at home when purchasing music games that require special controllers, and get the sequels or add-ons they may not have at home.) It won the Video Game Librarian's Bookmark award. Available: www.rockband.com

Figure 5SG.28. *Rock Band 2*

The Simpsons Game (EA, 2007). Also available for Nintendo DS, PS2, PSP, Wii, and Xbox 360. Action. Rated T for Alcohol and Tobacco Reference, Animated Blood, Cartoon Violence, Crude Humor, Language, and Suggestive Themes.

Stuck in video game purgatory, America's favorite animated family must battle their way through Simpsonized versions of video games, drawing on characteristics for their video game superpowers. Humor abounds at pop culture references and spoofs of franchises, including *EverQuest*, *Final Fantasy*, and *Halo*. Available: www.ea.com/simpsons/

SoulCalibur IV* (Namco, 2008). Also available for Xbox 360. Adventure. Rated T for Animated Blood, Mild Language, Suggestive Themes, and Violence.

This adventure fighting game features characters from the previous titles in the series as well as to-be-announced special guest appearances. Available: www.soulcalibur.com

Spider-Man 3 (Activision, 2007). Also available for Wii. Action. Rated T for Animated Blood and Violence.

> The game follows the plot of the film, *Spider-Man 3*, as the player takes on the role of Peter Parker/Spider-Man/Venom, fighting all manner of evil in New York City. Available: www.activision.com/index.html#gamepage|en_US|gameId:Spiderman3&brandId:Spiderman

Tekken 5: Dark Resurrection (Namco, 2007). Also available for PSP. Action. Rated T for Crude Humor, Suggestive Themes, Tobacco Reference, Violence, and Mild Language.

> In this arcade-style combat game, players have over 30 characters to choose from. Players must earn money to further customize their characters. Available: www.namcoband aigames.com/games/tekken5dr

Adult Games for Young Adults

This category includes complex video games intended for an adult audience, featuring mature content that has a high appeal for teens.

Beowulf (Ubisoft, 2007). Also available for PC, PSP, and Xbox 360. Action. Rated M for Blood, Intense Violence, Partial Nudity, and Sexual Themes.

> Based on the film adaption of the epic poem, the game adds 30 years of history, allowing gamers to play elements from the Norse warrior's life not shown in the film. Available: www.ubi.com/US/Games/Info.aspx?pId=5875

Bourne Conspiracy* (Sierra, 2008). Also available for Xbox 360. Action. Rated T for Blood, Mild Language, Use of Alcohol and Tobacco, and Violence.

> Robert Ludlum's Jason Bourne goes digital in this spy game based on Ludlum's hit thriller novels. Available: www.activision.com/index.html#gamepage|en_US|gameId:bourne Conspiracy&brandId:bourne

Devil May Cry 4* (Capcom, 2008). Also available for PC and Xbox 360. Fighting. Rated M for Sexual Themes, Violence, Blood, and Language.

> Old-school button-mashing pays off in this cinematic game of demon slaying. Available: http://devilmaycry.com

Fallout 3* (Bethesda Softworks, 2008). Also available for PC and Xbox 360. Action. Rated M for Blood and Gore, Intense Violence, Sexual Themes, Strong Language, and Use of Drugs.

> As the resident of an underground complex the player was born in, the player emerges to explore postapocalyptic society peopled with interesting characters. Violently bloody, but the vast world to explore, the choose-your-own-adventure style of play, and the collection of side missions ensures hours of engagement. Somber colors add to the barren feel of the landscape in *Fallout 3* (see Figure 5SG.29). It won the Video Game Librarian's Bookmark award. Available: http://fallout.bethsoft.com

Figure 5SG.29. *Fallout 3* Screenshot

Source: Photo by Beth Gallaway.

Fight Night Round 3 (EA, 2007). Also available for PS2, PSP, Xbox, and Xbox 360. Sports. Rated T for Blood, Mild Language, Violence, and Suggestive Themes.

Players create a customizable character and fight in historical matches in this multiplayer boxing game. Expand your collection with a similar fighting title, *Def Jam: Icon* (EA, 2007). *Fight Night Round 3* won BAFTA's Best Sports Game award. Available: www.ea.com/games/ fight-night-round-3

Guitar Hero: World Tour* (Activision, 2008). Also available for PC, PS2, PS2, Wii, and Xbox 360. Rhythm. Rated T for Lyrics and Mild Suggestive Themes.

This edition adds new bands, new tracks ,and new instruments to the popular music franchise. Expand your collection with *Guitar Hero: Rocks the 80s* (Activision, 2007) and *Guitar Hero: Aerosmith: Walk This Way* (Activision, 2008), with inventive gameplay that progresses as a historical tour of Aerosmith's career, spanning recreations of venues that were career highlights from opening acts to world superstars. Available: www.guitar hero.com

LOST: Via Domus* (Ubisoft, 2008). Also available for PC and Xbox 360. Action/ adventure. Rated T for Alcohol and Tobacco Reference, Blood, Mild Language, and Violence.

This edition extends the premise of the TV series *LOST* by placing the player on the Island as passenger with amnesia, fighting for survival, making alliances, and helping unravel the mystery of the island. It features both familiar locations and new places to explore. Available: http://lostgame.us.ubi.com

Medal of Honor: Airborne (EA Games, 2007). Also available for PC and Xbox 360. Action. Rated T for Violence.

This World War II–themed first person shooter game features a whole new arsenal of weapons. Available: www.ea.com/moh/airborne

Metal Gear Solid 4* (Konami, 2008). Action. Rated M for Blood, Crude Humor, Strong Language, Suggestive Themes, and Violence.

This tactical first person shooter game is set just a few years in the future. It features new moves, new weapons, and familiar characters—Solid Snake gets deployed in the Middle East to stop Liquid Ocelot. Because this title wraps up the series, purchasing older games in the series, available for PS2, is highly recommended. *Metal Gear Solid 4* won the Video Game Librarian's Bookmark award. Available: www.konami.com/games/mgs4

Ninja Gaiden: Sigma (Tecmo, 2007). Action. Rated M for Blood and Gore, Intense Violence, Partial Nudity, and Suggestive Themes.

Players can experience the story from the point of view of a male or female ninja, with new moves and weapons. Available: http://ninjagaidengame.com/ninjaGaiden/top.html

Unreal Tournament 3 (Epic/GT Interactive, 2007). Also available for PC and Xbox 360. Action. Rated M for Animated Blood and Gore and Animated Violence.

Unreal Tournament 3 is a turn-by-turn, human versus alien fighting game featuring multiple modes of play and a large arsenal of weapons. Available: www.unrealtournament3 .com

Sony PlayStation Portable

The PlayStation Portable, Sony's handheld mobile gaming device, debuted in 2005 and retails for about $199.99 (see Figure 5SG.30). It also plays movies and music files. The on-board WiFi allows gamers to connect to one another remotely over the PSP's network. A complete catalog of games is online at www.us.playstation.com/PSP.

Figure 5SG.30. PSP and Games

Games for Tweens

The BIGS (2K Sports, 2007). Also available for PS2, PS3, Wii, and Xbox 360. Sports. Rated E for Mild Violence.

> This game has it all: simple controls and a quick learning curve, all the favorite teams, and expert commentary from the voices of baseball. Minigames help players improve their pitching and hitting. In career mode, players can take their rookies to MVP status. Major League Baseball endorses this game. Available: http://2ksports.com/games/thebigs

Dungeon Maker: Hunting Grounds (2007). Role playing. Rated E10+ for Fantasy Violence and Mild Suggestive Themes.

> Players create their own dungeon and then play through it with spells and the weapons at their disposal to defeat enemies. Available: www.dungeonmakerhuntingground.com

*flOw** (SCEA, 2008). Also available for PC and PS3. Puzzle. Rated E.

> Players choose one of five creatures to navigate through a unique environment. The game is highly customizable and adaptive to the users' level. Available: www.us.playstation.com/flOw

Lemmings (SCEA, 2006). Also available for PS2 and PS3. Puzzle. Rated E for Mild Cartoon Violence.

> Players shepherd lemmings across 100 levels, utilizing the unique skills of individual lemmings to ward off danger. Available: www.us.playstation.com/Lemmings

LocoRoco (Sony, 2006). Puzzle. Rated E for Comic Mischief.

> Alien Moja troops invade the peaceful world inhabited by the LocoRoco and their friends, the Mui Mui. It won BAFTA's Strategy Game of the Year award. Available: www.locoroco.com

MotoGP (Namco, 2006). Racing simulation. Rated E.

> This motorcycle racing game with realistic physics features professional riders. Available: www.namcobandaigames.com/games/motogp_psp

NBA 2K8 (2K Sports, 2007). Also available for PS2, PS3, and Xbox 360. Sports. Rated E.

> In minigames, players can improve their skills, manage their franchise, or play their favorite hoop stars down to their signature moves. Available: www.2ksports.com/games/nba2k8

Pac-Man World Rally (Namco, 2006). Also available for GameCube, PC, and PS2. Racing simulation. Rated E for Mild Cartoon Violence.

This Kart racing game features Namco characters, some exclusive to the PSP. Available: www.mobygames.com/game/psp/pac-man-world-rally

Patapon (Sony, 2008). Action. Rated E.

The Patapons have returned to Earthend in search of a Mighty One to lead them—by drumming. Abstract, artsy graphics, original music, and multiple modes of gameplay (missions and minigames) made this a GameSpot and IGN Editor's Pick of 2008. Available: www.us.playstation.com/Patapon

Games for Teens

Beats (SCEA, 2007). Music. Rated E.

Players can import songs from personal music collections and create rhythm games—or compose from a free selection—and then upload and share original compositions. Available: www.us.playstation.com/PSP/Games/Beats

Bomberman (Konami, 2006). Action. Rated E for Mild Cartoon Violence.

Through 100 levels of the classic game, Bomberman must protect his planet from alien invaders. Expand your collection with *Bomberman: Land** (Konami, 2008). Available: www.hudsonentertainment.com/gamedetail.php?game-id=29&console=1

Final Fantasy Tactics: The War of the Lions (Square Enix, 2007). Role-playing. Rated T for Blood, Drug Reference, Fantasy Violence, and Mild Suggestive Themes.

This *Final Fantasy* title features new character classes, new multiplayer modes, and the same gorgeous graphics and rich storytelling. Expand your collection with *The War of the Lions* (Square Enix, 2007) and *Final Fantasy VII: Crises Core* (Square Enix, 2008). Available: http://na.square-enix.com/fftactics

MediEvil: Resurrection (SCEA, 2005). Action. Rated T for Animated Blood and Violence.

Players fight against an army of undead or play 700 minigames. Cartoonish styling and quirky characters, like a cowardly hero, make this immensely appealing. Available: www.us .playstation.com/MediEvilResurrection

Pursuit Force: Extreme Justice (SCEA, 2007). Also available for PS2. Action. Rated T for Alcohol and Tobacco Reference, Mild Language, and Violence.

Players use land, air, and sea vehicles to track down and arrest street criminals. Available: www.us.playstation.com/pursuitforce

Star Wars Battlefront: Renegade Squadron (Lucas Arts, 2007). Action. Rated T for Violence.

A rogue team of warriors led by Han Solo participates in a series of space battles across the galaxy in the war of the rebels versus the Alliance. The story is set in the Star Wars universe between *A New Hope* and *Return of the Jedi*. Available: www.lucasarts.com/games/sw battlefrontrenegadesquadron

Street Fighter Alpha 3 MAX (Capcom, 2006). Fighter. Rated T for Violence.

This is a classic 2D side-scrolling fighter game. Available: www.us.playstation.com/PSP/
Games/Street_Fighter_Alpha_3_MAX

Transformers: The Game (Hasbro, 2007). Also available for Nintendo DS, PC, PS2,
PS3, and Xbox 360. Action. Rated T for Violence.

As an Autobot or a Decepticon, players interact with or destroy the world in this sandbox-
style game that follows the plot of the *Transformers* blockbuster movie. Available: www
.transformersgame.com

Wipeout: Pure (SCEA, 2006). Racing simulation. Rated E.

Gameplay is futuristic-styled combat racing. Expand your collection with *Wipeout: Pulse*
(SCEA, 2007), featuring new weapons and tracks. Available: www.wipeoutpure.com

Adult Games for Young Adults

This category includes complex video games intended for an adult audience, featuring
mature content that has a high appeal for teens.

Arthur Maclean's Mercury (Ignition Entertainment, 2005). Puzzle. Rated E.

Players slide a slippery ball of mercury through
a number of paths and mazes. Designed to
take advantage of PSP's unique capabilities,
Mercury offers several types of games, all
multiplayer, with music, amazingly realistic
graphics, and tilt action play (see Figure
5SG.31). Each level adds a new challenge.
Expand your collection with *Mercury Melt-
down* (Ignition Entertainment, 2006) and
Mercury Remixed (Ignition Entertainment,
2006). Available: www.us.playstation.com/
PSP/Games/Mercury

**Figure 5SG.31. *Mercury
Game***

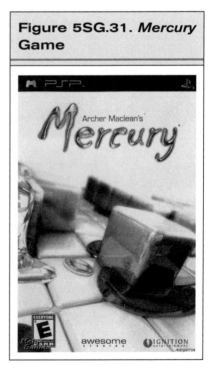

Brothers in Arms: D-Day (Ubisoft, 2006).
Action. Rated M for Blood and Gore, Strong
Language, and Violence.

As either a corporal or a sergeant in the
Normandy invasion of World War II, players
fight their way through recreations of historic
battles. This is a multiplayer game, with team-
based combat. Available: www.ubi.com/US/
Games/Info.aspx?pID=5064

Dead Head Fred (D3Publisher, 2007). Action. Rated M for Blood and Gore, Intense
Violence, Mature Humor, and Strong Language.

A decapitated private eye is resurrected to solve his own murder, using the decapitated
heads of his enemies to find clues. Gory, but the unique story with its horror mystery
theme and comic tones equals high appeal. Available: www.deadheadfred.net

Infected (Majesco, 2005). Action. Rated M for Blood and Gore, Intense Violence, and Strong Language.

A virus has turned New Yorkers into zombies, just in time for the holidays. Players evacuate healthy citizens and slay the infected ones. Available: www.infected.com

Midway Arcade Treasures: Extended Play (Midway, 2005). Arcade. Rated M for Blood and Gore and Violence.

Classic arcade games include *Spy Hunter, Paperboy, Joust, Marble Madness, Gauntlet,* and *Mortal Kombat,* some with multiplayer action. Available: www.midwayarcade.com/us/Game_ MidwayArcadeTreasuresExtendedPlay.html

---

Circulate as a Kit

Books with companion tapes, language CDs accompanying workbooks, and puzzles packaged into kits and toys are nothing new at libraries across the country. Package specialty controllers in a heavy duty plastic hanging bag and barcode each part to keep track of the pieces. These games will need special packaging:

Nerf N-Strike (EA, 2008). Action. Rated E10+ for Fantasy Violence.

This is a shooter game without bullets or blood! The Wii remote tucks into a Nerf Switch Shot EX-3 blaster, which is then used to "fire" Nerf missiles through the storyline (see Figure 5SG.32). Gameplay progresses without the player needing to navigate the character. Available: www.hasbro.com/nerf/ en-US/shop/details.cfm?guid=942892DE-6D40-1014- 8BF0-9EFBF894F9D4&product_ id=22851

Figure 5SG.32. *Nerf* *N-Strike* **Game and Controller**	*Guitar Hero: On Tour** (Activision, 2008). Music. Rated E10+ for Lyrics. This handheld version of the popular rhythm game features classic and contemporary rock, punk, and pop songs. It comes with a special four-button controller (see Figure 5SG.33). Available: www.guitar hero.com/ghot/

Figure 5SG.33. *Guitar Hero: World Tour*

Source: "Details: Nerf N-Strike Game for Wii with Switch Shot EX-3 Blaster." Hasbro, 2008. http://www.hasbro.com/ shop/details .cfm?guid=942892DE-6D40-1014-8BF0- 9EFBF894F9D4& product_id=22851&src= endeca (accessed: April 16, 2009).

Source: Photo by Beth Gallaway.

Valkyrie Profile: Lenneth (Square Enix, 2006). Role-playing. Rated T for Suggestive Themes, Use of Alcohol, Fantasy Violence, and Language.

> A female Valkyrie is responsible for transporting lost souls to Valhalla in this revisioning of a popular PS1 game with a Norse mythology theme. It is recommended for fans of *Final Fantasy* games. Expand your collection with *Valkyrie Profile: Silmeria* (Square Enix, 2006). Available: http://na.square-enix.com/valkyrieprofile

Digital Collections

Subscription Services

Subscription services are Web sites where you sign up to purchase streaming or downloadable content. Figure 5SG.34 lists several popular services.

Figure 5SG.34. Video Game Subscription Services

Title	Publisher	Scope	Cost	URL
GameTap	Turner Broadcasting	900+ video games for PC including titles from Sega, Commodore, 64 & Intellivision consoles	$6.95 $9.95/month	www.gametap.com
Games On Demand: Unlimited	Comcast	500+ PC games, rated E10+, T, & M	$14.95/ month	http://gamesoduser .comcast.net/games ondemand/unlimited .html
Games on Demand: Kids Play	Comcast	170+ PC games rated EC & E	$7.95/month	http://gamesoduser .comcast.net/games ondemand/kids .html
OverDrive		70 productivity edutainment, and casual games for PCs	To be announced	www.overdrive.com/ products/dlr/media formats/games.asp
Shockwave Unlimited	Atom Entertainment	400 PC games	$4.95–$9.95	

Source: Table by Beth Gallaway.

Digital Downloads

Digital downloads are games to download and install on library computers. Some games are also available for consoles; hence, the publisher submitted the game to the ESRB for a rating. Traditionally, Web-based games don't carry ratings; games with

Figure 5SG.35. Games to Download—Services

Title	Publisher	Scope	Cost	URL
Direct To Drive	IGN	PC Titles rated E-M; maybe backed up and archived on CD	$20–$49.99	www/direct2drive.com
PlayFirst	Viacom	Unrated Mac & PC games	$9.95–$19.95	www.playfirst.com

Source: Table by Beth Gallaway.

online play components carry a disclaimer that gameplay may change online. Figure 5SG.35 lists two services that sell downloadable games.

Downloads for Tweens

Bookworm (PopCap, 2006). Puzzle.

> Players create words from letters in this word game. Available: www.popcap.com/gamesfree/bookworm

Lemonade Tycoon (Jamdat, 2008).

> Players run a virtual lemonade stand in this management simulation. Available: www.shockwave.com/gamelanding/lemonade.jsp

Line Rider (Media Mayhem, 2007). Action.

> Players draw a route filled with ramps, hills, and jumps for a virtual sledder to follow. Previous incarnations of the game include a bike, and content may change seasonally. This is a content creation game; users are invited to post video footage of their landscapes. Available: http://linerider.com

Oregon Trail Edition 5 (Broderbund, 2006). Life simulation.

> In this classic historical simulation game, the goal is to get the Conestoga wagon to Oregon, avoiding obstacles such as dysentery. Available: www.oregontrail.org/download-free-oregon-trail.htm

Pirates of the Caribbean (Disney, 2008). Role-playing.

> This free pirate-themed game is based on the *Pirates of the Caribbean* Disney films. Players create and customize their own pirate and ship, recruit a crew, and accomplish quests in search of fame and fortune. Available: http://apps.pirates.go.com/pirates/v3/welcome

WolfQuest (Minnesota Zoo, 2009). Life simulation game.

> Designed for players aged nine to adult, *WolfQuest* teaches wolf behavior, conservation, and ecology through engaging gameplay and social interactions (see Figure 5SG.36, top of next page). Players join a wolf pack made up of friends or non-player character (NPC) wolves and explore the complex interactions within a pack. Available: www.wolfquest.org

Figure 5SG.36. *WolfQuest* Web site

Available: http://www.wolfquest.org (accessed: April 16, 2009).

Downloads for Teens

Command & Conquer (Virgin Interactive, 2007). Also available for PC. Strategy. Rated T for Animated Violence.

Players control the rivaling Brotherhood of Nod or the Global Defense Initiative over a dozen or more missions. Available: www.gamespot.com/pc/strategy/commandconquer/download.html?sid=6178099

Diner Dash (PopCap, 2006). Management simulation.

Players help waitress Flo welcome, seat, and serve customers in this waitressing simulation game that rewards the ability to multitask. Available: www.playfirst.com/game/dinerdash

Iced (Break Through Production, 2008). Strategy.

This is a serious game about deportation. Available: www.icedgame.com

Maple Story (Nexon, 2005). Role-playing.

This is a 2D, side-scrolling fantasy massively multiplayer online game. Available: www.maplestory.com

Science Mystery (Ken Eklund, 2008). Strategy.

Unique illustrated mysteries are written in second person, integrating science into a suspenseful storyline. Players will build their logic and problem solving skills. Available: http://sciencemystery.com

Step Mania (Sourceforge, 2006). Music.

> *Dance Dance Revolution* for the fingers... or plug in a USB pad. Available: www.stepmania .com

Adult Downloads for Young Adults

This category includes complex video games intended for an adult audience, featuring mature content that has a high appeal for teens.

America's Army: Special Forces (Ubisoft, 2003). Also available for PC, PS2, and Xbox. Action. Rated T for Blood and Violence.

> This is the civilian version of a military game developed to test and train soldiers in warfare and battle tactics. Available: www.americasarmy.com

Bejeweled 2 (PopCap, 2008). Puzzle.

> Players swap gems in this puzzle game. Available: http://popcap.com/games/bejeweled2

The DaVinci Code (2K Games, 2006). Also available for PS2 and Xbox. Puzzle. Rated T for Teen for Blood, Language, and Violence.

> This game is based on the best-selling novel and film about the quest for the Holy Grail intertwined with a murder mystery. Available: www.2kgames.com/davincicode

Dyson (Rudolf Kremers, 2008). Strategy.

> Players remotely command semiautonomous self-replicating mining machines in order to take over an entire asteroid belt. Abstract drawings propel the game (see Figure 5SG.37). Available: www.gamespot.com/pc/strategy/dyson/download.html?sid=6202144

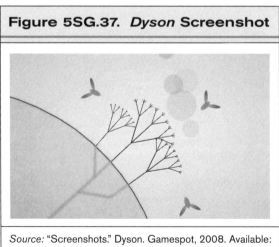

Figure 5SG.37. *Dyson* Screenshot

Source: "Screenshots." Dyson. Gamespot, 2008. Available:
www.gamespot.com/pc/strategy/dyson/download.html?
sid=6202144 (accessed: April 16, 2009).

The Endless Forest (Tale of Tales BVBA, 2004–2007). Role-playing.

> Players take on the role of a deer and communicate with one another through sounds and body language. Available: http://tale-of-tales.com/TheEndlessForest

Objection! (Transmedia, 2008). Management simulation.

This game was designed for law students to sharpen their courtroom skills. Available: www.objection.com

Snood (Word of Mouse, 1999). Puzzle.

Shoot matched Snoods—three of kind (or more)—to make the Snoods disappear, freeing up lines. Word of Mouse has a variety of other games based on Snoods. Available: www.snoodworld.com

Web-Based Games

Web-based games are games played over the Internet via a standard Web browser such as Firefox, Internet Explorer, Opera, and Safari. Games are played online, with no file downloading required.

Plug-ins for Web-Based Games

Usually, Web-based games require plug-ins—additional free software to install to your browser so the animations in the game can be viewed and the game can be played. A few of the common plug-ins required are described. Some plug-ins have security issues or allow streaming media, which can create bandwidth issues; talk to your technology staff before installing.

DirectX 10 (Microsoft, 2008).

DirectX 10 enhances graphical details like lighting and weather to create a more realistic gameplay experience. It is limited to PCs running Windows. Available: www.games forwindows.com/en-US/aboutgfw/pages/directx10-a.aspx

Flash Player 10 (Adobe, 2008).

Flash Player displays content created with Flash CS4 Professional, a software program that is used to design animated Web pages and interactive applications like games. It is available for Internet Explorer, Firefox, Opera, and Safari Web browsers. Available: http:// get.adobe.com/flashplayer

Java Runtime Environment (Sun Microsystems, 2007).

The Java plug-in creates a connection between your browser and the Java platform to enable applets, like games, on to be run within the browser instead of downloading and installing the game. It is available for Internet Explorer, Firefox, Opera, and Safari Web browsers. Available: http://java.sun.com/products/plugin

Shockwave Player 11 (Adobe, 2008).

The Shockwave Player displays content created with Adobe Director® software, including high-performance multiplayer games, interactive 3D product simulations, online entertainment, and training applications. It is available for Internet Explorer, Firefox, Opera, and Safari Web browsers. Available: http://get.adobe.com/shockwave

Adobe developed the Shockwave Web site (see Figure 5SG.38) to feature games and films built with Adobe Director. The site includes single and multiplayer games for the Web and short animated films. Game categories include Action and Arcade, Adventure, Card and Board, Jigsaws, Kids, Music and Photos, Puzzle Games, Racing, Shooters, Sports, Strategy, and Word Games. Available: http://getadobe.com/shockwave

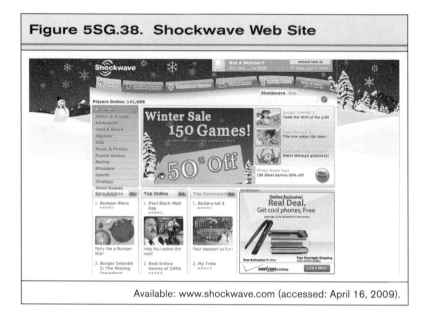

Figure 5SG.38. Shockwave Web Site

Available: www.shockwave.com (accessed: April 16, 2009).

Games for Tweens

Adventure Quest (Artix Entertainment, LLC, 2006). Role-playing.

> Players can defeat over 600 enemies, earning new armor, weapons, and spells to assist them in combat in a fantasy realm. Available: www.battleon.com

Aliens Must Die (LongAnimal, 2008). Action.

> This is a space shooter game, similar to *Asteroids* but 3D. Available: www.kongregate.com/games/robotJAM/aliens-must-die-the-jupiter-wars

Bella Sara (Hidden City Games, 2009). Also available for Nintendo DS and in card form. Life simulation.

> Players choose a foal and care for their virtual pet, earning horseshoes by playing puzzle and trivia games (see Figure 5SG.39, see next page). This gender-specific game is focused on building positive self-esteem in young girls through affirmations. Available: www.bellasara.com

Cartoon Network: Games (Turner, 2008). Arcade, Action, Strategy.

> This Web site contains more than 200 games based on Cartoon Network shows. Available: www.cartoonnetwork.com/games

Club Penguin (Disney, 2008). Action, Arcade, Puzzle.

> This game includes minigames and social networking with Penguin avatars. Available: www.clubpenguin.com

Defend Your Castle (XGen Studios, 2008). Also available as a WiiWare download. Strategy.

> Players defend their castle from dawn 'til dusk! Available: www.xgenstudios.com/play/castle

Figure 5SG.39. *Bella Sara* **Screenshot**

Source: "My Horse Stall." Bella Sara. Hidden City Games, 2009. Available: www.bella sara.com/myhorsestall.aspx?ref=headnav&lcid=EN (accessed: April 16, 2009).

flOw (Jenova Chen, 2008). Also available for PSP. Life simulation.

Players start as plankton, grow by eating, and avoid being eaten. The game features simple, beautiful graphics and lovely ambient music (see Figure 5SG.40). Available: http://intihuatani.usc.edu/cloud/flowing

Figure 5SG.40. *flOw* **Screenshot**

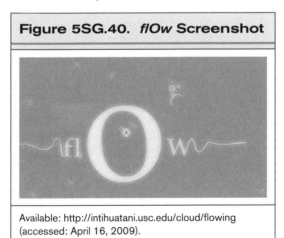

Available: http://intihuatani.usc.edu/cloud/flowing (accessed: April 16, 2009).

Girls Go Tech (Girl Scouts of the United States of America, 2004). Puzzle.

The Girl Scouts of America offer interactive games that fit their themes: multiculturalism, communication, arts, music, and science. Available: www.girlsgotech.org

Games to Enhance School Curriculums for Tweens

BBC School Games (BBC, 2002). Edutainment.

Numerous games feature citizenship, history, languages, literacy, math, and science subjects organized by age ranges 4–7, 7–11, and 11–16. Available: www.bbc.co.uk/schools/games

Caduceus (Fablevision, 2008). Puzzle.

As a novice healer newly graduated from the Alterican College of Alchemy, the player is sent into field to fight a disease that is ravaging the land, earning the pieces of the magical Caduceus: a healing staff with snakes, wings, and jewel. The game was designed to impart altruism and compassion, while also testing skills of logic, reason, and creativity. Available: www.educationarcade.org/node/349

Fun Brain (Pearson Education, Inc. 2002). Various.

Games include edutainment arcade and e-books for K–8 and teachers. Available: www.funbrain.com

Learning Vocabulary Fun (www.vocabulary.co.il, 2008). Puzzle.

Vocabulary building matching games include word searches, crosswords, and other word puzzles (see Figure 5SG.41). Designed for English as a Second Language students, the games are useful for students of all ages. Available: www.vocabulary.co.il

Figure 5SG.41. *Learning Vocabulary Fun*

Available: www.vocabulary.co.il (accessed: April 16, 2009).

Mr. Nussbaum (Greg Nussbaum, 2008). Puzzle.

Over 60 interactive edutainment games for grades K–8 include topics like ecology, math, science, and history. Available: www.mrnussbaum.com/gamescode.htm

Quest Atlantis (Indiana University, 2009). Strategy.

Games for elementary and middle school students are based on the concept of social responsibility. Available: http://atlantis.crlt.indiana.edu

Games to Enhance School Curriculums for Teens

Ayiti: The Game of Life (Global Kids, 2008). Life simulation.

Global Kids, an organization to transform urban youth, teamed up with Gamelab to create Ayiti. In this game, players make decisions on how to spend their sparse resources to provide their Haitian family the necessities: food, clothing, shelter, education, and recreation (see Figure 5SG.42). Available: www.gamelab.com/game/ayiti

Figure 5SG.42. *Ayiti* Screenshot

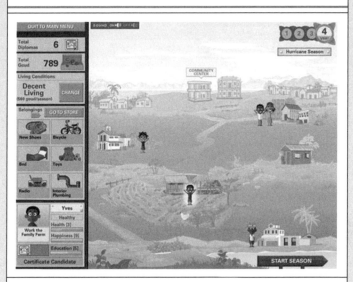

Source: "Ayiti Screenshots." *Ayiti: The Game of Life.* Gamelab, LLC, 2008. Available: www.gamelab.com/files/ayiti_screen_2.jpg (accessed: April 16, 2009).

Darfur is Dying (Networks on Campus, 2008). Life simulation.

Players keep the refugee camp stable in the face of many threats in this serious game about genocide. Available: www.darfurisdying.com.

Free Rice (FreeRice, 2008). Word.

Ten grains of rice are donated by the World Food Bank via sponsors. Players learn how to make a difference in the world while building their vocabulary for the SATs in this multiple choice game. Available: www.freerice.com

Immune Attack (American Federation of Scientists, 2008). Strategy.

This game introduces basic concepts of human immunology to high school and entry-level college students. Available: http://fas.org/immuneattack

Jefferson Labs: Games & Puzzles (Thomas Jefferson National Accelerator Facility, Office of Science Education, 2008). Puzzles.

Subjects include general science, math, and chemistry. Available: http://education.jlab.org/indexpages/elementgames.php

LEGO: Play: Games (Lego, 2009). Action, Construction, Puzzle.

Rendered in LEGO bricks, games are based on themed sets (Mission to Mars, Castle) and popular licensed franchises (*Indiana Jones*). Games for preschoolers also provided. Available: http://play.lego.com/en-us/games/default.aspx

Planet Cruncher (Rock Solid Arcade, 2008). Action.

Players draw loops around planets to make them explode and then collect the crystal particles left behind. Available: www.rocksolidarcade.com/games/planetcruncher.

Games for Teens

Bob the Blob (Flash Gem, 2006). Action.

Bob the Blob is sucked into a third dimension while eating his hamburger and must navigate his way out in this cute platformer. Available: www.addictinggames.com/blobbob.html

David & Goliath Arcade (David & Goliath, 2006). Arcade.

There are several games in the *David & Goliath* series: *Boys Are Stupid*, *Jack the Nerd*, and *Goodbye Kitty*, a spoof based on the Hello Kitty character. Available: www.davidand goliathtees.com/index.php?mode=DLG

Gaia Online (GAIA Interactive, 2004). Multiple.

In the worldwide Gaia online community, players customize avatars by playing games for points to purchase items for the avatar. Available: www.gaiaonline.com

i made this. you play this. we are enemies (Jason Nelson, 2008). Action.

In this platformer game, players advance through levels that are based on popular Web sites (such and Google and Yahoo!). Available: www.secrettechnology.com/madethis/enemy6 .html

PlayFirst (PlayFirst, 2005). Action, arcade, puzzle, strategy.

PlayFirst publishes highly original casual games for multiple platforms, with free trials and downloadable content. Available: www.playfirst.com

RuneScape (Jagex LTD, 1999). Role-playing.

In this free fantasy massively multiplayer online game, the ultimate goal is to acquire the most money to earn the winged headpiece. Available: www.runescape.com

Adult Games for Young Adults

This category includes complex games intended for an adult audience, featuring mature content that has a high appeal for teens.

Games for Change (Games for Change, 2004). Action, simulation, strategy, management.

As part of the Serious Games Initiative, *Games for Change* uses games to explore the management and leadership challenges the public sector faces in education, training, health, and public policy. Available: www.gamesforchange.org

IFiction (Dave Walton, 2007). Adventure.

Also called *Interactive Fiction*, this archive contains more than 250 text adventure games. Available: www.ifiction.org

Kingdom of Loathing (Asymmetric Publications, 2006). Role-playing.

Kingdom of Loathing is a free, comical (with tongue planted firmly in cheek), turn-based, text-based adventure game played alone or in groups (see Figure 5SG.43). Available: www.kingdomofloathing.com

---

Figure 5SG.43. *Kingdom of Loathing* Screenshot

Places to go, People to see

The Kingdom is broad and deep. Visit such picturesque zones as:

The Barrel full of Barrels	The Misspelled Cemetary	The Orcish Frat House	The Bugbear Bakery

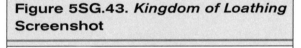

Danger!

The Kingdom contains scores of terrifying monsters. Among them are:

 The ferocious Sabre-Toothed Lime!

 The menacing Booze Giant!

 And hordes of fierce Ninja Snowmen!

Source: What is KoL? Kingdom of Loathing. Asymmetric Publications, LLC 2008. www2.kingdomofloathing.com/static.php?id=whatiskol (accessed: April 16, 2009).

Orisinal (Ferry Halim, 2001). Puzzle.

Minigames are beautifully illustrated. Available: www.ferryhalim.com/orisinal

Pogo (EA, 2006). Action, arcade, puzzle.

This site contains over 100 free, downloadable games. Players can win tokens to exchange for cash. Available: www.pogo.com

RoboKill (Rock Solid Arcade, 2008). Action.

The premise is a simple premise: kill robots! Available: www.rocksolidarcade.com/games/robokill

SetGame (Set Enterprises. 2000). Puzzle. Also available in card form.

This site offers pattern recognition games. Available: www.setgame.com

Untangle (Chris Benjaminsen, 2008). Puzzle.

Players untangle the lines that create a shape by dragging from fixed points. Ambient music adds to the experience. The goal is to locate six sets of three from the 16 cells by selecting three cells to create a set. Available: www.ebaumsworld.com/games/play/63028/

Weekday Warrior (Bungie, 2007). Life simulation.

This online adventure game is set in a corporate office. Available: http://students.guildhall .smu.edu/~weekdaywarrior/contents/html/home.html

Weffriddles. Puzzle.

Weffriddles is an html-coded, text-based series of logic puzzles. Figure 5SG.44 shows the rules. The answer is the name of the next Web page. Available: www.weffriddles.com

---

Figure 5SG.44. *Weffriddles* Screenshot

So. Glad you could make it. Let's go over some rules, shall we?

1. This isn't a puzzle, per se. It's actually a series of puzzles. Some will be obvious right away, some will not be so obvious... Most of the levels' challenge really relies on what kind of thinker you are. Do not get discouraged; these are supposed to be challenging.

2. No spoilers. If you've beaten a level, and you're talking to someone who hasn't, don't go and tell them how to beat it. It's no fun for the people who haven't beaten it yet to be told the answer. In that same vein, it's against the rules to go looking for spoilers. It's much more satisfying to get the answers yourself.

3. Most of the time, the answer will replace the part of the URL *just before* the .html. You are going to want to put .html after every answer, or else you may not get the page you're looking for.

4. Sometimes you will need outside knowledge to beat a level... I try to keep things untechnical, but in a game like this, some situations are unavoidable. It is recommended that in another tab/window, you keep open your favorite search engine, so you can go find the knowledge you need.

5. No spoilers. Seriously.

6. Try having fun at this. All the levels are fair. If you find the answer, it will be quite obvious that you got the answer. Guessing wildly really doesn't help at all.

7. If you're ready to start, then go ahead. Don't get frustrated... Sometimes the answers are just waiting in the dark.

Available: www.weffriddles.com/level1.html (accessed: April 16, 2009).

Yahoo! Games (Yahoo, 2009). Puzzle, strategy.

Games include chess, checkers, and bridge. Many pit the player against an online opponent and integrate chat features. Available: http://games.yahoo.com.

Library-Themed Games

The Goodhue Codex (LAPL, 2006). Strategy.

Solve a mystery set in the Los Angeles Public Library. Available: www.lapl.org/ya/game

Library Arcade: Within Range (Carnegie Melon, 2007). Management simulation.

Arrange books in Library of Congress shelf order. Available: www.library.cmu.edu/Libraries/etc/index.html

Library Arcade: I'll Get It! (Carnegie Melon, 2007). Management simulation.

Deliver the right resource for the reference question. Available: www.library.cmu.edu/Libraries/etc/index.html

Chapter 6

Level 6:
The Future of Games

Projected Growth

Gaming is not a passing fad. According to the NPD Group, a 35-year-old market research company that provides consumer and retail information for a wide range of industries including entertainment (which includes computer and video games), total revenue for games, consoles, and accessories has been on the rise, jumping 18 percent to $12.5 billion in 2006[1] and to $18.8 billion in 2007, a 43 percent increase.[2] In 2005, gaming revenue was expected to triple to over $13 billion in 2011,[3] and that figure has already been surpassed. Industry data from Datamonitor in 2006 suggested that video games would generate $21.9 billion in hardware and software revenue by 2008.[4] As predicted, game sales in the United States for January through May 2008 were 6.58 billion; it is anticipated that games sales will top $21–$23 billion in the United States in 2008.[5] John Gaudiosi of WRAL Local Tech Wire predicts that with the increasingly high price of gas, people will continue to spend money on home entertainment,[6] like games, instead of traveling for vacations or driving to movie theaters and the like.

Gaming is not going away. In fact, its popularity and saturation continue to grow. For all libraries, this means (at the very least!) keeping gaming on the radar, purchasing crossover materials, and allowing access to online games for patrons of all ages. For many libraries, it means recognizing games as a legitimate format and offering game services, programs, and collections.

Console Gaming

Video game consoles will continue to evolve. "Next–generation" consoles are the latest, most advanced game consoles: the Microsoft Xbox 360 debuted in late fall 2005, and the Nintendo Wii and Sony PlayStation 3 (PS3) hit shelves in fall 2006. Perhaps because of the "everything is in beta" premise of Web 2.0,[7] manufacturers continue to look for ways to upgrade their consoles.

All of the next-generation consoles connect to the Internet. Owners can create user profiles and buy points to purchase games, upgrades, and demos. With a subscription, owners can get arcade-style games, first crack at new games, and exclusive titles. For libraries, this means making sure someone on staff (or a gamer patron who you radically trust) needs to maintain the user profile, download updates, purchase new content, and possibly be responsible for creating a third space in the online network.

Online Content

Microsoft: Xbox Live (https://xbox.com/live). Cost: Silver level, free; Gold level, $49.99/year.

A free account includes a gamer profile, a friends list for sending text and voice messages, access to the Xbox Live Marketplace (which features an arcade, demos, and trailers), and access to massively multiplayer online games (MMOGs). The upgrade enhances feedback options, friends list capability, and multiplayer gameplay and provides access to exclusive content in the Marketplace. Xbox 360 profiles will be incorporating avatars to represent players in a variety of interactive and passive ways.

Nintendo: Mii/Wii Shop/WiiWare (www.nintendo.com/wii/wiiware). Cost: Wii Shop is free to browse; content is valued in Wii Points.

Nintendo offers a virtual console that allows users to download classics for a number of systems (NES, SNES, N64, NEOGEO, Sega Genesis, and TurboGrafx 16). Modern games, many by independent publishers, are available via WiiWare (see Figure 6.1). Wii users can create their own avatars, known as Miis, which represent them in video games and can be sent to friends' Wiis over the Internet. Nintendo's Web site hosts a step-by-step-video tutorial on how to download WiiWare games to your Wii console. The Wii also offers weather and mail.

Figure 6.1. WiiWare Screenshot

Source: www.nintendo.com/wii/wiiware (accessed: April 16, 2009).

Sony: Sony Online Entertainment (SOE) (www.station.sony.com). Cost: free to subscribe.

Players create a profile to use on the Web and on their consoles. They can access blogs and podcasts, keep all of their SOE games automatically updated, download and play great free and subscription-based games, manage their friends list, and chat with their friends across all SOE games.

Libraries are beginning to maintain an online presence in social-networking sites like MySpace, Facebook, and Second Life, and they should consider joining gaming sites like Xbox Live and Sony Online Entertainment (SOE). The advent of SOE's much anticipated *Home* software will make creating a multimedia third-dimensional (3D) space a reality.

Luckily the trend of downloadable games means increased coverage, online and in print, of Internet-only games, so selecting these games will become less of a challenge. Currently GameStop's magazine, *Game Informer* (www.gameinformer .com), dedicates one page to downloadable games, and all of the major magazines dedicate online space to downloaded content reviews.

According to VG Chartz, a sales statistics Web site that provides the most accurate, up to date, and comprehensive video game sell-through charts in the world, Nintendo is leading the pack for units sold in both the console and handheld divisions (see Figure 6.2). At the time of this writing, the DS continues to outsell the PlayStation Portable (PSP) by more than two to one, holding 68.4 percent of the market.[8] The Wii is outselling the PS3 more than two to one, holding 48.9 percent of the market, with the Xbox360 and PS3 holding 29.8 percent and 21.6 percent, respectively.[9]

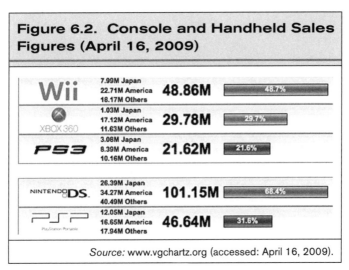

Figure 6.2. Console and Handheld Sales Figures (April 16, 2009)

Wii	7.99M Japan 22.71M America 18.17M Others	**48.86M**	48.7%
XBOX 360	1.03M Japan 17.12M America 11.63M Others	**29.78M**	29.7%
PS3	3.08M Japan 8.39M America 10.16M Others	**21.62M**	21.6%
NINTENDO DS.	26.39M Japan 34.27M America 40.49M Others	**101.15M**	68.4%
PlayStation Portable	12.05M Japan 16.65M America 17.94M Others	**46.64M**	31.6%

Source: www.vgchartz.org (accessed: April 16, 2009).

Mobile Games

Cell phone games, like console, arcade, and computer games, have evolved from simple 2D two-color graphics to full-color 3D games, rich in plot and story. A *Business Week* article in 2006 covered the history of cell phone gaming, which in just ten years had grown in leaps and bounds. The article concluded:

> It has become fairly obvious that mobile gaming is the next frontier in portable gaming, as worldwide mobile games download revenue is set to hit $8.4 billion by 2010, according to the Screen Digest study.[10]

Many multiplayer games are played over the cell phone provider network, and this trend will continue. One issue is that not every game is available for every phone. At Apple computer's developer's conference in spring 2008, *Super Monkey Ball* for the iPhone was introduced, incorporating tilting the phone to roll the ball (see Figure 6.3), and in July 2008, Activision ported *Guitar Hero* to the Nokia cell phone. As of April 2009, the iTunes store hosted over 8,000 games; games dominate downloaded applications.[11]

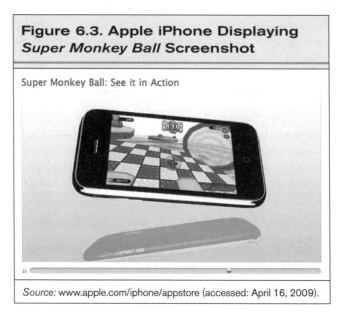

Figure 6.3. Apple iPhone Displaying *Super Monkey Ball* Screenshot

Super Monkey Ball: See it in Action

Source: www.apple.com/iphone/appstore (accessed: April 16, 2009).

Mobile gaming revenue is expected to quadruple from $2.6 billion in 2006 to $11.2 billion by 2010.[12] According to M:Metrics, 98.4 million people in the United States and Western Europe are playing mobile games.[13] M:Metrics further reports that in the United States 22 percent of cell phone owners played cell phone games in the last quarter of 2007, and the majority of games were native to the phone, not downloaded and installed or played over a live Internet connection.[14]

Lebanon and Thorntown Public Libraries in Boone County, Indiana, and the North Shore Public Library in Shoreham, New York, offer cell phone clinics, with teen volunteers who assist adults with storing phone numbers and text messaging. A next step for libraries might be to offer a program in which patrons bring in their cell phones to show and share games. Hosting a gaming event that incorporates use of smartphones may also be of interest, for example, a round of *Cruel 2 B Kind* (Jane McGonigal and Ian Bogost, 2006) in which teams check in via text messaging or a scavenger hunt that requires digital photos.

Internet Games and Digital Downloads

With ever-increasing access to higher bandwidths and high-speed Internet connections, more and more games will be downloaded and played digitally. WildTangent ORB (www.wildtangent.com) seeks to revolutionize PC gaming to make it more like console gaming. WildTangent has its own PC platform game development studio and has distribution agreements with Dell, HP, Gateway, and Toshiba, meaning that their proprietary PC Game Console for direct to desktop games is bundled to 25 million new consumer PCs annually. Their gaming portal, WildGames (www.wildgames .com; see Figure 6.4) hosts 20 million players worldwide who play 250 million game sessions a month, and it supports over 8,300 affiliates from top online game developers like HipSoft, PlayFirst, Sandlot, and PopCap.[15] Using virtual tokens called "WildCoins," gamers purchase sessions of ad-free gaming. Instead of having to buy a subscription, players pay only for their actual playtime. The company also has a try and buy model in which games can be purchased for $19.95.

Figure 6.4. WildTangent's Gaming Portal

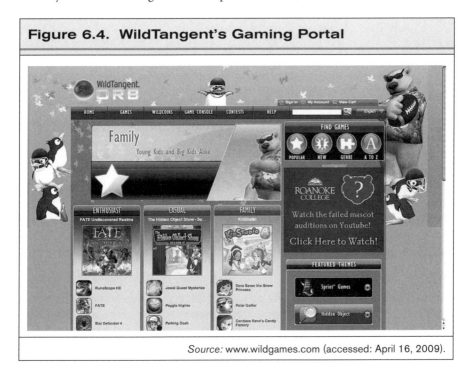

Source: www.wildgames.com (accessed: April 16, 2009).

PC Gaming

Is PC gaming on the decline or on the rise? *PC World* argues that PC gaming is not dead.[16] However, it may stabilize or even decrease as mobile gaming and Internet-ready consoles usage increase. It is much easier to design games for a console than a PC, because a console standardizes the graphics, sound, and gameplay; games for PCs have to adapt to a wide range of operating systems and graphics and sound cards.

One interesting trend is the porting of traditional PC game series like *The Sims* and *Civilization* to consoles. Consoles have the ability to offer memory for storage of game data, although they generally use keyboards for a variety of complex commands.

More and more cross platform porting is expected. For libraries, this means incorporating PC games into services, programs, and collections and possibly purchasing subscription services or digital downloads for in-house or at-home use.

Subscription Services

Games acquired from subscription services are "DRM (digital rights management) free," which means you can download a title again if you lose it from your computer, can install it on multiple machines, and can play offline. Plus, your purchase may include supplementary materials like walkthroughs.

MMOGs

MMOG Chart, an online Web site that tracks users of online games, reports that *Lineage* peaked at just over 3 million users in late 2003; *EverQuest* (989 Studios–1999) just barely got beyond the 500,000 mark; and *World of Warcraft* hit 6.5 million players in summer 2006[17] and passed 11 million players in October 2008.[18] According to a December 2008 Nielsen report, almost 20 percent of PC gaming is dedicated to *World of Warcraft*, and the average user spends 823 minutes a week playing—that's nearly 14 hours a week.[19] Similar popular titles range from *RuneScape* and *Guild Wars* (which has free and fee models) to subscription titles like *City of Heroes/City of Villains* (NCSoft, 2006) for PC.

Although it's a challenge for a library to provide access to subscription games like *World of Warcraft*, programming can be built around MMOGs for the PC. Offering LAN (local area network) parties so community members can come and play together socially is an easy solution that requires only power strips, Internet access, and dismantling library filters that block high-bandwidth applications. *LAN Party: Hosting the Ultimate Frag Fest* by William Steinmetz (John Wiley and Sons, 2004) is a good resource for more information on LAN games and program structures.

Virtual Worlds

Virtual worlds are not games by any stretch of the imagination. Unlike games, virtual worlds do not have goals, objectives, or structured play. They are more like building block toys, created for the purpose of amusement and diversion. The user creates his or her own experience that may or may not include playing games, chatting, listening to music, role-playing, fashion design building, and computer programming. The virtual world Web site Second Life (http://secondlife.com) grew in leaps and bounds. Launched in 2003, it had 11 million users in 2007; this increased to 14.5 million by the end of July 2008.[20] However, elimination of gambling, the influx of commercial businesses like Toyota, and major problems with software instability mean that numbers of users are now decreasing. The June 2008 release of an open source client for creating 3D worlds, *OpenSim*, has offered potential users more control over a buggy software. Google debuted their browser-based 3D virtual world, *Lively*, in June 2008, but it was short-lived, shutting down in November 2008.

Philip Rosedale, the founder and former CEO of Linden Lab, said of Second Life to *Wired* in 2004: "I'm not building a game.... I'm building a new country."[21] The country apparently has space for a library. In April 2006, Alliance Library System (ALS) in Illinois purchased a plot of land in *Second Life* to build a virtual library that might attract Illinois residents and act as a referral to local physical libraries (see Figure 6.5). The project was a "response to a shift in people of all ages from media consumers to media creators.... [T]hey want to create and contribute, not just consume."[22] The project has grown by leaps and bounds, with a virtual reference desk staffed several nights a week by volunteer reference librarians from all over the world, programs and events that include bibliographic instruction, professional development for librarians, book discussions, and virtual author visits. EBSCO and OCLC have offered trials to databases and World Cat, and partners include in-world newspapers, writing groups, e-book creators and artists, as well as organizations like Tech Soup. With over 500 dedicated volunteers and 50 islands, ALS has invited participation from other libraries to ascertain what digital residents want in a twenty-first-century virtual library—and then build it.

Figure 6.5. "Den of Inquiry." *Info Island International* Screenshot

Source: Alliance Virtual Library. Available: www.slurl.com/secondlife/Info%20Island%20 International/144/248/34 (accessed: April 16, 2009).

The *Second Life Library* is a perfect example of the culmination of delivering services to patrons who live online, of meeting users where they are, of trying pilot projects, of adapting to change, and of adopting content creation technologies. Although not a game with goals and objectives, *Second Life* shares many characteristics of video games. The challenge to create an avatar as a representation of oneself, the social networking and building of affinity groups, and the tendency to create and modify content in and around the world all pay tribute to video games. The interface and the ability to zoom in and out are designed for—and by—a generation that has grown up focusing on a screen while their hands manipulate a character.

In 2006, Steven Johnson, Technology Writer for *Wired*, predicted that virtual worlds will converge in the next ten years. "One way or another, consolidation is all but inevitable. A single, pervasive environment will emerge, uniting the separate powers of today's virtual societies."[23] No matter what platform libraries choose to get involved with, using the communication tools, software, and currency of their virtual world of choice will be good practice for what's to come.

Device as Platform: Controllers That Play Games

Qmotions (www.qmotions.com) introduced a golf club–shaped controller in 2004 to work with EA Sports' *Tiger Woods PGA Tour 2004* (EA, 2003)(see Figure 6.6) and *EyeToy*'s PS2-compatible camera, sensitive to light and motion. A version of the controller is now available for PC *EyeToy* games.

Figure 6.6. Qmotions Golf Club Controller

Source: www.qmotions.com/golf_product.html (accessed: April 16, 2009).

In 2005, RedOctane's *Guitar Hero* and *Namco's Taiko: Drum Master* introduced controllers shaped like musical instruments, and XaviX Games introduced a baseball bat–shaped controller and ball that allow the player to bat and pitch at the console's motion sensor. Video games now move players off the couch to dance, drum, exercise, and mimic sports and other activities. These items commanded a high price when new, but as technology evolves, these unique gadgets are slipping into the mainstream.

Edutainment software is pursuing a more game-like approach. In 2006, Fisher-Price introduced a plug-and-play product, I Can Play Piano, to teach children aged

4–8 the basics of reading notes and playing them on a keyboard (see Figure 6.7). A color-coded key electronic piano plugs directly into the RCA jacks of most televisions.

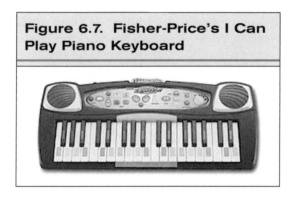

Figure 6.7. Fisher-Price's I Can Play Piano Keyboard

Modeled after *Piano Wizard* software created by Allegro, I Can Play Piano is accompanied by a cartridge containing eight songs (ranging from childhood favorites such as "Row, Row, Row Your Boat" to classics such as "Fur Elise"). Cartoonish static backdrops depict the song, and the shapes of the notes support the theme; for example, "Heart and Soul" shows a canoodling couple, and the notes are heart shaped. Each song can be played at four levels. In Level 1, players match the colored shapes that scroll up from the bottom of the screen with the colored squares on the keyboard. In Level 2, the colored shapes scroll from right to left. In Level 3, the shapes become regular colored notes, and in Level 4, the colors disappear, leaving white notes for white keys and black notes for sharps and flats. Each song can be played in three modes—right hand, left hand, and both hands—and the keyboard can emulate five different instruments.

The variety of play can keep a child occupied for hours, and the drive to best one's score creates engagement in the sometimes tedious practice process that creates tension between parent and child. Songs can be slowed down or speeded up. Timing is critical, because if the player is off by a quarter beat, no sound emerges from the piano. Instead of allowing the player to hear and correct a missed note, only correct notes are played. There is no indication of how long each note should be played, and musical notations, such as rests, are not introduced. The software is billed as being "just like a video game," because the software tracks the number of correct notes played and displays the top score of the session and the current score. While the challenging feel, interactivity, and intuitive interface are game-like, I Can Play Piano is simply good edutainment software for a generation of children who prefer games as their primary form of entertainment. It has the added advantage of play without the TV connection, for practice or original composition, and can be battery operated.

A true video game style would not allow the player to move freely from level to level; there is no advancement reward for improvement or perfect playing. Each song continues to the end, regardless of how well the player does (compared to Konami's

Dance Dance Revolution in which missed steps cause the player to "fail" and the song to end. The minigames consist of a "banger" game (accompaniment is provided, and four notes are recommended for an impromptu jam session) and a matching game (colored cars drive across the screen, and the player presses the correspondingly colored key). There are no practices drills, listening exercises, or quizzes to associate the notes with the colors. After playing through all the songs on all the levels, I didn't feel like I was associating the shape of the middle C note with the middle C on the keyboard; I was still reading the letter on the note itself or relying on memory to play the song as I knew it should sound. A fifth level, with no lettered notes, would elevate the stakes.

At present there are eight other game cartridges for I Can Play Piano, five of which incorporate trademarked icons such as Dora the Explorer, Scooby Doo, and Barbie. Advanced learners can go on to the *Piano Wizard* software. A similar software with a guitar controller debuted about a year later.

Games on the iPod/iTunes

Games finally debuted in the iTunes store in fall 2006 with the launch of iTunes 7. Retailing for $4.99, they are compatible with iPod classic, third-generation iPod nano, or fifth-generation iPod. Apple's new attentiveness to gaming was further reflected at the 2008 World Wide Developers Conference where Sega demonstrated *Super Monkey Ball*, a console game with over 100 levels that has been ported to the iPhone.[24] The intuitive interface of the phone lends itself well to the complex game controls; for example, titling the device makes the Monkey Ball roll. Pangea Software has ported two games to the iPhone: *Enigmo*, a physics-based puzzle game, and the 3D racing game *Cro-Mag Rally* in which the iPhone becomes the steering wheel.

Predictions for Games

Convergence

Increased convergence of mediums is expected. Look for not only games based on films, and films based on games, but more films *made* from games in the form of machinima. Game characters will cross over into more books. Bands will continue to use video games as a new venue to get their music out, and music from games will become an increasing part of the soundtrack of our lives. The acquisition of Harmonix by MTV is very interesting—the merging of music video and musical video games.

Graphics and gameplay will become increasingly realistic. By summer 2006, 60-plus leading publishers and developers had adopted the new Ageia PhysX into over 100 new games.[25] The PhysX chip performs the calculations of rigid-body dynamics (everything from the motion of water and clothing to the interaction and destruction of objects) hundreds of times faster than current chipsets.[26] Now Phys-X is being incorporated into graphics cards.

Content

Serious gaming will continue to increase. Games will employ ethical decisions and center on political, racial, historical, and socioeconomic premises. Academic, school, and special libraries will be more likely to give serious games the time of day. It's likely that major game publishers may not be interested in creating serious games. Independent publishers may see a renaissance, and game design will explode with users creating content, much like YouTube has taken off for video bloggers and blogging for amateur journalists.

More women will get involved in game design, resulting in stronger female characters, fewer stereotypical portrayals of women, and more games that are creation based rather than destruction based. Sony's revolutionary Sony G.I.R.L. (Games in Real Life) game design competition for female gamers features a prize that is a paid internship at Sony Online Entertainment and a $10,000 scholarship to attend the Art Institutes School (see Figure 6.8). This is just one way the industry is seeking to diversify.

Figure 6.8. Sony G.I.R.L. Competition

Julia Brasil of San Francisco won the 2008 G.I.R.L. Game Design Competition.

Source: www.station.sony.com/girl (accessed: April 16, 2009).

Virtual Worlds

Social and economic activity will continue to migrate to virtual worlds like Second Life, a 3D online community that is entirely user created. Creating an avatar, building a space, and incorporating media will only become easier as presences in virtual worlds become more ubiquitous. For libraries, this may mean using 3D spaces to develop interactive, highly visual, digital branches in order to reach patrons or offer services—and showing support for new technologies by offering a gaming experience for all!

Notes

1. NPD Group. "2006 U.S. Video Game and PC Game Retail Sales Reach $13.5 Billion Exceeding Previous Record Set in 2002 by Over 1.7 Billion." Port Washington, NY: NPD Group (January 19, 2007). Available: www.npd.com/press/releases/press_070119.html (accessed: April 22, 2009).
2. NPD Group. "2007 U.S. Video Game and PC Game Sales Exceed $18.8 Billion Marking Third Consecutive Year of Record-Breaking Sales." Port Washington, NY: NPD Group (January 31, 2008). Available: www.npd.com/press/releases/press_080131b.html (accessed: April 22, 2009).
3. DFC Intelligence. *The Online Game Market*. San Diego: DFC Intelligence (June 2006). Available: www.dfcint.com/game_report/Online_Game_toc.html (accessed: April 22, 2009).
4. Datamonitor. "Next Generation Video Games Consoles." New York: Datamonitor (October 12, 2005). Available: http://datamonitor-market-research.com/Merchant2/merchant.mvc?Screen=PROD&Product_Code=BFTC1208&Category_Code= (accessed: April 22, 2009).
5. Hefflinger, Mark. "Report: U.S. Game Sales Up 37% in May to $1.12 Billion." Digital Media Wire Daily (June 13, 2008). Available: www.dmwmedia.com/news/2008/06/13/report%3A-u.s.-game-sales-37%25-may-%241.12-billion (accessed: April 22, 2009).
6. Gaudiosi, John. "Videogame Sales Continue to Increase at Torrid Pace." Raleigh, NC: WRAL Local Tech Wire (June 20, 2008). Available: http://localtechwire.com/business/local_tech_wire/news/story/3076645 (accessed: April 22, 2009).
7. O'Reilly, Tim. "What is Web 2.0? Design Patterns and Business Models for the Next Generation of Software." O'Reillynet.com (September 30, 2005). Available: www.oreilly net.com/pub/a/oreilly/tim/news/2005/09/30/what-is-web-20.html (accessed: April 22, 2009).
8. VGChartz.com (April 22, 2009). Available: http://vgchartz.com (accessed: April 22, 2009).
9. Ibid.
10. Graft, Kris. "Analysis: History of Cell Phone Gaming." *Business Week*, January 22, 2006. Available: www.businessweek.com/innovate/content/jan2006/id20060122_077129.htm (accessed: April 22, 2009).
11. Informa Telecoms & Media. "Mobile Games 2nd Edition Strategic Report Explores the Entire Mobile Games Value Chain." London: Informa Telecoms & Media (July 2006). Available: http://shop.telecoms.com/marlin/30000000861/MARKT_EFFORT/marketing id/20001256794/?proceed=true&MarEntityId=1156130307005&entHash=10023abf620 (accessed: April 22, 2009).
12. M:Metrics. "Press Release: M:Metrics Reports Mixed Fortunes for Mobile Games Industry." Seattle: M:Metrics (February 18, 2008). Available: www.mmetrics.com/press/PressRelease.aspx?article=20080219-gamesindustry (accessed: April 22, 2009).

13. Ibid.
14. Ibid.
15. WildTangent. "About Us: Company Background" (April 22, 2009). Available: http:// about.wildtangent.com/about (accessed: April 22, 2009).
16. Peckham, Matt. "What Dying Industry? The PC Gaming Alliance Interview, Part One." PC World (April 15, 2009). Available: www.pcworld.com/article/163105/what_dying_industry_ the_pc_gaming_alliance_interview_part_one.html (accessed: April 22, 2009).
17. Gamespot. "Blizzard Entertainment Presents Latest Additions to World of Warcraft Expansion at E3" (May 10, 2006). Available: www.gamespot.com/pc/rpg/worldofwarcraft exp1/news.html?sid=6150779&mode=press&print=1 (accessed: April 22, 2009).
18. Blizzard Entertainment. "Press Release: World of Warcraft Surpasses 11 Million Subscribers." Irvine, CA: Blizzard Entertainment (October 28, 2008). Available: www.blizzard.com/us/ press/081028.html (accessed: April 22, 2009).
19. The Nielsen Company. "The State of the Video Gamer: PC Game and Video Game Console Usage Fourth Quarter 2008" (April 9, 2009). Available: URL to "http://blog .nielsen.com/nielsenwire/wp-content/uploads/2009/04/stateofvgamer_040909_fnl.pdf (accessed April 22, 2009).
20. Linden Lab. "Economic Statistics." San Francisco: Linden Lab (July 28, 2008). Available: http://secondlife.com/whatis/economy_stats.php (accessed: April 22, 2009).
21. Terdiman, Daniel. "Fun in Following the Money." Wired, May 8, 2004. Available: www.wired.com/gaming/gamingreviews/news/2004/05/63363 (accessed: April 22, 2009).
22. Bell, Lori, Tom Peters, and Kitty Pope. "Enjoying Your First Life? Why Not Add a Second? Developing Library Services in Second Life." Serious Games Source, June 30, 2006.
23. Johnson, Steven. "When Virtual Worlds Collide." Wired, April 2006. Available: www .wired.com/wired/archive/14.04/collide.html (accessed: April 22, 2009).
24. MacWorld. "WWDC 2008 Keynote—Live Update." MacWorld.com (June 9, 2008). Available: www.macworld.com/article/133798/2008/06/wwdckeynote.html (accessed: April 22, 2009).
25. Shilov, Anton. "Ageia Tests Next-Generation PhysX Accelerators." XBt Laboratories (August 30, 2007). Available: www.xbitlabs.com/news/multimedia/display/20070830161921 .html (accessed: April 22, 2009).
26. "Update: Startup Develops 'Physics Accelerator' Chip." ExtremeTech.com (March 8, 2005). Available: www.extremetech.com/article2/0,1558,1773957,00.asp?kc=ETRSS02129TX1K 0000532 (accessed: April 22, 2009).

Bonus Round 6:
Video Game Review, Mad Libs Style

In the _____ _____ video game, _____,
         (adjective)   (genre)   (title)

the hero _____ adventures through _____. Set in the year
         (name of person in room)   (place)

_____, you must use your _____ power of the _____,
(number)   (adverb)   (animal)

you must _____ a variety of _____ in level one. If you
              (verb)   (plural noun)

discover _____, you advance to level _____, a _____
             (place)   (number)   (noun)

full of _____ and _____. You must locate the _____
        (plural noun)   (plural noun)   (noun)

and bring it to _____ before the timer runs out to earn a
                  (name of person in room)

_____. Your success brings you to level _____, a _____.
   (noun)   (number)   (noun)

The obstacles are even tougher: _____ a gang of _____ and collect
                                    (verb)   (plural noun)

_____ _____. Turn in the _____ to
 (number)   (plural noun)   (same plural noun)

_____ to unlock the gates that hold back the boss, _____.
(name of person in room)   (name of celebrity)

_____ the boss in the _____ to _____
     (verb)   (body part)   (verb)

him and win the game! This game is rated _____ for _____
                                           (ESRB rating)   (adjective)

excitement, _____ humor, and _____
               (adjective)   (adverb)

_____.
(plural noun)

Glossary

action game: A game focused on fast-moving action. Includes fighting games and shooting games, such as *Super Smash Bros. Brawl* (Nintendo, 2008).

add-on: User-created software that allows the user to extend and customize the game.

adventure game: A game focused on exploring, such as *Super Paper Mario* (Nintendo, 2007).

aerial view: A perspective from an omniscient point of view, looking down at the gameplay, such as in *Starcraft* (Blizzard, 1998).

artificial intelligence (AI): Computer-generated characters for the player to interact with.

console: Electronic equipment that reads and plays game software. A console requires a controller and a display.

construction game: A game focused on creating buildings or systems, such as *RollerCoaster Tycoon 3* (Atari, 2005).

controller: The hardware through which the player interacts with the game on a screen, such as a keyboard, joystick, mouse, floor pad, steering wheel, wand, or even a motion-sensitive camera that is activated by the player.

display: Any screen for viewing gameplay.

Easter egg: A hidden object that is extraneous to gameplay intended to amuse the designer and reward the investigative and inventive player.

edutainment: A game primarily focused on delivering information rather than fun.

EyeToy: PlayStation 2–compatible camera sensitive to light and motion, used as a video game controller as well as a digital camera for still and motion shots.

first person shooter (FPS): A game in which the primary perspective of action is down the barrel of a gun or other weapon. FPS games can be fiercely competitive, military themed, suspenseful, horrific, and sometimes historical in nature.

forum: An online communication tool, usually in the format of a bulletin board with threaded topics, provided for game support; information from the publisher/ designer; Q&As; and user-created content related to the game, such as fan fiction, cheat codes, and game reviews.

game engine: The core software that allows the game to run on a platform. Typical components include a graphic renderer, physics engine, scripting, animation, and AI.

gaming: The act of playing a video game. "Gaming" in this book always refers to the act of playing video games and never to casino gambling! "Games" are those that are played through an electronic medium:
- On a Web site or downloaded from a Web site
- On a CD, CD-ROM, or DVD played on a computer
- On a CD, CD-ROM, or DVD played on a computer with an Internet connection required
- On a CD, CD-ROM, DVD, or cartridge on a standalone console, requiring a television or other monitor
- On a CD, CD-ROM, DVD, or cartridge on a standalone console, requiring a television or other monitor and a live Internet connection
- On a handheld device such as a Palm Pilot, cell phone, smart phone, or other type of personal system

goal: What the player has to accomplish in the game. Winning or beating the game is often the goal; sometimes there are benchmarks along the way, such as collecting items, improving skills, and discovering or unlocking new content.

guild: A group of characters in the game that have joined to play together. Sometimes called a clan.

hacking: Running a code within the game with the exploitative intent to change the outcome or enhance the experience.

handheld: A small electronic device for playing games, such as a Palm Pilot, a cell phone, an iPhone, or a personal portable game system such as the Sony PlayStation Portable or the Nintendo Game Boy or DS.

hardware: Physical equipment that runs the software. Consoles, controllers, and hard drives are examples of hardware.

isometric: A game perspective in which the action takes place on a diagonal, to look three dimensional, such as in *The Sims* (EA, 2000).

life simulation: A game focused on managing people, animals, or biological systems, such as *Bella Sara* (Codemasters, 2008).

machinima: A type of film made by recording video game play, editing clips together to create a story, and inserting an audio soundtrack. Machinima may be short films, music videos, commercials, or even periodic episodes.

manual: Instruction book that accompanies the game. Contents often include the premise for the action and a plot outline, a diagram explaining the controller buttons and knobs, and a definition of the basic gameplay and rules.

massively multiplayer online game (MMOG): A style of game that requires players to log on to a server via the Internet to interact with other real players in real time.

MMOGs are massive because players can number in the hundreds of thousands at a time. Characters and other game elements are stored on the server, not on the players' personal console or computer.

minigame: A short arcade-, action-, or puzzle-type game, often designed to improve skills needed in the main game. A minigame is like a subplot.

mobile gaming: Playing games on portable electronic devices, such as cell phones or handheld game consoles.

modding: Changing or "modifying" game content to make the game do or include something it wasn't intended to. For example, a player might export a red couch from *The Sims* (EA, 2000) into a graphics program, re-color it blue, and reimport it into the game.

music game: A game focused on music and rhythm.

next gen: Refers to the evolution of video games and consoles. "Next gen" is short for "next generation," the upcoming replacements for current models.

obstacles: Things that impede the player's progress in a game, such as lack of skill, knowledge, resources, power, or tools.

party: A small group of characters in the game with unique skills who make up a team and work together for a specific goal or mission.

PC bang: Korean version of a LAN (local area network) gaming center in which multiple computers are connected to each other via a LAN connection for the purpose of playing multiplayer computer games; largely responsible for the growth of online communities.

platform: industry jargon for console, computer, browser, or handheld, referring to the type of device a game is played on. Examples include Microsoft's Xbox and Xbox 360; Nintendo's Wii and GameCube; Sony's PlayStation 2 and PlayStation 3; personal computers (PCs, Macs, Linux); handhelds (Nintendo DS and PlayStation Portable); and mobiles (cell phone, smart phone, handheld computer, PDAs).

platformer: A style in which the gameplay is focused on moving from point to point, such as used in *Super Paper Mario* (Nintendo, 2007). The game can be two or three dimensional.

possibility space: Game environment that allows the player to make choices with a variety of outcomes.

puzzle: A game focused on problem solving, such as *Bejeweled 2* (PopCap, 2004). Gameplay generally involves linking objects or information, deciphering a code, or analyzing a sequence.

quest: An assignment, mission, or activity that must be completed to advance in a role-playing or action game.

rails: Advancement of the game is automatic rather than player controlled, such as the toilet plunger minigame in *Rayman Raving Rabbids* (Ubisoft, 2006).

rating: A code designed to provide accurate and objective information about the content of computer and video games so that one can make an informed purchase decision. For example, ratings by the Entertainment Software Ratings Board (ESRB) assess content appropriateness by age and are based on approximately 40 elements.

real time: Continuous, simultaneous actions occur in the game, regardless of whether a player is logged into it or not.

role-playing game (RPG): A game that requires players to define a set of characteristics for an avatar and choose their actions, attitude, and speech based on the persona they've created. A popular style of play for games in the fantasy and science fiction genres.

sandbox: A style of game in which the action progresses in nonlinear fashion—the player creates the story, as in *Grand Theft Auto IV* (Rockstar, 2008).

side-scroller: A style of game in which the action progresses horizontally in a linear fashion, such as in the online MMOG *Maple Story* (Hexon, 2005).

simulation: Electronic modeling of a system (such as a social, historical, business, or biological system) with experimental manipulation of variables for different outcomes, such as *The Sims 2* (EA, 2004).

software: The computer coding that renders the graphics, text, sound, and action of the gameplay experience. The software may come packaged on a CD, CD-ROM, cartridge, or diskette or in digital file format.

soundtrack: The audio that accompanies a video game, including dialogue, music, and sound effects. Songs are often packaged separately in CD format.

sports games: A game in which the gameplay is based on a physical sport, such as auto racing, baseball, golf, wrestling, or, as in *Madden NFL 2009* (EA, 2008), football.

strategy game: A game that requires methodical testing of a hypothesis and critical thinking skills, such as *Civilization IV* (2K Games, 2005).

strategy guide: Sometimes called a "cheat book," strategy guides assist new and struggling players and include cheat codes, walkthroughs, and Easter eggs.

tools: Items in the game that players use to overcome obstacles and achieve goals. Examples include skills, experience, weapons, armor, vehicles, spells, and signature moves.

turn-based game: A game in which a player makes a decision or executes an action followed by a period for assessment or reaction from the AI.

video game: A type of game that requires software (the coding for the game); a unit to decipher the code and render it into multimedia text, audio, and graphics; a screen for image display; and a controller used by the player to manipulate the characters and objects in the game. Examples include arcade games and games played on a console, on a personal computer such as a laptop, on the Internet, or on a handheld or mobile device.

walkthrough: A step-by-step resource guide to a game, provided to help players improve their skills and scores. May be online or in print format, with or without photos. A walkthrough is a type of strategy guide.

Annotated Bibliography

Books

Ahl, David H. 1979. *BASIC Computer Games*. Morristown, NJ: Creative Computing Press. Available: www.atariarchives.org/basicgames (accessed: April 22, 2009).

Online in its entirety; tells how to program computer games in BASIC.

Beck, John C. and Mitchell Wade. 2004. *Got Game? How the Gamer Generation Is Reshaping Business Forever*. Cambridge, MA: Harvard Business School Press.

Examines the video game industry through a business lens, looking closely at generational differences and skills learned from playing games.

Bettleheim, Bruno. 1923. *Psychological Types: The Psychology of the Individuation*. New York: Harcourt Brace.

Discusses personality traits.

Bettelheim, Bruno. 1976. *The Uses of Enchantment: The Meaning and Importance of Fairy Tales*. New York: Knopf.

Discusses, from a Jungian point of view, the need for violence in stories as a form of catharsis, even for very young children.

Bettleheim, Bruno. 1987. *A Good Enough Parent: A Book on Child Rearing*. New York: Knopf.

Parenting book from a psychoanalyst's perspective.

Burnham, Van. 2001. *Supercade: A Visual History of the Video Game Age 1971–1984*. Cambridge MA: MIT Press.

Illustrated history of video games.

Cassell, Justine and Henry Jenkins, eds. 1999. *From Barbie to Mortal Kombat: Gender and Computer Games*. Cambridge: MIT Press.

Examines the video game industry through a gender lens.

Castro, Radford. 2004. *Let Me Play: Stories of Gaming and Emulation*. Tucson, AZ: Hats Off Press.

Biography of an enthusiastic long-time gamer.

Castronova, Edward. 2005. *Synthetic Worlds: The Business and Culture of Online Games.* Chicago: University of Chicago Press.

Examines the video game industry through an economic lens, looking closely at the virtual economies in *Second Life* (Linden Lab, 2003) and *EverQuest* (989 Studios – 1999), among other games.

Chaplin, Heather and Aaron Ruby. 2005. *Smartbomb: The Quest for Art, Entertainment, and Big Bucks in the Video Game Revolution.* Chapel Hill, NC: Algonquin Books.

Examines the video game industry through a financial lens.

Compton, Shanna. 2004. *Gamers: Writers, Artists and Programmers on the Pleasures of Pixels.* Brooklyn, NY: Soft Skull Press.

Essays by gamers on the gaming experience, from arcade classics to massively multiplayer online games.

DeMaria, Rusel and Johnny Lee Wilson. 2002. *High Score! The Illustrated History of Electronic Games.* Berkeley: McGraw-Hill Osborne Media.

Thorough but now dated graphical timeline of video game milestones.

Freeman, David and Will Wright. 2003. *Creating Emotion in Games: The Craft and Art of Emotioneering.* Indianapolis: New Riders.

How to design games that evoke an emotional response.

Gee, James Paul. 2003. *What Video Games Have to Teach Us About Learning and Literacy.* New York: Palgrave McMillan.

Identifies over 30 principles that can be learned from games, including rewards for practice and developing affinity groups.

Goldstein, Jeffrey. 1998. *Why We Watch: The Attractions of Violent Entertainment.* New York: Oxford University Press, pp. 53–68.

Discusses the cathartic purpose of violence in multimedia.

Gosnety, John W. 2005. *Beyond Reality: A Guide to Alternate Reality Gaming.* Boston: Thomson Course Technology.

Covers alternate reality games (ARGs) that go beyond boards and consoles (ARGs are a blend of scavenger hunt and mystery and use multimedia clues to present a premise for the players to investigate).

Greenfield, P.M. 1984. *Mind and Media: The Effects of Television, Computers and Video Games.* Cambridge, MA: Harvard University Press.

Suggests exploring ways media can be used to promote social growth and critical thinking skills.

Howe, Neil and William Strauss. 2000. *Millennials Rising: The Next Great Generation.* New York: Vintage/Random House.

Biography of the generation of children born between 1982 and 2000.

Johnson, Steven. 2005. *Everything Bad Is Good for You: How Today's Pop Culture Is Actually Making Us Smarter.* New York: Riverhead Books.

Examines pop culture and its effects on processing information, critical thinking, and storytelling.

Jones, Gerard and Lynn Ponton. 2003. *Killing Monsters: Why Children Need Fantasy, Super Heroes, and Make-Believe Violence*. New York: Basic Books.

Argues for the need for catharsis through simulated violence.

Kent, Steven L. 2001. *The Ultimate History of Video Games: From Pong to Pokémon*. Rosevilla, CA: Prima Publishing.

History of the first 25 years of video games.

King, Brad and John Borland. 2003. *Dungeons and Dreamers: The Rise of Computer Game Culture From Geek to Chic*. Berkeley: McGraw-Hill Osborne Media.

History of the first 25 years of gaming, from underground to mainstream.

King, Lucien, ed. 2002. *Game On: The History and Culture of Videogames*. London: Laurence King.

Illustrated history of video games from a global perspective.

Kushner, David. 2003. *Masters of Doom: How Two Guys Created an Empire and Transformed Pop Culture*. New York: Random House.

Biographical sketch of game designer/programmers Carmack and Romero, their company id Software, and their best-selling games *Wolfenstein*, *Doom*, and *Quake*.

Kutner, Lawrence and Cheryl K. Olson. 2008. *Grand Theft Childhood: The Surprising Truth About Violent Video Games and What Parents Can Do*. New York: Simon & Schuster.

Results from a survey of 1,200 middle school students and focus group interviews with parents and children. Findings include youth play violent games for cathartic effect.

Neiburger, Eli. 2007. *Gamers at the Library*. Chicago: ALA Editions.

Advocates for gaming at the library, with model, tried and trued programs and tournaments.

Pesce, Mark. 2000. *The Playful World: How Technology Is Transforming Our Imagination*. New York: Ballantine.

Examines the history of play and how play is essential to learning.

Pierce, Jennifer Brubeck. 2007. *Sex, Brains, and Video Games: A Librarian's Guide to Teens in the Twenty-first Century*. Chicago: ALA.

An academic look at why teens act the way they do.

Prensky, Mark. 2004. *Digital Game-based Learning*. Berkeley: McGraw Hill.

Game designers describe how video games were used to teach and train in a variety of situations.

Prensky, Mark. 2006. *Don't Bother Me, Mom—I'm Learning!: How Computer and Video Games Are Preparing Your Kids for Twenty-first Century Success and How You Can Help*. St. Paul: Paragon House Publishers.

Guide to video games for parents, with assurances that gaming is good for youth.

Ray, Sheri Graner. 2003. *Gender Inclusive Game Design: Expanding the Market.* Hingham, MA: Charles River Media.

Examines the history of girls and games and encourages designers and publishers to consider female players.

Rolling, Andrew and Dave Morris. 2002. *Game Architecture and Design.* Scottsdale, AZ: Coriolis.

Game design textbook focuses on getting from concept to finished product.

Salen, Katie, ed. 2007. *The Ecology of Games: Connecting Youth, Games & Learning.* Cambridge, MA: MIT Press.

Maps the way game elements coexist to create a harmonious whole and investigates the different and overlapping roles players take on as participants, observers, and creators.

Salen, Katie and Eric Zimmerman. 2003. Rules of Play: Game Design Fundamentals. Cambridge, MA: MIT Press.

Game design theory textbook.

Salen, Katie and Eric Zimmerman. 2005. *The Game Design Reader: A Rules of Play Anthology.* Cambridge, MA: MIT Press.

Collection of articles on game design theory and game criticism.

Sawyer, Ben. 2003. *Monster Gaming: The Complete How-to Guide for Becoming a Hardcore Gamer.* Phoenix: Paraglyph Press.

Covers the hobby of gaming, including equipment, modding, competing, and more.

Sefton-Green, Julian, ed. 1998. *Digital Diversions: Youth Culture in the Age of Multimedia.* London: UCL Press.

Examines the impact of technology on youth from a cultural and social perspective.

Steinmetz, William. 2004. *LAN Party: Hosting the Ultimate Fragfest.* Indianapolis: Wiley.

Step-by-step directions for networking computers and hosting LAN parties.

Wardrip-Fruin, Noah and Pat Harrigan, eds. 2004. *First Person: New Media as Story, Performance, and Game.* Cambridge, MA: MIT Press.

Makes a case for video games as a medium for electronic storytelling.

Wolf, Mark J.P., ed. 2002. *Video Games: In the Beginning.* Austin: University of Texas Press.

Analyzes video games as an electronic medium.

Wolf, Mark J.P. 2003. *The Video Game Theory Reader.* London: Routledge.

Collection of articles on game theory. A sequel, The Video Game Theory Reader 2, was published in 2008.

Articles

American Psychological Association. "The Psychiatric Effects of Media Violence." *Healthy Minds*. Available: www.healthyminds.org/mediaviolence.cfm (accessed: April 22, 2009).

Includes the Association's position statement on violent media and tips for parents on how to limit the media's influence on their children.

Anderson, Craig. "Violent Video Games: The Myths, the Facts, and Unanswered Questions." American Psychological Association. Available: www.apa.org/science/psa/sb-anderson.html (accessed: April 22, 2009).

Addresses myths that violent video games do *not* lead to aggressive behavior.

Anderson, C.A. and B.J. Bushman. 2001. "Effects of Violent Video Games on Aggressive Behavior, Aggressive Cognition, Aggressive Affect, Physiological Arousal, and Prosocial Behavior: A Meta-Analytic Review of the Scientific Literature." *Psychological Science* 12, no. 5: 353–359.

Findings in a review of the research conclude that violent video games increase aggressive behavior in children and young adults and decrease pro-social behavior.

Anderson, Craig A. and Karen E. Dill. 2000. "Video Games and Aggressive Thoughts, Feelings, and Behavior in the Laboratory and in Life." *Journal of Personality and Social Psychology* 78: 772–790.

Results from two studies demonstrate that exposure to violent video games increases aggressive behavior and leads to delinquency and lower academic achievement.

Barack, Lauren. 2005. "Gaming at Your Library." *School Library Journal* 51, no. 7: 22. Available: www.schoollibraryjournal.com/article/CA621772.html (accessed: April 22, 2009).

Addresses the growing trend of gaming in libraries.

Barker, Alison. "Study Uses Video Games to Fight Obesity." *Associated Press*, April 2, 2005. Available: www.usatoday.com/news/nation/2005-04-02-obesity-video-game_x.htm (accessed: April 22, 2009).

West Virginia Public Employees Insurance Agency recruits youth to participate in an at-home study using the video game *Dance Dance Revolution* to increase activity.

Barnett, M.A., C.D. Vitaglione, K.K. Harper, S.W. Ouackenbush, L.A. Steadman, and B.S. Valdez. 1997. "Late Adolescents' Experiences with and Attitudes Toward Video Games." *Journal of Applied Social Psychology* 27: 1316–1334.

Results of a survey of 229 15- to 19-year-olds about video game–relevant experiences, preferences, and attitudes.

Bavelier, Daphne and Shawn Green. *Psychological Science*, March 14, 2006. Available: http://handle.dtic.mil/100.2/ADA444148 (accessed: April 22, 2009).

Argues that action video games increase vision up to 20 percent.

Bell, Lori, Tom Peters, and Kitty Pope. "Enjoying Your First Life? Why Not Add a Second? Developing Library Services in *Second Life*." *Serious Games Source*, June 30, 2006. Available: http://seriousgamessource.com/features/feature_063006_second_life_library.php (accessed: April 22, 2009).

   Describes the Alliance Library System's Second Life Library project in April 2006.

Bellis, Mary. "The History of Computer & Video Games." About.com. Available: http://inventors.about.com/library/inventors/blcomputer_videogames.htm (accessed: April 22, 2009).

   Computer and video game history, including early arcade machines and home consoles.

Blizzard Entertainment. "Press Release: *World of Warcraft* Surpasses 11 Million Subscribers," October 28, 2008. Available: http://www.blizzard.com/us/press/081028.html (accessed: April 22, 2009).

   Press release announces new peak in subscriptions.

Blumberg, F.C. 1998. "Developmental Differences at Play: Children's Selective Attention and Performance in Video Games." *Journal of Applied Developmental Psychology* 19, no. 4: 615–624.

   Provides insight into children's goals and motivation for learning in the context of video games.

Blumberg, F. 2000. "The Effects of Children's Goals for Learning on Video Game Performance." *Journal of Applied Developmental Psychology* 21, no. 6: 641–653.

   Findings highlight the efficacy of video games on the goals of learning for children.

Bower, Bruce. 2005. "Possible Worlds: Imagination Gets Its Dues as a Real World Thinking Tool." *Science News* 167, no. 23: 200–202. Available: www.phschool.com/science/science_news/articles/possible_worlds.html (accessed: April 22, 2009).

   Discusses the vitality of imagination and play.

Brand, Stewart. "*Spacewar*: Fanatic Life and Symbolic Death Among the Computer Bums." *Rolling Stone*, December 7, 1972. Available: www.wheels.org/spacewar/stone/rolling_stone.html (accessed: April 22, 2009).

   Describes one of the first video games and computing in the 1960s and early 1970s.

Braun, Linda W. 2004. "What's in a Game?" *VOYA* vol 27(6) (August): 189.

   Explores the possibility of video games in libraries as a new trend.

Card, Orson Scott. "Civilization Watch: Brain Training." *The Rhinoceros Times* (Greensboro, NC), June 26, 2005. Available: www.ornery.org/essays/warwatch/2005-06-26-1.html (accessed: April 22, 2009).

   Addresses using video games to exercise the brain and improve mnemonic, visual, and audio skills.

Castaldi, Chris. "Universal Game Model: Starting the Conversation about Games and Education" (2009). University of Advancing Technology, Phoenix, AZ.

   Thesis on five common elements of video games, tied to how people learn and apply new information.

CNN. "Japanese Cartoon Triggers Seizures in Hundreds of Children," December 1997. Available: www.cnn.com/WORLD/9712/17/video.seizures.update (accessed: April 22, 2009).

Reports that a *Pokémon* episode triggered seizures in over 600 Japanese children.

Cohen, Patricia. "Video Game Becomes Spectator Sport." *New York Times*, April 11, 2009. Available: www.nytimes.com/2009/04/12/sports/othersports/12star.html?_r=2 (accessed: April 22, 2009).

Covers the startup of collegiate competitive intramural video gaming with the classis strategy game, StarCraft (Blizzard, 1998).

Cox, Deena. 2006. "Games Foster Learning." *i.e. magazine* Spring: 38–39. Available: http://dlsystems.us/readings/NTFL_1/Games_Foster_Learning.pdf (accessed: April 22, 2009).

Interview with video game designer Marc Prensky.

Cross, Jason. 2005. "The Big Shakeup: Game Consoles Bulk Up." *PC Magazine* (August 9): 98. Available: www.pcmag.com/article2/0,2817,1836182,00.asp (April 22, 2009).

Predictions for the next generation of video game consoles.

Data Monitor. "Next Generation Video Games Consoles," October 12, 2005. Available: http://datamonitor-market-research.com/Merchant2/merchant.mvc?Screen= PROD&Product_Code=BFTC1208&Category_Code=(accessed: April 22, 2009).

Predictions about the three seventh-generation consoles.

Dede, Chris. 2006. "Virtual Reality of Learning." *i.e. magazine* (2006): 40–41. Available: http://dlsystems.us/resources/Virtual%20Reality%20of%20Learning.pdf (accessed: April 22, 2009).

Discusses how media can be used in education.

DeLoche, Melissa. "Library Filling a Niche." *Joplin Globe*, June 6, 2005.

Library responds to increased interest in games and increased number of teen computer users by opening the computer lab to teens to play games three times a week.

DFC Intelligence. "Online Game Market," June 2006. Available: www.dfcint.com/ game_report/Online_Game_toc.html (accessed: April 22, 2009).

Comprehensive analysis of the online gaming market, with updated forecasts every six months.

Dill, K.E., and J.C. Dill. 1998. "Video Game Violence: A Review of the Empirical Literature." *Aggression and Violent Behavior* 3: 407–428.

Bibliography of research on violent video games and aggressive behavior; findings demonstrate the need for additional research.

Dodero, Camille. "Games People Play: An Axe to Grind." *Boston Phoenix*, May 6, 2005. Available: http://bostonphoenix.com/boston/news_features/other_stories/ multi-page/documents/05133995.asp (accessed: April 22, 2009).

Reviews *Guitar Hero* and discusses its relationship to the music industry.

Doshi, Ameet. 2005. "Gaming Could Improve Information Literacy." *Computers in Libraries* (May): 15–17. Available: www.infotoday.com/cilmag/may06/Doshi.shtml (accessed: April 22, 2009).

Strategizes how to incorporate gaming experiences to teach library skills, such as locating, analyzing, and organizing information.

Durkin, K. and B. Barber. 2002. "Not So Doomed: Computer Game Play and Positive Adolescent Development." *Applied Developmental Psychology* 23: 373–392. Available: www.rcgd.isr.umich.edu/garp/articles/durkin02.pdf (accessed: April 22, 2009).

Examines the positive effects of video game play on high school students.

Egenfeldt Nielsen, S. 2005. *Beyond Edutainment: Exploring the Educational Potential of Computer Games.* PhD. dissertation. IT-University of Copenhagen, February, 2005. Available: www.learninginvideogames.com/research-and-papers/beyond-edutainment-a-dissertation-by-simon-egenfeldt-nielsen (accessed: April 22, 2009).

Presents a variety of unique perspectives on educational media and nonelectronic games, focusing on edutainment titles; then examines educational theory and computer games research to present alternatives to edutainment.

Entertainment Software Association. *Essential Facts About the Computer and Game Industry.* Entertainment Software Association (2008). Available: http://theesa.com/facts/pdfs/ESA_EF_2008.pdf (accessed: April 22, 2009).

Results of annual survey on who plays what.

Flanagan, Mary. 1999. "Digital Stars Are Here to Stay." *Convergence: The Journal of Research into New Media Technologies.* Available: www.maryflanagan.com/articles/convergence.pdf (accessed: April 22, 2009).

Flanagan, Mary. "Hyperbodies, Hyperknowledge: Women in Games, Women in Cyberpunk, and Strategies of Resistance." *Reload: Rethinking Women + Cyberculture.* MIT Press, pp. 425–454. Available: www.maryflanagan.com/articles/ReloadHyperbodies .pdf (accessed: April 22, 2009).

Addresses the experience and portrayal of women in cyberculture.

Flanagan, Mary. 2001. "Mobile Identities, Digital Stars, and Post-Cinematic Selves." *Wide Angle: Issue on Digitality and the Memory of Cinema* 21, no. 3 (Spring). Available: http://muse .jhu.edu/journals/wide_angle/v021/21.1flanagan.html (accessed: April 22, 2009).

Discusses women's use of technology.

Flynn, Shawn. "Video Games Lure Youth to the Library." *News 14* (Charlotte, NC), July 22, 2005. Available: www.news.com (accessed: April 22, 2009).

Library dangles video games as a carrot to increase library use.

Frazier, Anita. The NPD Group, Port Washington, NY. 2008. Available: www.npd group.com (accessed: April 22, 2009).

Group provides consumer and retail market research information for a wide range of industries; publishes quarterly information on various industries, including entertainment, electronics, and computers.

Funk, J.B. et al. 1999. "The Attitudes Towards Violence Scale: A Measure for Adolescents." *Journal of Interpersonal Violence* 14, 1123–1136.

Evaluates the impact of violence prevention programs.

Funk, J.B. et al. 2003. "Violence Exposure in Real-Life, Video Games, Television, Movies, and the Internet: Is There Desensitization?" Department of Psychology, University of Toledo, Ohio.

Study to determine if video game violence was associated with (lower) empathy. Findings: The active nature of playing video games resulted in negative impact; causality was not investigated.

Funk, J.B., G. Flores, D.D. Buchman, and J.N. Germann. 1999. "Rating Electronic Games: Violence Is in the Eye of the Beholder." *Youth & Society* 30, 283–312.

Compares game ratings and consumer perceptions of titles; findings indicate a discrepancy with games that display cartoon violence and call for a revision of the ratings systems for all entertainment media.

Funk, J.B., J. Hagan, and J. Schimming. 1999. "Children and Electronic Games: A Comparison of Parent and Child Perceptions of Children's Habits and Preferences in a United States Sample." *Psychological Reports* 85, 883–888.

Examines parents' and children's perceptions of video games and game ratings.

Gamespot. "Blizzard Entertainment Presents Latest Additions to World of Warcraft Expansion at E3" (May 10, 2006). Available: www.gamespot.com/pc/rpg/worldofwar craftexp1/news.html?sid=6150779&mode=press&print=1 (accessed: April 22, 2009).

Describes the newest features being added to *World of Warcraft: The Burning Crusade.*

Gardner, Howard. "Frames of Mind: The Theory of Multiple Intelligences." Available: www.howardgardner.com/Papers/documents/MI%20at%2025%20%204-15-08%202.doc (accessed: April 16, 2009).

Gardner discusses his theory of how people learn differently.

Gauder, Brad. "Gaming in the College. Using Interactive Technology to Enhance Learning." *OCLC Newsletter.* Dublin, OH: Online Computer Library Service (2004). Available: www.oclc.org/news/publications/newsletters/oclc/2004/265/gamers.html (accessed: April 22, 2009).

Looks at using video games for instruction.

Gaudiosi, John. "Videogame Sales Continue to Increase at Torrid Pace." *TechWire*, June 20, 2008. Available: http://localtechwire.com/business/local_tech_wire/news/story/3076645 (accessed: April 22, 2009).

Article on the video game industry predicts that by January 1, 2009, U.S. game sales could tally $21 to $23 billion.

Graft, Kris. "Analysis: History of Cell Phone Gaming." *Business Week*, January 22, 2006. Available: www.businessweek.com/innovate/content/jan2006/id20060122_077129.htm (accessed: April 22, 2009).

Outlines history of cell phone gaming.

Gray, Charles. "Video Games Projected on Downtown Building." *WTOC*, March 21, 2005. Available: www.wtoctv.com/global/story.asp?s=3107143 (accessed: April 22, 2009).

Pac-Man, Pong, and Asteroids displayed on building in Savannah, Georgia.

Grossman, Lev, and Kristina Dell. "From Geek to Chic in 33 Years: Three Decades After Video Games Invaded Our Space, It's Finally Hip to Be Square." *Time*, May 23, 2005. Available: www.time.com/time/magazine/article/0,9171,1061499,00.html (accessed: April 22, 2009).

Provides a timeline of significant events in videogame history.

Hawkins, Donald T. and Barbara Brinko. "Gaming: The Next Hot Technology for Libraries?" *Information Today*, June 2006. Available: www.time.com/time/magazine/article/0,9171,1061499,00.html (accessed: April 22, 2009).

Brief time line of video game milestones from 1972 to 2005.

Helmrich, Erin and Eli Neiburger. 2005. "Video Games as a Service: Hosting Tournaments at Your Library." *VOYA* 27, no. 6: 450–453. Available: http://pdfs.voya.com/VO/YA2/VOYA200502VideoGames.pdf (accessed: April 22, 2009).

How-to article (including glossary) from a public library perspective.

High, Kamau. "Cross Media Franchises: Video Games Battle to Climb Up a Level on to the Big Screen." *Financial Times*, March 7, 2006, p. 8.

Discusses transition of games to film.

Hitch, Leslie and Jim Duncan. "Games in Higher Ed: When *Halo 2*, *Civilization VI* and Xbox 360 Come to Campus." Boulder, CO: EDUCASE, Evolving Technologies Committee, August 15, 2002. Available: http://net.educause.edu/ir/library/pdf/DEC0503.pdf (accessed: April 22, 2009).

Examines the potential for gaming in academic coursework and academic libraries.

Hopkins, Gary. "Celebrate the Century: Search the Web for U.S. History of the 1980s." Lesson Planning Channel Education World (2000). Available: www.education-world.com/a_lesson/lesson215.shtml (accessed: April 22, 2009).

Describes the rise of the video game industry in the 1980s.

Informa Telecoms & Media. "Mobile Games: Strategic Report Explores the Entire Mobile Games Value Chain." Informa Telecoms & Media (2006). Available: http://shop.telecoms.com/marlin/30000000861/MARKT_EFFORT/marketingid/20001256794/?proceed=true&MarEntityId=1156130307005&entHash=10023abf620 (accessed: April 22, 2009).

Article on mobile gaming, with industry predictions.

Izzolo, Corrine. "The PCMag Dream Home: Game Room." *PC Magazine*, April 2, 2008. Available: www.pcmag.com/article2/0,2817,2281059,00.asp (accessed: April 22, 2009).

Projects for turning a spare room into a gaming room.

Jana, Renee. "Harnessing the Power of Video Games." MSNBC, August 22, 2006. Available: www.msnbc.msn.com/id/14468654/ (accessed: April 22, 2009).

Looks at the trend of using video games for health purposes, including pain management.

Jenkins, Henry. "Reality Bytes: Eight Myths About Video Games Debunked." *The Video Game Revolution*. PBS. Available: www.pbs.org/kcts/videogamerevolution/impact/myths.html (accessed: April 22, 2009).

Examines myths about video games.

Johnson, Steven. 2005. "This Is Your Brain on Video Games." *Discover* 26(7), 38(6). Available: http://discovermagazine.com/2007/brain/video-games (accessed: April 22, 2009).

Examines the value of the video game medium as mental enrichment.

Johnson, Steven. "When Virtual Worlds Collide." *Wired*, April 2006. Available: www.wired.com/wired/archive/14.04/collide.html (accessed: April 22, 2009).

Article about convergence of digital three-dimensional worlds and video games.

Jones, Steve. "Let the Games Begin: Gaming Technology and Entertainment Among College Students." *Pew Internet and American Life Report*, July 6, 2003. Available: www.pewinternet.org/PPF/r/93/report_display.asp (accessed: April 22, 2009).

Examines impact of college students' use of video, computer, and online games on their everyday life.

Kelly, Kevin, and Howard Rheingold. "The Dragon Ate My Homework." Wired. Issue 1.03 July/August 1993. Available: www.wired.com/wired/archive/1.03/muds.html (accessed: April 22, 2009).

Covers the history of multi-user dimensions (MUDs).

King, Brad. "Educators Turn to Games for Help." *Wired*, August 2, 2003. Available: http://wired-vig.wired.com/news/print/0,1294,59855,00.html (accessed: April 22, 2009).

Describes the creation of the Digital Media Laboratory.

Kirsh, SJ. 1998. "Seeing the World Through *Mortal Kombat*–Colored Glasses: Violent Video Games and the Development of a Short-Term Hostile Attribution Bias." *Childhood* 5, no. 2: 177–184.

Findings suggest that playing violent video games leads to development of a hostile attribution bias.

Konigkramer, Lisa. "NPD: US Videogame Sales Total 21.33 Bil in 2008, Wii Play Top Selling Game." El33t OnLine (2008). Available: www.el33tonLine.com/past/2009/1/16/npd_us_videogame_sales_total/ (accessed: April 22, 2009).

Presents NPD gaming research statistics.

Krupa, John. "Rogers: Dance Game Revolutionizes Middle School Student's PE." *NWA News.com*, February 24, 2006. Available: www.nwanews.com/adg/News/146745 (accessed: April 22, 2009).

Dance Dance Revolution finds its way to physical education classes in Arkansas schools.

Lenhart, Amanda. "Teen Content Creators and Consumers." Pew Internet & American Life Project (November 2, 2005). Available: www.pewinternet.org/Reports/ 2005/Teen-Content-Creators-and-Consumers.aspx (accessed: April 22, 2009).

Report on how teens add content to the Internet

Lenhart, Amanda. "Teens and Technology." Pew Internet & American Life Project (July 27, 2005). Available: www.pewinternet.org/Reports/2005/Teens-and-Technology .aspx (accessed: April 22, 2009).

Lenhart, Amanda et al. "Teens, Video Games and Civics." Pew Internet & American Life Project (September 2008). Available: www://pewinternet.org/Reports/2008/ Teens-Video-Games-and-Clinics.aspx (accessed: April 22, 2009).

Report that demonstrates teens who play civic games are civic minded.

Linden, Zee. "Second Life Virtual World Expands 44% in Q2." Linden Lab (July 28, 2008). Available: http://blog.secondlife.com/2008/07/08/second-life-virtual-world-expands-35-in-q2/ (accessed April 22, 2009).

Presents data on the expansion of land mass, user hours, user-to-user transactions, volume, and in-world businesses.

Linden Lab. "Economic Statistics." Linden Lab (July 28, 2008). Available: http:// secondlife.com/whatis/economy_stats.php (accessed: April 22, 2009).

Monthly statistical report of Linden Lab metrics.

Maragos, Nich. "Gaming + Culture: Digital Delivery." *PC Magazine*, April 11 2006. Available: www.pcmag.com/article2/0,2817,1936249,00.asp (accessed: April 22, 2009).

Briefly discusses using the Internet to distribute digital games.

McLester, Susan. 2005. "Game Plan." *Technology & Learning*, 26, no. 4 (October 15): 20–24. Available: www.techlearning.com/showArticle.php?articleID=171202908 (accessed: April 22, 2009).

Focusing on the Education Arcade, summarizes use of video games in education.

McGraw, Tammy, Krista Burdette, and Kristine Chadwick. "The Effects of a Consumer Oriented Multimedia Games on the Reading Disorders of Children with ADHD." British Columbia: Simon Fraser University (2005). Available: http://ir. lib.sfu.ca/handle/1892/1631 (accessed: April 22, 2009).

Research paper on *Dance Dance Revolution* (*DDR*) and pattern recognition; concludes that playing *DDR* may increase reading comprehension of students with attention deficit hyperactivity disorder on standardized tests.

McLester, Susan. 2005. "Game Plan, Part 2: Student Gamecraft." *Technology & Learning* 26, no. 3 (November 15): 18–26. Available: www.techlearning.com/show Article.php?articleID=173601950 (accessed: April 22, 2009).

Examines what kids learn when they create their own video games.

M:Metrics. "Press Release: M:Metrics Reports Mixed Fortunes for Mobile Games Industry." Seattle: M:Metrics (February 18, 2008). Available: www.mmetrics.com/press/ PressRelease.aspx?article=20080219-gamesindustry (accessed: April 22, 2009).
Discusses mobile gaming.

Mobclix (April 22, 2009). Available: http://mobclix.com/appstore/1 (accessed April 22, 2009).
Provides data on iPhone applications.

Myers, David. 1991. "Computer Game Semiotics." *Play and Culture* 4: 334–345. Available: www.loyno.edu/~dmyers/F99%20classes/Myers1991_ComputerGame Semiotics/Page1.htm (accessed: April 22, 2009).
Explores symbols in computer gameplay.

National Middle School Association Research Summaries. "Young Adolescents' Developmental Characteristics" (1996). Available: www.nmsa.org/Research/Research Summaries/DevelopmentalCharacteristics/tabid/1414/Default.aspxx (accessed: April 16, 2009).
Research summary on the physical, intellectual, moral/ethical, emotional/psychological, and social developmental characteristics of youth and their implications for practice.

The Nielsen Company. "The State of the Video Gamer: PC Game and Video Game Console Usage Fourth Quarter 2008" (April 9, 2009). Available: http://blog.nielsen. com/nielsenwire/wp-content/uploads/2009/04/stateofvgamer_040909_fnl.pdf (accessed: April 22, 2009).
Report on games people play, on consoles and online.

Norton-Meier, Lori. 2005. "Joining the Video Game Literacy Club: A Reluctant Mother Tries to Join the Flow." *Journal of Adolescent & Adult Literacy* 48, no. 5 (February 2005): 428–432. Available: www.reading.org/publications/journals/jaal/ v48/i5abstracts/JAAL-48-5-Norton-Meier.html (accessed: April 22, 2009).
Video game literacy from a parent's point of view.

NPD Group. "2007 U.S. Video Game and PC Game Sales Exceed $18.8 Billion Marking Third Consecutive Year of Record-breaking Sales." Port Washington, NY: NPD Group (January 31, 2008). Available: www.npd.com/press/releases/press_ 080131b.html (accessed: April 22, 2009).
Discusses video game industry sales.

Olson, C.K., L.A. Kutner, and E.V. Beresin. "Children and Video Games: How Much Do We Know?" *Psychiatric Times* (October 2007). Available: www.psychiatrictimes .com/display/article/10168/54191 (accessed: April 22, 2009).
Addresses concern that violent video games turn ordinary children and adolescents into violent people in the real world; analyzes school shooting incidents and finds no evidence of a link between violent games and real-world attacks.

O'Reilly, Tim. "What Is Web 2.0? Design Patterns and Business Models for the Next Generation of Software." O'Reillynet.com (September 30, 2005). Available:

www.oreillynet.com/pub/a/oreilly/tim/news/2005/09/30/what-is-web-20.html
(accessed: April 22, 2009).

Explains the concept of Web 2.0.

Parungoa, Robert. 2006. "Asianness in Video Games." Sociology Department,
University of British Columbia, Vancouver, BC, Canada.

Thesis discusses ethnicity in video games.

Patton, Zach. "Dance Dance Obesity Revolution!" Governing.Com (January 26,
2006). Available: http://13thfloor.governing.com/2006/01/dance_dance_obe.html
(accessed: April 16, 2009).

Article about schools incorporating DDR as part of gym class.

Peckham, Matt. "What Dying Industry? The PC Gaming Alliance Interview, Part
One." PC World, April 15, 2009. Available: www.pcworld.com/article/163105/what_
dying_industry_the_pc_gaming_alliance_interview_part_one.html (accessed: April
22, 2009).

Interview with Intel Director of Gaming Randy Stude about the state and future of the PC
gaming industry.

Philips, Amy and Becky Spilver. 2006. "Gaming: Console Video Games." *School
Library Journal* (June): 91–94. Available: www.schoollibraryjournal.com/article/
CA6404359.html (accessed: April 22, 2009).

Reviews video games; provides information about the Wii and PlayStation 3 for library
purchase.

Rosenbloom, Stephanie. "Sorry Boys, This Is Our Domain." New York Times,
February 21, 2008. Available: www.nytimes.com/2008/02/21/fashion/21webgirls.htm
(accessed: April 22, 2009).

Examines content creation, gender and cyberculture.

Rosser, James C., et al. 2006. "The Use of a 'Hybrid' Trainer in an Established
Laproscopic Skills Program." *JSLS, Journal of the Society of Laproendoscopic Surgeons*
10, no. 1: 4–10. Available: www.ingentaconnect.com/content/sls/jsls/2006/00000010/
00000001/art00002 (accessed: April 16, 2009).

Results of study on using handheld video games to improve surgical skills.

Rosser, James C., et al. 2007. "The Impact of Video Games on Training Surgeons in
the 21st Century." *Archives of Surgery* 142, no. 2: 181–186. Available: http://archsurg
.highwire.org/cgi/content/abstract/142/2/181 (accessed: April 16, 2009).

Results of study on using handheld video games to improve surgical skills.

Ryan, Richard M. 2006. "The Motivational Pull of Video Games: A Self-Determination
Theory Approach." *Motivation & Emotion* 30, no. 4. 347–363. Available: www
.springerlink.com/content/h8u63440vl4q6534 (accessed: April 22, 2009).

Examines the motivation for computer game play and the effects of game play on one's
well-being.

Sawyer, Ben and Kurt Squire. "Dr. Pac-Man? Smart and Healthy Video Games." Transcript of live chat, July 13, 2005. Sponsored by Connect for Kids, Web site of the Forum for Youth Investment, Washington, DC. Available: www.connectforkids.org/ node/3203 (accessed: April 22, 2009).

> Interview with Kurt Squire of Education Arcade and author/gaming researcher Ben Sawyer on the health values of video games.

Scalzo, John. "The Video Game Librarian." Gaming Target, a Web-based Discussion Forum. February 25, 2005. Available: www.gamingtarget.com/article.php?artid=3982 (accessed: April 22, 2009).

> Addresses adding video games to circulating library collections.

Scalzo, John. "The Video Game Librarian: Book 'em!" Gaming Target, a Web-based Discussion Forum. July 20, 2005. Available: www.gamingtarget.com/article.php? artid=4470 (accessed: April 22, 2009).

> Recommends several books about gaming and strategy guides for library collections.

Scalzo, John. "The Video Game Librarian: Breaking the M-rated Barrier." Gaming Target, a Web-based Discussion Forum. April 26, 2005. Available: www.gamingtarget .com/article.php?artid=5221 (accessed: April 22, 2009).

> Discusses hosting collections for adult gamers.

Scalzo, John. "The Video Game Librarian: Choosing a Next-Generation Console." Gaming Target, a Web-based Discussion Forum. December 21, 2007. Available: www.gamingtarget.com/article.php?artid=8051 (accessed: April 22, 2009).

> How to select one of the newer consoles for your library.

Scalzo, John. "The Video Game Librarian: GameFest at the Bloomington Public Library." Gaming Target, a Web-based Discussion Forum. August 26, 2005. Available: www.gamingtarget.com/article.php?artip=4579 (accessed: April 22, 2009).

> Interview with Kelly Czarnecki about gaming programs at the Bloomington (IL) Public Library.

Scalzo, John. "The Video Game Librarian: The Novel Approach" Gaming Target, a Web-based Discussion Forum. September 26, 2005. Available: www.gamingtarget .com/article.php?artid=4652 (accessed: April 22, 2009).

> Addresses books made into video games.

Scalzo, John. "The Video Game Librarian: Six Months Later." Gaming Target, a Web-based Discussion Forum. June 24, 2005. Available: www.gamingtarget.com/ article.php?artid=4411 (accessed: April 22, 2009).

> Follow-up article on adding video games to circulating library collections.

Scheers, Julia. "The Quest to End Video Game Addiction." *Wired News*, December 5, 2001. Available: www.wired.com/news/gamers/0,2101,48479,00.html (accessed: April 22, 2009).

> Examines the question of gaming addiction, specifically with regard to the massively multiplayer online game *EverQuest*.

Schiesel, Seth. "P.E. Classes Turn to Video Game That Works Legs." *New York Times*, April 30, 2007. Available: www.nytimes.com/2007/04/30/health/30exer.html (accessed: April 16, 2009).

Article about schools incorporating DDR as part of gym class.

Sinclair, Brendan. "Student Thesis Pegs Video Games as Racist." GameSpot. Blog. Posted July 24, 2006. Available: www.gamespot.com/ps2/action/grandtheftauto3/news.html?sid=6154591 (accessed: April 22, 2009).

Interview with Robert Parungao, who examines four popular video games, evaluates the portrayal of players from different ethnic backgrounds, and concludes that stereotypes abound.

Springen, Karen. "This Is Your Brain on Violence." MSNBC, November 28, 2006. Available: www.newsweek.com/id/44720/output/print (accessed: April 22, 2009).

Looks at the first study of the direct effects of video games on teen brains; documents functional differences between violent and nonviolent play.

Squire, Kurt. 2004. *Replaying History: Learning World History Through Playing Civilization III*. PhD dissertation. Curriculum & Instruction, School of Education, University of Wisconsin Madison, 2004. Available: http://website.education.wisc.edu/kdsquire/dissertation.html (accessed: April 22, 2009).

Three case studies in which *Civilization III* was used as the basis for a unit on world history in urban learning environments.

Squire, Kurt and Constance Steinkuehler. 2005. "Meet the Gamers: They Research, Teach, Learn, and Collaborate. So Far, Without Libraries." *Library Journal*, 130, no. 7 (April 15): 38. Available: www.libraryjournal.com/article/CA516033.html (accessed: April 22, 2009).

Advocates for library services to gamers.

Steinkuehler, Constance. 2007. "Massively Multiplayer Online Gaming as a Constellation of Literacy Practices." *E-Learning* 4, no. 3: 297–318. Available: http://dx.doi.org/10.2304/elea.2007.4.3.297 (accessed: April 22, 2009).

Examines massively multiplayer online gaming, arguing that activities are not replacing literacy activities but rather are literacy activities.

Storey, Tom. "The Big Bang." *OCLC Newsletter*. Dublin, OH: Online Computer Library Center (2005). Available: www.oclc.org/news/publications/newsletters/oclc/2005/267/thebigbang.htm (accessed: April 22, 2009).

Examines differences between the gamer and boomer generations.

"Startup Develops 'Physics Accelerator' Chip." ExtremeTech, Blog Discussion Thread, March 8, 2005. Available: www.extremetech.com/article2/0,1558,1773957,00.asp?kc=ETRSS02129TX1K0000532 (accessed: April 22, 2009).

Discusses refinements in video game physics.

Terdiman, Daniel. "Fun in Following the Money." *Wired*, May 8, 2004. Available: www.wired.com/gaming/gamingreviews/news/2004/63363 (accessed: April 22, 2009).

Briefly describes the economy of *Star Wars Galaxies*.

van Schie, E.G.M. and O. Wiegman. 1997. "Children and Video Games: Leisure Activities, Aggression, Social Integration, and School Performance." *Journal of Applied Social Psychology* 27: 1175–1194. Available: http://www3.interscience.wiley .com/journal/119167361/abstract (accessed: April 22, 2009).

> In a study of over 300 junior high school students, playing video games did not appear to take place at the expense of the children's other leisure activities, social integration, and school performance.

Vered, Karen Orr. 1998 "Beyond Barbie: Fashioning a Market in Interactive Games for Girls." In *Millennium Girls: Today's Girls Around the World*, edited by Sherrie Inness. New York: Roman & Littlefield: 169–191.

> Looks at games girls prefer; concludes that girls seem to prefer games in which creation is a part of the narrative structure and that young girls may be shying away from computers/ technology because of boys and boy behavior surrounding computers/technology.

Vered, Karen Orr. 1998. "Blue Group Boys Play Incredible Machine, Girls Play Hopscotch: Social Discourse and Gendered Play at the Computer." In *Digital Diversions: Youth Culture in the Age of Multimedia*, edited by Julian Sefton-Green. London: UCL Press: 43–61.

> Examines gender differences in computer use and software preferences.

Wang, X. and A.C. Perry. 2006. Metabolic and Physiological Responses to Video Game Play in a Group of 7–10-Year-Old Boys. *Archives of Pediatric and Adolescent Medicine* 160: 411–415.

> Examines physiological parameters in boys playing video games.

Warlick, David. 2005. "The New Literacies." *Scholastic Administrator* (March–April). Available: http://content.scholastic.com/browse/article.jsp?id=263 (accessed: April 22, 2009).

> Asserts that today's students need to know not only how to read, write, and do arithmetic but also how to find, analyze, and organize information, how to apply it, and how to share it—in an ethical manner.

West Virginia Department of Education. West Virginia Board of Education Policy 2520.6: 21st Century Physical Education 5–12 Content Standards and Objectives for West Virginia Schools (March 19, 2007). Available: http://wvde.state.wv.us/policies/ p2520.6_ne.doc-2007-03-19 (accessed: April 16, 2009).

> Adoption of DDR into gym classes in West Virginia.

Whelan, Debra Lau. 2005. "Let the Games Begin! Researchers Say That Computer Games Are Crucial to Learning—And About to Hit Schools in a Big Way." *School Library Journal* 51, no. 4: 40 (4). Available: www.schoollibraryjournal.com/article/ CA514020.html (accessed: April 22, 2009).

> Describes how schools are integrating video games into learning.

Wiegman, O. and E.G.M. van Schie. 1998. "Video Game Playing and Its Relations with Aggressive and Prosocial Behaviour." *British Journal of Social Psychology* 37: 367–378.

> Study of 278 middle school–aged boys and girls focusing on video games, aggression, and prosocial behavior finds no significant relationship between video game use in general and aggressive behavior, but a significant negative relationship with prosocial behavior was supported.

Wilson, Heather 2005. "Gaming for Librarians: An Introduction." *VOYA* 26, no. 6: 446–449. Available: http://pdfs.voya.com/VO/YA2/VOYA200502YA101.pdf (accessed: April 22, 2009).

> Defines different types of gaming experiences teens have outside of libraries and challenges librarians to offer gaming as a service to teens.

Wilson, Lee. 2007. "Getting It Wrong: Slaying Myths About Video Games (Part 1)." *Technology & Learning* 28, no. 2: 16 (5). Available: www.techlearning.com/story/showArticle.php?articleID=196604665 (accessed: April 22, 2009).

> Dispenses with the myths that all video games are about hand–eye coordination and that games are all about violence and sex.

Wilson, Lee. 2007. "Getting It Wrong: Slaying Myths About Video Games (Part 2)." *Technology & Learning* 28, no. 3: 30 (4). Available: www.techlearning.com/showArticle.php?articleID=196604734 (accessed: April 22, 2009).

> Dispenses with the myths that all educational video games are terrible, that kids should play without teacher intervention, and that there is no research documenting games for learning.

Woodcock, Bruce Sterling. "MMOG Subscribers 200,000+ ." MMOG Chart. 2008. Available: www.mmogchart.com/Chart1.html (accessed: April 22, 2009).

> Analyzes massively multiplayer online games.

Yang, S.P. and G. Graham. 2005. "Project Game. Gaming Activities for More Exercise." *Research Quarterly for Exercise and Sport* 671, suppl 1: A-96.

> Research study demonstrates that playing the video game Dance Dance Revolution increases heartbeats to 100–160 beats per minute.

Yates, Simeon J. and Karen Littleton. 1999. "Understanding Computer Game Cultures: A Situated Approach." *Information, Media & Society* 2, no. 4: 566–583. Available: www.ingentaconnect.com/content/routledg/rics/1999/00000002/00000004/art00010 (accessed: April 22, 2009).

> Examines video game players and video game culture through a psychological lens.

Yee, Nicholas. "The Norrathian Scrolls: A Study of *EverQuest*" (version 2.5; 2001). Available: www.nickyee.com/eqt/report.html (accessed: April 22, 2009).

> Research project investigates player demographics, play style, and other aspects of *EverQuest*.

Yi, Matthew. "Playing Games in School/Using Videos Helps Students Love to Learn Their Lessons." *The San Francisco Chronicle*, February 20, 2006. Available: www.sfgate.com/c/a/2006/02/20/BUG86H9SBD1.DTL (accessed: April 16, 2009).

> Article about schools incorporating DDR as part of gym class.

Index

279

About the Author

Beth Gallaway is convinced that playing *Hangman* on her cousin's Atari when she was five helped her learn to read and spell. The first system her family owned was the Nintendo Entertainment System, with the game *Super Mario Brothers*, and she came in second (with 189 points!) in a *Tetris* competition sponsored by a local video store in the early 1990s. Growing up playing *Oregon Trail*, *Agent USA*, *Joust*, *Mickey's Space Adventure*, and *Super Mario Brothers* led to pursuit of *Sim City* and *Myst* in college. A creative writing major and avid reader, she sees video games as just a new form of storytelling.

All the game-playing paved the way for accepting video games as another format for recreation and information. After graduating from Simmons Graduate School of Library and Information Science in 1998, Beth landed a job as a YA Librarian at the Haverhill (MA) Public Library. On the library's guided access teen portal, she linked to online games for teens to play and to cheat code Web sites and recommended strategy guides for purchase for the YA nonfiction collection. Young gamers in the community responded by asking for a circulating game collection, and Beth facilitated a Gaming Club that researched the pros and cons and put together a title list and collection policy for the director to review and approve. By treating reference questions about cheat codes for games seriously, Beth befriended adult gamers who donated gaming magazines to the library's collection.

As a Massachusetts trainer and consultant for youth services in the Metrowest region, Beth attended a session on video games facilitated by Linda Braun that made her realize supporting gamers in the library was not the norm. In her consultant role, she did free gaming programs at member libraries and fielded many questions about gaming at the library.

Beth was named a *Library Journal* Mover and Shaker in 2006 for her work in advocating for video games in libraries. In July 2007, she started her own library consulting and training business, Information Goddess Consulting, specializing in gaming, technology, and youth services. Beth delivers continuing education workshops to librarians, in person and online, speaks at conferences in the United States and Canada, and provides dynamic and interactive technology, creative writing, and gaming programs to library patrons of all ages. More information about Beth's consulting is available online at http://information goddess.info.

305

Beth has been hired to teach continuing education classes to librarians for Infopeople (San Mateo, CA), Simmons Graduate School of Library Science, and YALSA (Young Adult Library Services Association), as well as the Connecticut State Library, the MA Regional Library System, and the Arizona State Library, among others. She has been a repeat presenter at conferences for the Cape Cod and Islands Library Association, the New England Library Association, and the Missouri Library Association. She also does staff development at individual libraries in New England. Beth is a YALSA-certified Serving the Underserved (SUS) trainer. Her favorite game is *Rock Band 2* (MTV Games, 2008); she plays a level 74 human paladin named Phoibe on the Kirin Tor Server in *World of Warcraft* (Blizzard, 2004).